Learning to Argue in Higher Education

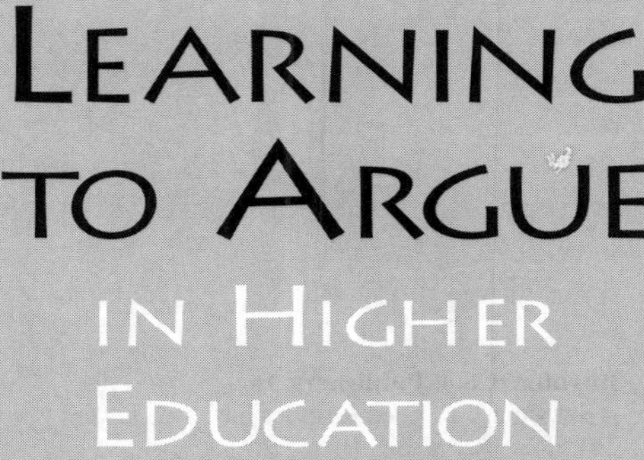

Learning to Argue in Higher Education

Edited by Sally Mitchell and Richard Andrew

Boynton/Cook
Heinemann

Boynton/Cook Publishers, Inc.
A subsidiary of Reed Elsevier Inc.
361 Hanover Street
Portsmouth, NH 03801–3912
www.boyntoncook.com

Offices and agents throughout the world

The author and publisher wish to thank those who have generously given permission to reprint borrowed material:

Cover photograph courtesy of the *South China Morning Post.*

Photographs of Hunstanton School by Alison and Peter Smithson courtesy of *Architects' Journal* and Peter Smithson.

Photograph of Japanese Storehouse by Alison and Peter Smithson courtesy of Peter Smithson.

Library of Congress Cataloging-in-Publication Data

CIP data is on file with the Library of Congress.
ISBN: 0-86709-498-2

Editor: Lisa Luedeke
Production coordination: Sonja Chapman
Production service: Lisa Garboski, bookworks
Cover design: Joni Doherty, Joni Doherty Design
Manufacturing: Deanna Richardson

Printed in the United States of America on acid-free paper

04 03 02 01 00 DA 1 2 3 4 5

Contents

Acknowledgments *vii*

From a Student
Amanda Jacobs *ix*

Introduction: Learning to Argue in Higher Education
Richard Andrews *1*

1 Innocent Concepts? A Paradigmatic Approach to Argument
Aram Eisenschitz *15*

2 Rhetoric and Architecture
Peter Medway *26*

3 Blinded by the Enlightenment: Epistemological Constraints and Pedagogical Restraints in the Pursuit of "Critical" Thinking
Doug Sweet and Deborah Swanson *40*

4 Improving Argument by Parts
Mike Riddle *53*

5 "A Workable Balance": Self and Sources in Argumentative Writing
Nicholas Groom *65*

6 "I Don't Have to Argue My Design—the Visual Speaks for Itself": A Case Study of Mediated Activity in an Introductory Mechanical Engineering Course
Maureen Mathison *74*

7 Context Cues Cognitio: Writing, Rhetoric, and Legal Argumentation
Paul Maharg *85*

8 Eager Interpreters: Student Writers and the Art of Writing Research
Claire Woods *96*

9 Citation as an Argumentation Strategy in the Reflective Writing of Work-Based Learning Students
Carol Costley and Kathy Doncaster *107*

10 Teaching Writing Theory as Liberatory Practice: Helping Students Chart the Dangerous Waters of Academic Discourse Across the Disciplines in Higher Education
Catherine Davidson *118*

11 "Argument" as a Term in Talk About Student Writing
Janet Giltrow *129*

12 Putting Argument into the Mainstream
Sally Mitchell *146*

Bibliography *155*

Notes on Contributors *173*

Acknowledgments

The editors would like to thank the following for their help and support in the making of this book: Maria Paschali, for administration of the 1997 conference at Middlesex University that gave rise to most of the papers that appear in the collection and for her subsequent work on permissions and other aspects of the management of the project; Jackie Lison of The University of Hull for work on the electronic formatting of chapters and on the bibliography; The Leverhulme Trust, for funding the four-year project "Improving the Quality of Argument in Higher Education" from 1995 to 1999; the steering committee of the project; colleagues at Middlesex University and The University of Hull for supporting the project and other work on argument between 1987 and 1999; Lisa Luedeke at Heinemann-Boynton/Cook for editorial encouragement and advice; Lisa Garboski of bookworks for her meticulous editing; and the anonymous reviewers of the original proposal to the publisher, who provided an important critique of earlier conceptions of the book.

From a Student

Amanda Jacobs

It's summer. My head and hands are in the washing machine, and I am hastily disentangling a pair of red socks from an otherwise white wash when the postman squashes a large brown DO NOT BEND envelope through the door. We tussle. Yes . . . it's the degree certificate. I haven't saved the whites but I am certified—a graduate. Crumpled and a trifle water-stained, it now has its place amongst other precious pieces of paper that mark out my over forty, nearer fifty, years alongside birth certificates, passports, and student loan repayment forms. Barely a year ago now, overdue bags of books were returned to the library, final submissions stamped in acceptance . . . and I recall the heavy silence of the exam hall. In recollection, for this "mature" undergraduate with young family, that student time was on the one hand an oasis of separateness, but also crucially a time of connection through argument.

No! I don't remember the detail of my disparate studies. But, I do recall the process. Indeed, it intrigued me at the time which is why, I guess, for my final short dissertation I chose to ask the question, "What are the expectations and perceptions of argument for a group of mature women students in relation to their studies?" Initially formulated as a response to the fairly chaotic experience of attempting to negotiate a path through a modular degree, further issues had arisen during courses concerned with educational research and argument that I had undertaken with both Richard Andrews and Sally Mitchell. It was with their support and guidance that I began to frame and structure the research.

My small-scale investigation had been prompted by a number of concerns. During the two-and-a-half years spent as a mature student engaged in study for a multidisciplinary degree I had become increasingly aware of argument; its centrality to discovery (the construction of knowledge), learning, and change. Within a broadly political framework argument, however defined, is instigated, shaped, and directed by the context within which the individual is operating—

their present, experience of the past and perceptions of a future. These, in turn, are linked to the societal and structural edifices which impact upon our individual lives. Taken to one extreme, the late twentieth century has witnessed the emergence of the notion that there can be no argument about the way in which societies should be structured: with the break-up of the USSR there is no apparent viable, proven alternative to liberal capitalist democracies which will support inevitable economic and cultural globalization. Consequently, social structures, of which education is a part, are molded to fit. In England, Higher Education is currently being fundamentally restructured, not just in terms of funding and organization of learning, but in terms of purpose. Combined, these factors must impact on how students are encouraged to engage within different discourses and with argument itself. Concern is illustrated by discussion of the role, construction, and assessment of argument within the academy (Myerson 1995). In other words, if there is general acceptance that there is but one right political and economic system what is the impact on the process of argument? Does this give primacy to the adversarial mode of argument, a cornerstone for rational and objective epistemology?

Challenge to this "way of knowing" has come partly from feminist discourse. My enquiry was influenced by questions that emanate from this perspective; that have sought to acknowledge and explain a gender difference in construction of knowledge and means of argument. Older women (i.e., over 21) are increasingly represented within the Higher Education student population but their combined experiences both as women and mature students are comparatively unexplored. Analysis of degree results revealed that whilst women students take a high proportion of high degrees, they achieve proportionately fewer top class degrees than men. Taking into account the probable complexity of their personal lives (i.e., managing families, paid work, general levels of confidence, previous education), it seemed still appropriate to ask why this should be the case? It seems only too convenient and neat to assume that failure to fulfil potential is to be located within women or explained as a result of social pressures. Are there not questions to be asked about the processes in higher education that mature women students are required to engage with? If academic written argument is a core undergraduate activity and dominant form of assessment, is there a mismatch for this group of students and the form of what is, predominately, adversarial argument?[1]

Such questions motivated my study but my findings questioned any notion of homogeneity within the group of mature women students, as individual responses from participants were clearly dependent on life experiences. These, in turn, reflected attitudes to both the understanding and reported ability and confidence to utilize academic argument. Some common issues between the two small focus groups I conducted did, however, emerge. Crucially, there appeared to be a strong connection between early personal experiences of verbal argument, methods of negotiation at this stage, and resulting self-esteem. Almost without exception participants needed encouragement to challenge ideas they encountered in their academic writing—to feel they had the right to do so. They needed the confidence that they were worthy of holding an opinion and that the opinion itself would have worth (the degree to which this featured depended on life experiences). Despite the recent academic success of girls and young women, teaching staff within the university would, it seems, still need to remain alert to the academic insecurities of their older students.

What Tenney and Annas (1996) call "being good"—abiding by the rules—was seen initially by a number of participants as of overriding importance in the construction of argument. There were a number of examples given in the focus groups where, in discussion of their work they felt as Tenney and Annas (1996) suggest, ". . . . sometimes disassociated from the positions they are taking; they may be uncomfortable with the act of positioning themselves and making assertions; and they may feel they are engaging in an unethical act if they argue for positions they do not believe in." One participant, for example, had developed a way of, as she described, "putting myself in a box." Indeed, in discussion, participants illustrated the process of constructing and writing argument in emotive terms indicating that although they were engaged in what was presented as a logical, objective, neutral activity, in actuality the "doing" of it was a matter of personal and emotional commitment seldom acknowledged in the learning environment. However, participants generally appeared to acknowledge their own development, their increasing capacity to negotiate a place for themselves within an argument, and their excitement at being able to do so. Although seldom expressed as such by participants, it could be interpreted as the excitement of connection and creativity. As one student said,

> . . . I can argue better on paper than I can in class . . . possibly, like H, I'm more comfortable with a pen and I think basically that might be stemming from the way we were brought up and lives we've led and the environment of our family . . . I can read all the historians and then as I'm writing it down it clicks and you get this real surge . . . and you can place yourself and you have to rush to get it all down.

The investigation revealed no hesitancy or reluctance on the students' part to engage in adversarial argument, but rather, highlighted the difficulties of inclusion in the process.

Note

1. It is important to note that whilst, for the purposes of my dissertation, I chose to concentrate on mature women students, the questions would seem to cross the gender divide; a brief glance at recent statistics from Middlesex University revealed that of those students receiving an unclassified/pass degree, 2.7 percent were women mature students, while 11.7 percent were mature men students.

Learning to Argue in Higher Education

Introduction

Learning to Argue in Higher Education

Richard Andrews

This book is designed for lecturers, professors, and students in higher education who are interested in the practice of how to learn to argue better, in speech and in writing as well as in listening and reading/interpretation—and in other modes of communication. It is also for researchers who want to understand more fully the difficulties of marrying thought to expression in higher education, and the political constraints that shape our exchanges with each other in the business of teaching and learning at advanced levels.

There is an increasing interest in argumentation. The approach taken by the writers in this book isn't formulaic; rather it's based on inquiry and critique, and on shining some light on the practices and assumptions of composition at undergraduate and postgraduate levels. Increases in numbers of students in higher education across the world (e.g., in Britain from 8 percent to 35 percent in fifteen years; in Hong Kong from 10 percent to 20 percent in five years) have brought about some mismatches in the expectations of lecturers/professors [1] on the one hand, and students on the other. The book is partly an attempt to reveal those mismatches and to begin to do something about them.

There are also more practical ends in mind. Included in the book are new approaches to learning to argue in higher education; ones that are light in their pedagogical scaffolding but which are effective; and ones which avoid excessive taxonomies, jargon, or categorization.

The field of inquiry in the book is argumentation in education and learning. This field or arena or space for debate allows us and our contributors to draw on a number of different disciplines—among them education, linguistics, discourse studies, philosophy, rhetoric—and to invite the contributors to grapple with problems of composition in spaces that are real as well as virtual: classrooms, seminar rooms, lecture theaters, and in electronic communities.

Contexts for Studies in Argument in Higher Education

It is tempting, in surveying the literature on learning to argue in higher education, to categorize the work to date into North American, English/European, and, say, Australian approaches to the problem. Crudely, these approaches might break down, respectively, into a primarily *textual* approach to questions of how students learn to argue in the first years of college or university; a more discipline-based *contextual* approach, taking into account the social and political bases for discourse; and a *rhetorical* approach, in the contemporary senses of that term. The temptation has been resisted for a number of reasons. First, each of these continental "approaches," on closer examination, does not appear to be unified. For example, there are different traditions at play within North America as well as within the other continents; in Europe, for example, there is a strong strand of textual studies in argumentation, represented principally through the special interest groups in the EARLI network which take their founding methodological tools from linguistics, pragmatics, and dialectics; equally, in North America, there are strands of inquiry that focus on community rather than on text (e.g., the work of Linda Flower and others in and around Carnegie Mellon University in Pittsburgh). Second, there is international commerce in the debate on argumentation and on learning to argue, maintained through visiting lectures, common practice, and international gatherings of teachers, lecturers, and scholars.[2] Third, such geographical categorizing sets up a polemic that isn't productive; far more productive is the exploration of a diverse and complex field via common ground, i.e., the problem of helping lecturers and students see how the writing of argument in the higher education context can be improved.

Rather, it is possible to identify two main bodies of theory underpinning thinking about argument and through a Hegelian process of thesis and antithesis, to try to create a new synthesis that at the same time explores the interface between invention and arrangement in learning to argue on the one hand; and is sensitive to the different disciplines in which argument is operating on the other. These two main bodies of theory—which are international in scope and range—can be characterized as rhetorical and cognitive.[3] The first has its eye on the way languages are shaped to persuade, resolve, defend, and so on; the second focuses on the structure of thinking that goes into the formation of ideas in speech and in writing (or some other form of mark-making). To suggest that the two are anything but closely interrelated would be to deny the power of the arena which we are trying to explore (thoughts are rarely fully formed and *then* committed to paper via a series of technical/linguistic transformations); but it is useful to separate the major influences on the process of learning to argue at an advanced level in education.

Rhetorical Perspectives

From a rhetorical perspective, a point of reference can be identified as two of the books that emerged from the 1979 Canadian Council of Teachers of English conference at Carleton University (Freedman and Pringle 1980; Freedman, Pringle, and Yalden 1983). The conference which gave rise to these books established its identity as one which marked a move on from the 1966 Dartmouth conference, with its affirmation of personal identity at the heart of the writing process, and a reinvention of the classical tradition of rhetoric which had surfaced again in the States in the 1960s (see, for example, Corbett 1965) in relation to the need for compositional assistance for the large number of undergraduates entering the higher education system. It is important to note that the Carleton conference was not affirming the taxonomically-driven, textbook-producing rhetorical tradition; on the contrary, its major contribution was to restore *invention* to a central place in considerations of learning to write; hence the term "reinventing." The main thrust of the Freedman/Pringle enterprise was not to foreground argument, however; it was to broaden the scope of rhetoric to embrace the "poetic" as well as the "transactional" (essays by Britton appeared in both volumes). But the effect on the teaching of argument was clear: argumentation was as much drawing on the voices and expressiveness of the individual as were the more obviously expressive modes such as poetry and narrative. Such a conception of argument lent itself more to advocacy and positioning than the arid formulae of an older rhetoric, described by I. A. Richards as "the dreariest, and least profitable part of the waste that the unfortunate trawl through in freshman English" (quoted in Corbett 1965, 626–7).

Freedman and Pringle's contribution, in summary, was to reinvent the classical rhetorical tradition by restoring invention (*inventio*) to pride of place in the business of learning to write, and to foreground process rather than product. But there was (and to a certain extent is) still a gap to be filled in the reinvention of rhetoric. While style, memory and delivery had been the keystones of the post-Ramus rhetoric—and consequently brought about the downfall of rhetoric because they lacked the other two elements of invention and arrangement—there was still little in Freedman and Pringle on arrangement (*dispositio*). Indeed, this key element in any discussion of argumentation seemed also to be neglected in other writing on rhetoric. Kinneavy's (1980) survey of contemporary rhetorical approaches spends little time on it, though his chapter does contain an important section on argumentation in North America and Europe and concludes that "it may be that the twentieth century is the most persuasive of all centuries" (202). Nevertheless, he goes on, "the study of the organization of the parts of a discourse insofar as they relate to the teaching of composition has not been nearly as interesting a field as either general composition theory or invention and process" (218–9); the slippage is from invention and content to grammatical and lexical issues, thus leaving out the *compositional* act. Some of the most interesting issues about learning to argue in higher education are precisely where Kinneavy finds little to write about: at the interface of invention and arrangement. If, as Kinneavy suggests, "possibly the most telling empirical finding of [the twentieth] century in composition research relating to grammar has been the accumulated evidence that the isolated teaching of formal grammatical skills (traditional, structural or transformational) cannot be shown to bring any significant improvement in writing, reading or speaking skills" (220), such a conclusion is further testimony to the gap that has unhelpfully opened between grammar and composition, unbridged by any consideration of arrangement. Freedman and Pringle themselves (1985, quoted in Andrews 1992) noted very little revision in school writing in Ontario "above the level of the sentence" in their study of writing at grades 5, 8, and 12.

It is at the interface of invention and arrangement that rhetorical convention can get in the way of learning. What teachers teach, "assured of certain certainties" of academic convention like the academic essay and its appropriateness for arriving at grades (through its making explicit the knowledge that students have gained), may not be what best helps students to learn. There are thus discoursal differences between learning and teaching. Again, put crudely, teaching tends to favor explicit end products that can be assessed (and modularization exacerbates the move toward the assessible). Learners will favor a wider net of genres that allow informal and formal expression of the process and heuristics of learning as well as the demonstration of what has been learnt, i.e., everything from notes through personal logs and diaries, question-and-answer to fully-fledged narratives and arguments (see, for instance, Medway's chapter). Insensitivity to the range of genres required for learning can lead tutors/lecturers into blocking off the routes into learning.

There are other ways in which student attempts to learn and to argue can be blocked. In his chapter, Nicholas Groom discusses a balance between authorial voice and self on the one hand, and outside sources on the other. Finding an appropriate balance between these, the object of study *and* the anticipated audience is at the heart of the rhetorical problem of writing for assessment in higher education. Groom suggests a further balancing is required between cognitive and linguistic demands and concludes that the balance needs to shift to the former.

Learning to argue has been a central focus of work in school and higher education in projects that Sally Mitchell, other colleagues, and I have been engaged in between 1990 and 1999 (e.g., Mitchell 1994, 1996; Costello and Mitchell 1995; Andrews 1992, 1995). Our conception of rhetoric is close to social semiotics and critical literacy in that it takes into account the social and disciplinary context in which argument takes place, is interested in the interplay of visual and verbal codes, and has been concerned with the distribution and effects of power in argumentation. In such a conception of argument, it is rebirth rather than reinvention that characterizes the nature of contemporary rhetoric, *viz* a rhetoric characterized by dialogue, imagination, making, and an integrated relationship between invention, arrangement, memory, style, and presentation. Rhetoric, however, has been a key foundation to the research in that argument is foregrounded, as it was in Aristotelian conceptions of the art. The dialogic dimension, backed by the work of Bakhtin, informs the whole process—which might be called, in short, the "arts of discourse." Andrews (1992) attempts to set out the foundation for further work on argumentation and to address the importance of such a foundation in the theory and practice of learning to argue. In doing so, he attempts to steer a course between the reapplication of Aristotelian rhetoric to the needs of the contemporary writing classroom at university level (e.g., Corbett 1965; Cockcroft and Cockcroft 1992) on the one hand, and literary-driven models of argument as a process in the *spirit* of rhetoric (e.g., Leith and Myerson 1989) on the other, in which argument's association with dialogue, address (audience), and play figure prominently.[4]

In his chapter in the present book, Medway explores the connection between rhetoric and architecture, suggesting that both architectural design and the verbal justification of design decisions involve learning to argue. He does so by looking at the pedagogy of schools of architecture and by an investigation into the notions, held by many architects and students, that buildings "speak." Distinctions are drawn between surface and more fundamental views of rhetoric; these distinctions are mirrored in writing about architecture by architects and critics. What is stressed is that rhetoric, including argumentation, is one of the arts of the *practical;* and that both—in the way they inform and arise from the practical—are a manifestation of "a broader habit or ethic of *rationality.*"

Cognitive Perspectives

From a cognitive perspective, argumentation has a central place in higher education. It must be said at the outset, however, that thinking will be grounded not only in its social and political situations, but also in the specific disciplinary contexts in which it is asked to operate. Cognitive approaches to argumentation, then, should be context-specific.[5] The connection between cognition and argumentation will be a strong one, however, not least because cognition ("thinking") is seen to proceed from assumptions about rationality that underpin the processes of higher education. Graduates from the university are expected to be able to "think" creatively and imaginatively about their discipline but also more generally to be able to apply that creativity to different contexts. Learning to argue, then, could be seen to be a central purpose and activity of attendance at the university.

Toulmin, Rieke, and Janik (1984) is generally regarded as a key early text in the composing of argument at undergraduate level, at least in the U.S. *An Introduction to Reasoning* is concerned with the study of "practical reasoning and argumentation" (v), that is to say, an introduction "to ideas about rationality and criticism without requiring a mastery of any particular logical formalism" (ibid.). As Riddle (1997) says of Toulmin's seminal text, *The Uses of*

Argument (1958), it[6] marked "a move away from argument conceived of as fixed patterns of "technical logic" to argument regarded as a linguistic activity constrained by use in context" (1). The follow-up practical book, *An Introduction to Reasoning,* associates practical reasoning with "informal logic" and the delivery function of rhetoric (not a conception of rhetoric to which the present book subscribes, i.e., rhetoric as "dress").

In the broad field of practical reasoning and argumentation, then, Toulmin, Rieke, and Janik posit a basic pattern of analysis "suitable for application to arguments of all types and in all fields" (pv). The pattern of analysis is designed to test the soundness and strength of arguments: how are claims supported by reasons? How are those reasons to be evaluated? And what makes some arguments, such as trains of reasoning, better and others worse? The key elements of the model which is used to gauge the soundness of arguments, i.e., whether they hang together or not, can be depicted thus:

Figure 1-1
Toulmin's model 1

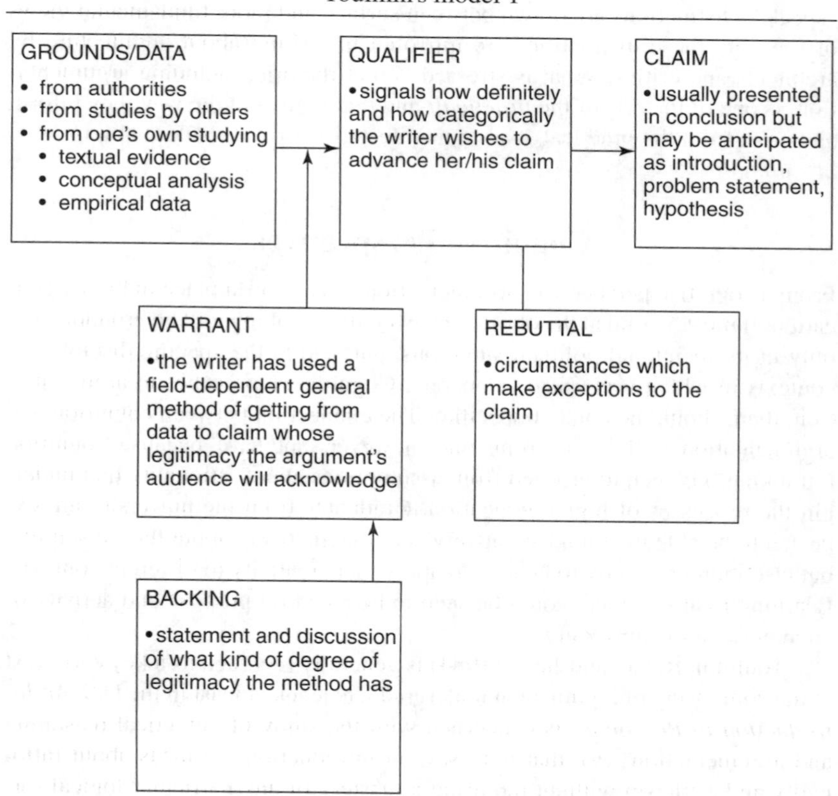

Briefly[7], claims are assertions or propositions; grounds are the evidence to support the claim, whether it is empirical or not; warrants and rules express the relationship between claims and grounds; and backing is the foundation for the warrants in disciplinary or other social bodies of knowledge, practice, and information. Qualifiers perform the function they denote: the qualification of a warrant, as indicated by phrases like "presumably" and "so far as the evidence goes." Rebuttals consist of the circumstances which make exceptions to the claim.

We have found that the model's veracity comes over more clearly if we turn the diagram on its side, rotating it by ninety degrees:

Figure 1-2
Toulmin's model 2

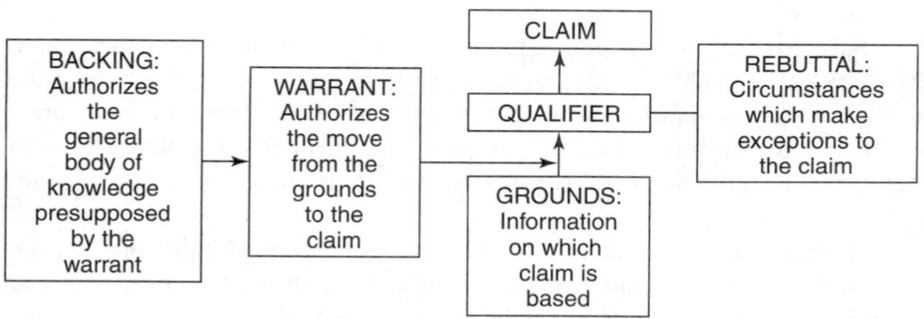

What such a reorientation suggests is that the underlying metaphor for the model is archaeological: the approach aims to dig below the surface of the verbal manifestations of the argument to reveal its soundness and strength. While there is explication of how arguments can be linked to each other, or arise from each other in "chains," the spirit of the model is analytical in a paradigmatic as opposed to syntagmatic way. That is to say, it digs and scrapes away at the surface representations of argument until it reveals the underlying layered *structure* of single arguments.[8]

There are other ways in which some chapters in the present book distinguish themselves from the approach of Toulmin, Rieke, and Janik. Toulmin et al. use the term "reasoning" for "the central activity of presenting reasons in support of a claim" (14) and as subsidiary to "argumentation" which they see as "the whole activity of making claims" and supporting and challenging them (ibid.). What they see as "rationality" strikes me as being more like an attitude than an operation of mind; and "argument" is seen as a "train of reasoning;" whereas this book sees argumentation as the process of arguing, and argument as the overall noun[9] describing the products of that process and manifesting itself in particular arguments. Argument and argumentation, from the point of view of this book, are subsidiary to rationality (the general web of discourses in which reason operates) and reasoning (the process of operation in those discourse worlds which might include, for example, mathematical reasoning as well as verbal reasoning). In short, argumentation—the main focus of our book as indicated in the title's use of the verb "to argue"—is subsidiary to reasoning.[10]

These are at least two ways, then, in which I would wish to refine the Toulmin, Rieke, and Janik model. There is much to go along with, however: the distinction between argument as inquiry and argument as advocacy; the useful distinction between generic, universal, field-invariant rules of procedure "that apply to rational criticism in all fields and forums" on the one hand, and field-dependent[11] elements of argument on the other. In a sense, while the present book is looking to chart ways of learning to argue in higher education in a generic fashion, the individual chapters take their own specific field in which to explore how students learn to argue, just as students themselves need to learn what the ground rules are in the different disciplines and modules in which they find themselves.

Furthermore, as Mitchell sets out in her interim report on the project "Improving the Quality of Argument in Higher Education," work by Higgins (1994), which attempts to explore the communicative contexts in which argument operates, adds to the picture; as does Toulmin et al.'s distinction between regular (rule-applying) and critical (rule-justifying) arguments (see Mitchell 1996, 12–17).

However, one misconception that has bedevilled composition practice and theory, especially in argumentation, might be said to be derived from an aspect of the Toulmin et al. model, namely the reification of a process as a product. The model, depicted earlier in its horizontal and vertical orientations, describes a process: the key elements are not the boxes or categories of analysis, important though they are to a scientific analysis of the process. Rather, the key elements as far as written and other forms of composition are concerned are the lines that join those boxes, i.e., the *action* of linking grounds to claims, or supporting the argument with warrants and backing.

A good example of a more creative application of Toulmin appears in work arising from the Leverhulme project, "Improving the quality of argument in higher education" (1995–1999). Mike Riddle describes a model developed from a study of models in the Toulmin tradition, but which looks at the dynamic relations of argument rather than the categorization of it (although the two are closely related). Rather than concentrate on backing, warrants, claims, and grounds, he looks at the relations between them and posits a model based on the syntactic terms "since," "then" and "because." When applied to the business of composition, Toulmin's ideas need to be transformed into an approach that is accessible and sensitive to the writing process.

In other words, *the act of arguing* is more dialogic and more contingent upon the contexts in which it is taking place than the Toulmin model of an *argument* enables us to see. The power relationship between protagonist and antagonist (proponent and respondent are milder terms) will be a major factor. The internal pressures behind composition, realizing themselves in blocks to writing or prejudices or predilections for particular modes of expression and forms of composition, will be another. Yet another will be the context in which the subject or discipline is framed (see Bazerman 1994, "Where is the classroom?"), whether it be institutional or not. Argument is particularly susceptible to context because it is essentially dialogic. It invites response in a way that narrative or lyric poetry often doesn't; its function is sometimes to heal rifts, sometimes to explore them, sometimes to engender them; but at all times one person's or one group's argued position depends on another's. Reification of interchange into "argument structure," as if the process were monologic, hardly stands up to contemporary dialogue theory (see Walton 1999).

The Dialogic Principle

The *dialogic*[12] nature of argument is well described in Riddle (1997):

> The singularity of argument lies in its mode of interaction. In non-argumentative modes, the form of the interaction is complete if receivers co-operate in the co-construction of meaning. In argumentative interactions the form is not achieved without active challenge to the construction of meaning represented by participants' positions. (4)[13]

This is not the place to repeat the case for seeing the dialogic principle at the core of argument (see, for example, Bakhtin 1981, 1986; Kaufer and Geisler 1991, 110ff; Andrews 1995; Riddle op. cit.), except to summarize the case by saying that dialogism manifests itself in argument in a number of ways. These include argument's openness to different points of view (sometimes opposed, sometimes tangential to each other, sometimes consensual where two points of view move to, or which move to and fro between consensus and conflict); its dynamic, interactive nature; its close association with conversation and drama; its predication on speech.

Let's take it as given that in higher education, students are inducted into a discipline (or a number of disciplines or professions) in which, by the time they attain degree level, they are expected to be able to argue in that discipline.[14] That is to say, although at the very beginning of the course or program, there may be a good deal of one-way communication, with the lecturer or professor "passing on" to the student the foundations of the subject, by the end of the course the student should be able to discuss and debate the subject with the lecturer or professor. In some disciplines, such dialogue takes place earlier, either because of the nature of the subject (e.g., philosophy, where argument is a *modus operandi*) or because it is is included earlier for pedagogic and interpretational advancement.

But much in the system of higher education works against either attainment of argumentation at the end of a program or use and exploration of argumentation during a program. One student Sally and I have both worked with complained that the size of an undergraduate group in which she found herself for a course on education research methods was too large to foster argument. Although the lecturer worked hard to break down a group of thirty students into smaller groups during the weekly sessions, the chances to run with an idea in a sustained way over a period of time were minimal. At the other end of the scale, small groups don't necessarily lend themselves to lively argument. Often they are dominated by one or two people who, as it were, demonstrate an argument to the rest of the group. Contributory reasons might be a lack of impetus or confidence on the part of the other students, or a lack of ability in the lecturer to engineer the learning so that everyone in a small group has a chance to make his or her voice heard. Furthermore, lecturers may not have made clear to students what the ground rules of the teaching sessions are: whether and how argumentation is expected.

Such tacit ground rules manifest themselves also in writing. The default genre in higher education—at least in the humanities—is the essay (Womack 1993). The essential problem is that the essay is a single-voiced genre that requires the student to weave together a number of other voices (authorities, references). I have experimented with different forms of writing for students to demonstrate to the lecturer that they have gained command of the subject or topic they are exploring. These include "dialogic writing" like symposia or script-writing, question-and-answer, Socratic dialogue, dissertations that interweave conventional essay sections with narrative, lyric sections, etc. Reports—a common genre in project work—often confuse students in that they don't know whether simply to report or whether to argue; often a mixed-mode work ensues, the criteria for judgement for which are sometimes not clear.

Dialogue theory (see Walton 1999) is helpful in setting out the different types of argument. Walton suggests six basic types of dialogue: persuasion, which results in resolutions or clarification of issues; inquiry, leading to the proof or disproving of a hypothesis; negotiation, leading toward a reasonable settlement; information-seeking, which far from being a simple process of transfer, often takes interactive form; deliberation, to decide the best course of action; and eristic or personal conflict, which often reveals the deeper basis of conflict or difference of values and positions. In pedagogy, dialogue is often used for demonstration purposes by lecturers who use student answers to questions in order to "demonstrate" knowledge in speech—rather than engaging in genuine dialogue. Although the types of argument suggested by Walton are not the only types, and real cases often exhibit a hybrid blend of types, these categories fulfil one part of the jigsaw of understanding what expectations are held by two parties. Where there is a mismatch of expectation and practice, poor communication and learning takes place.

One way in which the dialogic principle is explored in the current book is in the chapter by Eisenschitz. In discussing a course on town planning that ran within an innovative social science degree at a London university, he draws attention to the power and importance of dialectic in challenging accepted neo-liberal orthodoxies. The aim in providing an argumentative dimension to the course was to "recover the humanist ethos," and in the same way that Medway emphasizes the broader ethical and rational context, to restore "faith in human rationality and develop their [the students'] social and political imagination." This critical dimension is seen to be essential to any higher education discipline.

Different Voices, Different Disciplines

Berrill (1999) points out that ideas about learning to argue in higher education must take account of disciplinary differences because induction into a discipline partly means learning to argue within that discipline. She cites Young and Leinhardt (1998) who discuss the complexities of writing effective historical argumentation, a process which "requires students to transform both background and document knowledge, read and interpret historical documents, and manage discourse synthesis" (25). She also mentions Lave and Wenger's (1991) notion of legitimate participation in a community, and the problem of how "novices within a community are treated as legitimate participants while they learn community ways of thinking and acting" (Berrill 1999, 2). This problem manifests itself in the lecturer acting as the gatekeeper of disciplinary discourse who shuts the gate as well as opens it. And students whose degree courses involve more than one discipline may find themselves having to learn the ground rules of a number of different games. Where there is interdisciplinarity, there is scope for an exploration of differences in approach; but where there is only multidisciplinarity, there may be no integration of approaches or, indeed, any discussion at all of the different kinds of argument, kinds of evidence, and voices which are required and validated.

In the chapters that follow, contributors explore the issues set out in this introduction in a number of different disciplines.

Through examples of first-year undergraduate Law students grappling with issues of how to compose essays, Paul Maharg discusses the rhetoric of context and its impact on invention and arrangement in Law. He brings to bear research into legal communication and the rhetorical turn in legal studies on to the issues of how students cope with new—often mixed—genres in legal discourse. Learning to read and write in a professional discipline is suggested as tantamount to being inducted into at least the internal dynamics of that discipline: the particular relationships between evidence and claims/propositions, the status of logical discourse, and its influence by context.

Maureen Mathison argues for recognition of the importance of the visual and numerical (which often takes visual or graphic form) in the academic work of trainee engineers, even though the principal product for assessment is writing. She identifies a tension in engineering between the drive "for a product that works, not a final research report that describes it" on the one hand, and a need for explicitness in written and graphical form on the other. Writing prose is seen as ancillary to the real business of engineering: designing and making things that work. But Mathison proposes an increased sense of audience in the practice of engineering degree work so that students are required to convince others of the efficacy of their designs. When engineers argue, then, they will need to use words as well as visual and numerical evidence and the persuasive nature of the prototype and finished product.

Claire Woods, in her chapter on students as writers of ethnographic research, challenges the conventionally assumed chasm between narrative and argument, fiction and nonfiction by asking her first-year undergraduate students to study the work of travel writers, ethnographers, and literary journalists. Such a participant-observer approach to writing leads to expressive, analytical writing that bridges the chasm. It is writing "in the field" that is predicated on position and perspective. Because it takes a view, the underpinning tacit arguments can be revealed by degrees. Student work thus replicates what has been going on in ethnography for a number of years: an exploration of "the nature of ethnographic argumentation and the rhetoric of evidence" (Atkinson and Hammersley 1994, 254). Such relativization of the relationship between claims, grounds, warrants, and backing reveals the essential nature of the Toulmin model: that the evidence for a claim has no solid foundation; that good evidence—different in nature from discipline to discipline, context to context—is itself built on constructed foundation, and the earth in which such foundations are built is itself shifting.

Carol Costley and Kathy Doncaster, in their chapter on citation as argument strategy, explore how work-based learners draw on personal, professional, and academic experience as they cite sources to support or define their own emergent arguments. They describe a reflective action assignment on a program of work-based learning and how other voices are brought into the writer's argument not as evidence, but as points of reference for the developing case that is being made.

This introduction ends with a disclaimer and the prospect of a way forward. Studies in argumentation and rhetoric (and indeed other fields in social semiotics or linguistics) tend toward taxonomies. Such scientific categorizing is an important factor in clarifying the field. But it doesn't translate easily into ways of helping students speak, write, read, listen, or make in some other medium that verbal language. On the contrary, such taxonomies often lead, if followed slavishly, to wooden, formulaic composition. Janet Giltrow puts her finger on the problem that seeing argumentation as *argument* (i.e., the verb as a noun) can bring. She suggests that "argument" is too high a term for the apprentice writer at undergraduate level, tending to mystify induction into a discipline and higher education in general and disenfranchising many emergent student writers. She characterizes it as a text-type and an oppressive one. Her analysis comes from the North American school of genre as social action, preferring smaller, more specific text-types; it pinpoints the danger of reification of critical and creative processes into methods and conventions. Sweet and Swanson too, from a different perspective, suggest how the best-intentioned teachers "often reinforce epistemologies they'd be hard pressed to accept at face value." The writers of this chapter argue that students often effect their own erasure of the political from their thinking under the guise of undertaking "critical thinking" because the thinking is too close to the prejudices and predilections of the self. Such students are working within a myopic tradition that sees learning as a pursuit of the "truth"—but an "inert, visual, static, bipolar" version of it. These students, too, fall into the trap Giltrow identifies of trying to construct an "argument" after the fact.

Rather, the approach, as indicated by the title of the book, is to look not at teaching argumentative composition by textbook method but at *learning to argue;* in other words, the book is about argument *in verb:* the dynamics of argument in higher education. Consequently, there is no proposal to teach argument by formula, nor an assumption that argument is pervasive in higher education discourse (the notion that *all* discourse is persuasive, therefore it is all argumentative). It is the conditions in which argument might thrive in higher education which are the focus of interest, and how best to help students learn to identify the often tacit assumptions about argument that underpin and inform practice; furthermore, how best to help students and lecturers speak the same language and how best to argue in speech, writing, and other modes of communication. The aim is to develop a disposition to argue and to argue well; an encouragement of critical approaches to ideologies and ideas (and therefore a move away from affirmation to critique, in the most positive of lights—see Eisenschitz's chapter in the present book); the development of capability in students to imagine alternative positions and to listen carefully to the arguments put by others, complementing and challenging those positions as seems appropriate to the situation; and finally, providing students with a range of forms in which they might express their own distillations of arguments and their own new arguments. Essentially, then, learning to argue is fundamental to personal, social, institutional, and political transformation—whether that argument be for clarification, defence, assertion, or the breaking of new ground. That last function is the most important and is what links learning to argue with the potential for learning at undergraduate level.

Notes

1. From now on, the term "lecturers" will be used generally to refer to graduate teaching assistants, lecturers, associate professors, and professors who teach in higher education.

2. One such international conference, held at Middlesex University in London in September 1997, gave rise to many of the chapters in this book.

3. It is not possible to conceive of a complete synthesis. Perhaps "integration" would be a better word.

4. There is much more to say about the role of rhetoric in underpinning argument. For a full account of the rhetorical perspective, see Vickers (1988).

5. That is why this book does not focus on concepts of "argument structure" of the kind explored by Pinker (1989) and Grimshaw (1990), whose work is based on an assumption that the sentence or utterance is the unit of assessment, and that logical analyses of syntax reveal such structures.

6. Along with Perelman and Olbrecht-Tyteca's *La Nouvelle Rhetorique* (1958).

7. The exposition here is necessarily brief. For a full account of the model, readers are encouraged to refer to Toulmin, Rieke, and Janik (1984). For an excellent account of the macro-structural value of Toulmin's model in undergraduate writing, see Hegelund and Kock (1999).

8. However, I would not want to suggest that arguments have to *start* with a claim; the audience can be led to the claim, or the claim can emerge from the argument as a whole.

9. In this volume, Giltrow argues against the use of the term "argument" in the teaching of writing in higher education as "too high a term" to be useful to novices.

10. This is a dense paragraph in which I gloss over many interesting possible routes of exploration and contention. My proposition is that argument is not possible in a world which doesn't accept rationality and relativity; that's why it thrives where there is democracy, a willingness to achieve consensus, and an acceptance of relativity in personal, familial, social, and political affairs. I don't mean by rationality a world which is controlled and constrained by formulaic logic or dryly cerebral solutions to problems; on the contrary, my conception of rationality embraces feeling, passion and other orientations traditionally seen as *opposite* to rationality and (its servant) argument. Cf. Habermas (1984).

11. See Riddle (1997, 3)

12. I stop short of using the term a "dialectic," although there's much dialectical territory to be explored between the poles of rhetoric and logic.

13. See Bakhtin (1981, 1986), Andrews (1995, 52–77) and Riddle (1997 *pass.*) for exploration of dialogic forms of writing, often informed by speech.

14. Students seem to move from description through exposition to analysis and interpretation in each stage of their schooling and college/university education; such progression is built into the institutional expectation that frames education, and covers the whole education system as well as each phase of it.

1

Innocent Concepts? A Paradigmatic Approach to Argument

Aram Eisenschitz

Introduction

A liberal education has two faces. On the one hand it promises universal, neutral, and objective knowledge in the service of human enlightenment that provides understanding and empowerment. On the other hand, it is often a canon of received wisdom that provides a narrow training for technical problem solving and which reproduces the authority and hierarchical relations of the wider society. Argument, however, has the potential to counter these latter tendencies, to return a measure of autonomy and self-awareness to the learner, thereby reclaiming higher education as a means of expanding human choices and enhancing individual development. By its very nature argument is a force for democracy and social change and is inconsistent with the top-down nature of much education. It forces students to become active learners, making them aware of the competing paradigms which organize knowledge and requiring them to recognize and justify their own positions in the context of the range of social and political alternatives open to society. It also gives them a measure of self-consciousness and an ability to make choices which are likely to change them and certainly help them resist the determinist forces that shape our lives. In this chapter, I give an account of how we developed argument on a course on a town planning program that ran within a large and innovative social science degree at what was then Middlesex Polytechnic (Robinson 1991).

Why Paradigmatic Argument?

If we are to return to students a degree of autonomy, we have to recognize the political power of knowledge, a power reflected in the existence of a dominant paradigm. As Mannheim (1991, 3) argues,

> Strictly speaking it is incorrect to say that the single individual thinks. Rather it is more correct to insist that he participates in thinking further what other men have thought before him . . . on the one hand he finds a ready-made situation and on the other he finds in that situation preformed patterns of thought and conduct.

The "preformed patterns of thought" are transmitted by the dominant paradigm. Our aim, in the course we ran, was to overcome its adverse influence on critical thinking by identifying that paradigm in a subject area that displayed little independent thought and was swayed by rapidly changing fashions. Planning education, in our view, did little more than legitimate the claims of its practitioners for professional status. It made little attempt to evaluate the impact of planning upon society, adopting an approach to education that was both abstract and idealist. In fact as a series of routines around an ever-changing legislation planning is best learnt on the job. We decided to use the debates of social science to explain the issues that a century of urban intervention has thrown up and through that to develop an understanding of the processes and dilemmas of social change.

A further rationale for encouraging argument was planning's uncritical adoption of the neoliberal mantra "There is no Alternative." That phrase was blotting out a once-thriving debate over alternatives in urban policy by denying that we had control over our destiny. But the prime function of any study of society must be to show that we make our own history. Yet planning's capitulation to neoliberalism was a result of its pragmatism and apolitical professionalism which was threatening to obliterate the very purpose of intervention, namely the opening of social alternatives. Through argument we wanted to recover the humanist ethos, the faith in human rationality, and develop the students' social and political imagination rather than the sensibility of the accountant. As Mohan (1995, 129) argues, one aim of a geographical education should be to help the student break out from that triangle of home, school, and mall, a triangle of socializing institutions that so effectively stifles their imagination.

The biggest barrier to realizing this possibility is the circular relationship between knowledge of society and the dominant sources of power. As Harvey illustrates:

> The point is that social science formulates concepts, categories, relationships and methods which are not independent of the existing social relationships. As such, the concepts are the product of the very phenomena they are designed to describe. (Harvey 1973, 125)

Knowledge does not investigate society as much as confirm the key beliefs of hegemonic political interests. This circularity is the product of a dominant paradigm which defines what are acceptable concepts and theories through the medium of the conventional wisdom, but which tends to present itself as apolitical and timeless. It reinforces this power by appeals to a universal rationality that may be expressed by such means of legitimation as religion, nature, or the market. In that way it can obliterate social alternatives by undermining their assumptions without recourse to reason. It is precisely the existence of this power that underlines the importance of developing paradigmatic argument.

Argument can help expose the relationship between knowledge and economic and political power. Firstly, knowledge is fragmented into a myriad of specialisms and professions simply to reproduce those relationships. Our location on a social science course let us develop inter- rather than multidisciplinary teaching, enabling us to dissolve disciplinary boundaries and reconceptualize our subject areas. We found that what appeared to be spatial could be more appropriately analyzed as sociopolitical. Secondly, the emphasis upon the content of knowledge rather than the practice of learning hides the hierarchical social relations involved in gaining knowledge. These can be overcome if students are able to explore a holistic canvas themselves. Thirdly, introducing the notion of paradigms suggests to students that knowledge is not monolithic to be digested whole, but rather has to be probed.

By exposing the links between knowledge and power, argument helps to safeguard against the dangers of sinking beneath complacency and contentment that Galbraith (1992) so vividly illustrates. This is essentially a pluralist rationale for paradigmatic argument, a means of providing the "checks and balances" to the uncontrolled forces of economic change. But once we admit that knowledge is not neutral, a range of questions are opened: how does education socialize us and how do individuals gain their ideas? how is the social world constructed? how does the conventional wisdom influence the course of social change? how do forms of knowledge impose limitations to thought and action? The choice of concepts, for instance, predisposes the outcomes of debate; the notion of the inner city frames social issues in a physical manner which has significant implications for the way people think of the nature of capitalism. Or, taking an example from art appreciation, Berger (1972, chapter 1) argues that the conventional wisdom ignores the question of what makes good art while concentrating on contextual issues of authenticity. The consequence is a set of mystified assumptions about beauty, truth, genius, and so on that makes art increasingly remote to those not schooled in that language and which reinforces the exclusionary practices around it.

Concepts, and indeed the paradigms themselves, are not neutral lenses for studying society, but contribute to its formation. By investigating these relationships, argument may contribute towards human [illegible]tion, helping individuals use knowledge for human purposes; conversely it can also explain how the social organization of knowledge tends to oppose that aim. Such a defence is timely when there is an oversupply of graduates and higher education needs protection against elitist attempts to restrict it. The Right's battle cry, "When everybody is a graduate, nobody is," marks a society where education controls entry into the elite. But were the degree to mark a genuine commitment to argument, the power of the "preformed patterns of thought" would be reduced, thereby helping education to become a force for democratic social change (Rowe 1972).

Being critical does not mean setting up an alternative canon of knowledge but should focus on developing student consciousness. Berger (1972, 110–12) illustrates why this approach to argument is needed. All exceptional art, the art that is valued for its humanity, was produced through the artist's struggle with the language and the social relations that structured art's role in society. The artist had to "contest the norms of the art that had formed him. He had to see himself as a painter in a way that denied the seeing of a painter. That meant that he saw himself doing something that nobody else could foresee." Berger contrasts two Rembrandt self-portraits: one conventional and heartless, an advertisement for his own prestige, and the other in which he has turned around that tradition and used the painting to express the questions of existence, questions that the medium had excluded. In that portrait Rembrandt developed a degree of reflexivity about his art that let him override the limitations of a portraiture that did little more than confirm the status of the rising bourgeoisie. In the same way, critical argument in the humanities is essential to achieving enlightenment ideals of human development. If their aim is to open the range of choices to humans, the first step is to challenge the means whereby the hegemonic paradigm imposes itself upon us.

Levels of Argument

There are three levels at which skills of argument may be developed; these can be illustrated by the idea of enterprise, a concept that was central to the neoliberal diagnosis of British ills and which we used in the course.

1. Within the paradigm

Every concept lies within a particular paradigm which tries to make itself appear to be universally significant. This is often achieved by converting its key hypotheses to a set of accepted assumptions. The idea of enterprise was developed in the early 1980s in the context of programs to justify welfare cuts in areas with high unemployment. Explanations for regional deprivation focused upon a "culture of dependency" that had been created by the climate of welfare. But popular discourse—and vocational education—only examine the technical issues that this paradigm defines. The first critical task, however, is to investigate its internal coherence by identifying and testing its assumptions. Can entrepreneurs be created and does this alleviate regional economic problems?

The enterprise culture was indeed failing to absorb the unemployed, entrepreneurs were not being created from new groups, small firms were making a smaller-than-expected contribution to regeneration, and competition was often less important than cooperation in stimulating growth.

2. *Challenging the paradigm*

By identifying a set of ideas as a paradigm it may be historically, intellectually, and politically located and evaluated. This flies in the face of conventional wisdom since the hegemonic paradigm, as universally relevant, has no need to identify itself. Indeed the dominant positivist paradigms deny their power over the construction of knowledge or the practices governing its production. Nonetheless they reinforce the circularity between economic power and knowledge by creating a view of society that validates its central ideas. Each paradigm defines what is knowledge, how it is tested, and what makes it "correct," how problems are defined, what makes "good" and "bad" information, and why some opposition is acceptable and some not. Because of its influence over epistemology that allows it to decide on the rules of the game, a dominant paradigm is dislodged with difficulty, an illustration of why independence in argument is both necessary and difficult to achieve.

Enterprise's appeal in the 1980s lay in the approval it gave to ideas central to the neoliberal program. Its absence in certain areas provided politicians with a moral basis for using a deflationary economic strategy to free up the labor market and for replacing the welfare state with a culture of self-help. By creating entrepreneurs among vulnerable groups such as ethnic minorities or unemployed miners, these groups could escape poverty; furthermore, the cause of poverty could no longer be blamed upon capitalism but upon its absence, namely too little enterprise. This more critical evaluation was hidden from those who worked within the paradigm. To identify it, however, one would take a Kuhnian approach and start with the paradigm's inconsistencies identified in the previous section.

3. *Using other paradigms*

Any event can be explained by using any number of paradigms. Our aims were to equip students with the tools to evaluate competing explanations of social phenomenon, to choose the most appropriate for the task in hand and to defend that choice. If planners wish to increase regional prosperity then the relevance of enterprise depends upon whether one accepts the neoliberal diagnosis. Keynesianism, on the other hand, emphasizes the state and the large firm, while socialism and green politics avoid the concept altogether by raising a different set of questions about the nature of growth and human development. Each paradigm is constructed out of particular conjunctures of political and economic forces and has to be examined within that context. Every view, therefore, is "right" within the confines of its assumptions, but each set of assumptions needs situating and explaining.

Refining Argument

The following section illustrates how we introduced an awareness of these levels in our course. We had one-third of a student's time in their fourth and final year after their return from a year's work placement. The course's key elements included the progression of its aims, access to an emerging critical literature on urbanism, sufficient seminar time to discuss them, and assessment by essay and five thousand-word project. Students were also preparing a ten thousand-word dissertation on issues emerging from their placement and used the course to develop a critical perspective of that experience. The degree as a whole provided an integrated environment with a wide range of material to draw on, particularly in sociology, epistemology, method, and political philosophy. It was also organized in a progressive manner, restricting choice until the final year. Because students had all taken an extensive range of background courses, we were able to provide them with both the depth and breadth of knowledge necessary for developing argument.

Problems with Explanation

Students started with little awareness of paradigms in planning. Returning from placement they had often absorbed the professional problem-solving approach. Our first task was to make them aware of the problems of the conventional wisdom. In order to destabilize them, we asked them to evaluate some of the profession's set pieces, but instead of using the criteria chosen by planners we wanted them to develop and argue for their own criteria, drawing upon their wider knowledge of society. The intention was to show that it is not difficult to find alternative views of the impact and the causes of policy. Indeed "successes" such as green belts could be interpreted as failures if one used different criteria. This exercise also demonstrated how planners were able to exclude different ways of understanding society.

The second exercise to encourage argument dealt with the definition of problems. Instead of a universally relevant "problem" waiting to be solved, we wanted to demonstrate that by providing a learning environment unconstrained by disciplinary boundaries, we could demonstrate how problems are socially constructed. The "problem" of slums, for instance, could be regarded, from the slum-dweller's perspective, as a solution to the predicament that they found themselves in, just as single parenting is a rational response to the difficulty that unskilled men face in supporting a family in current inner-city labor markets. What appears superficially to be the problem—a physical object or a behavior pattern—is the result of a particular interpretation. This begged one of the course's central questions, the reasons for these differing interpretations. If concern with slums is really a problem of poverty why is it presented as a physical issue? With our roots in social theory we wanted students to link problem definition with the way the state uses the technical fix to reproduce the illusion that we are in control of society.

We then asked students to compare the rhetoric of policy with its impact evaluated against a wider choice of criteria. By asking of policy "who pays?" and "who profits?" they identified an alarming gap between its reformist intentions and its actual outcomes which at best could be labeled as social engineering. Students were struck by the planner's failure to acknowledge this gap and their faith in key beliefs like community, partnership, and enterprise, which inform policy yet which are rarely tested. Moreover these were normative beliefs, often expressing the values of the majority. Community in particular guides a range of policy from housing to policing and education. It became apparent that problems are defined with solutions in mind and that these solutions often articulate what is politically fashionable. This suggested that policy is less concerned with alleviating particular problems than with molding public discourse.

The Idea of the Paradigm

Having disabused students of common-sense views of problem solving, we wanted to show how the concepts, theories, and beliefs used in planning form different paradigms according to the politics of the time. One starting point was the identification of the "problem-solving paradigm" using the work of the American sociologist, C. Wright Mills (1970, 87–112). That reading was an eye-opener for students because it situated what they thought were universal attitudes to social problems in the values of small-town America. Using case studies of controversial redevelopment schemes we contrasted these attitudes with the rationalities of the other institutions and groups involved—poor residents, local business, central government, and so on. Each competing position depended upon a set of assumptions to create a closed world of discourse. Identifying these worlds set up issues which we referred to throughout the course, such as how one evaluates these positions, how the dominant paradigm is able to eclipse the others, and the role politics plays in constructing hegemonic ideas.

In order that students should see these relationships in practice, we took any of the fashionable concepts of the time and asked students to demonstrate not whether they were correct, but whether they helped to confirm neoliberal politics in people's minds by underwriting particular assumptions about the nature of society and acting as carriers of ideas about the "real world." Each assumption had to be questioned within its own terms. For instance enterprise justified itself by admitting the short-term pain that tax cuts would cause through reduced welfare and more privatization. Ultimately, however, everyone would benefit. Each clause in this argument could be tested. Do tax cuts increase motivation? Is enterprise the engine of growth? Does privatization benefit those on welfare? Does high welfare spending encourage economic decline? Do the benefits of growth "trickle down?" Do the underclass choose not to work? Do cuts in welfare reduce unemployment? Students had to look for evidence for these propositions, but what they found were problems with the choice of facts, with arbitrary interpretations of facts and behavior, and with the use of evidence. By showing the frailty of this argument and by identifying the political load carried by the concepts employed, this exercise raised serious doubts over the objectivity of social science.

Having identified neoliberalism in planning it was time to examine alternatives. We looked at contrasting interpretations of concepts like poverty, the state, and welfare in neoliberal and structuralist paradigms focusing on the issue of change, both in society and in the ideas that interpret it. Why were structuralist ideas replaced by neoliberalism? We wanted students to consider whether this paradigmatic shift reflected an advance in our knowledge or whether it was a consequence of political change. The outcome of this question has enormous implications for understanding both policy and the corresponding social theory. The practical outcome was to ask students to construct and to criticize policy-related statements couched in the language of different paradigms: "The country cannot afford to house the homeless;" "The middle class do not see why they should pay for the improvident behavior of groups who bring problems on themselves;" "Housing the homeless would be self-financing through increased productivity;" "Housing the homeless would weaken the work ethos with serious implications for the economic system."

Explaining Planning

The purpose of paradigmatic analysis was to identify and evaluate different explanations of planning and spatial patterns. We started from the position that there are no innocent explanatory concepts: they are given meaning by political forces. We firstly had to deal with a body of knowledge that mediates relations of power. Planning's engagement with class politics makes a critical analysis particularly difficult. Its political program, motivated by a fear of the poor and characterized by strategies of repression and cooption, is presented as a technical activity concerned above all with land use. To go beyond that interpretation one has to stand outside its assumptions. We therefore reminded students of the interpretations that they could use for explanation, in particular Keynesianism and Marxism.

Secondly we had to locate each paradigm within political and economic history. What types of planning have existed over time and what explanations can be applied? We encouraged students to apply previously encountered ideas: the breadth of the degree meant we provided a menu ranging from economic cycles to the politics of welfare, from the formation of liberalism to the history of poverty policy. We returned to policy analysis, using workshops to discuss articles that put forward a particular interpretation of contemporary policies or a particular analysis of the causes of urban change. The most useful articles were the "good, bad ones," that minority of articles that clearly represent a particular, if partial, position and which allow students to use their failings to refine their own powers of criticism.

Often the most illuminating work, work that clarified different paradigmatic positions and which linked ideas and politics, existed in other fields. The politics of food was one such area. Famine is often seen as the result of overpopulation and the physical amount of food produced, but the carrying capacity of land depends upon the social and political relationships that organize production and consumption (George 1976). Famine is the result of replacing traditional food production with cash cropping, often to produce grain for conversion into meat for the West. This paradigm focuses on land ownership and the influence of global financial flows upon agricultural policy. The idea of overpopulation as a natural phenomenon reflects the power of the landowners and the banks. Such writing gave students confidence to apply similar ideas to the urban setting.

By this time, students were using the seminars to explore the viability of new combinations of ideas in the context of the course readings. They had so much material to explain urban change that they often could not control the process. Although a common complaint was that we should have introduced this course earlier in the program, socializing them into the culture of planning was a necessary condition for this course. The way that students were bringing a wide range of ideas to analyze spatial issues confirmed our ideas about disciplinary fragmentation as a means of controlling knowledge and ultimately social power.

Rethinking the Problematic

One of the most rewarding—and difficult—aspects of developing skills of argument is dissolving one's starting point and developing alternative problematics. As we have seen a concept is locked within a paradigm by a set of assumptions; if those assumptions are challenged the concept may be undermined. Planning concepts are created by the demands of problem solving but they can be reinterpreted with different assumptions. The inner city, for example, may be an important concept but it has little theoretical justification. As a vehicle for articulating ideas of race or the underclass it is given meaning by the state's attitude to containing and marginalizing certain groups (Gans 1990). Faced with similar class problems over the centuries—working-class degeneration, the "breeding" of the "dangerous classes" and fears of contagion—society has responded in different ways. Contemporary strategy includes physically and socially separating the "deserving" from the "undeserving" poor so as to legitimate differential degrees of citizenship. By illustrating how urban policy replaces these social issues with a rhetoric of the physical, we were able to introduce new concepts with a greater explanatory value than those used by planners. Some, such as the reproduction of labor or notions of ideology and legitimation, had great purchase with students for that very reason. We were therefore able to return to the initial argument, that the spatial problematic was often constructed by wider social and political concerns.

For a student who had been on placement with a housing association, the dissertation would start with the empirical work they had done there. If that work were written for that institution it might identify the changes needed to meet the aims of policy such as "more resources" or "better information." But the course gave them ideas for reconceptualizing the housing association movement. An institutional focus, for instance, could show how it reflected tensions in the state's management of class relations. Or a political economy approach could analyze the progression of ideas for coping with the political threat inherent in cities, in this case the threat represented by council housing and the part played by housing associations in marginalizing local government.

Alternatively, a student working in an inner-city voluntary organization could examine how the idea of the underclass provides a political discourse through which we think about society; how it shapes ideas about citizenship, state, and the individual's relationship to society. Debates about the city and urban crisis are therefore not essentially about cities, but construct daily life and contribute to socialization; as Beauregard (1993) reminds us, they articulate basic social anxieties. The student's task is to unravel the hidden dimensions and underlying causes behind the symptoms. In both these examples they are radically rethinking their initial starting point. Such intellectual movement was our criterion for success, a movement that could be seen, for example, by students' ability to critically locate their placement organization or by their redrafting of the dissertation to incorporate new concepts to aid understanding.

The Implications for Argument

A modern economy is held back by the repressive industrial relations characteristic of the previous century. Since so much education reproduces and reinforces those relations it is increasingly at odds with contemporary demands. To some commentators the economy demands more abstract, conceptual, and unconventional thinking to meet the uncertainty and competitive pressures of a global economy (Reich 1991). The development of reflexive skills and the ability to argue across paradigms may therefore be more suitable for a knowledge-based economy in which specific vocational skills are increasingly transitory.

Compared to professional courses, our graduates looked to root causes rather than the symptoms of urban decay. They had the skills to develop multiple levels of understanding which helped them cope with the frustrations of the job. Since the task of regulating development is so often one-sided our graduates at least knew why knocking their heads against a wall should give them a headache. Argument gives students freedom—not the freedom of modularized choices—but the confidence and intellectual autonomy to interrogate bodies of knowledge by choosing methods and concepts, to overcome academic fragmentation and thereby to reinterpret familiar landscapes and make abstract ideas real. Above all, it makes them aware of the wider implications of the ideas that are in daily use and unafraid to challenge the conventional wisdom. Argument, consequently, encourages the social change that makes for fundamental differences in the world. As A. J. P. Taylor puts it:

> Conformity may give you a quiet life; it may even bring you a University Chair. But all change in history, all advance, comes from the nonconformists. If there had been no trouble-makers, no Dissenters, we should still be living in caves. . . . A man may disagree with a particular line of British foreign policy, while still accepting its general assumptions. The Dissenter repudiates its aims, its methods, its principles. (quoted in Wrigley 1989, 112)

2

Rhetoric and Architecture

Peter Medway

I am going to be making a case about argument in architectural education. Why should any nonarchitect care? Why would most readers of this book want to know about argument in such a specific context? My claim, as you might expect, is that lessons of general value to teachers are to be gained from a pedagogy that is highly untypical of university disciplines. I propose not simply—indeed, not mainly—that schools of architecture produce an ability to argue, but that this ability stems from the essentially rhetorical nature of design. And I want to suggest that we should be thinking of argument in more inclusive terms, as a manifestation of a broader habit or ethic of *rationality*. Architecture (ideally, at any rate) embodies that ethic in its *nonverbal* practice—in design; and the frequent manifestations of verbal argument in the written and (mainly) spoken dialogue of the school of architecture are attempts to reflect and communicate a "reasoned judgment" whose primary mode of operation is tacit and unarticulated.

It may reassure readers to know that this insight has come as a surprise to me. I am primarily a "language person" who have spent a large part of my professional lifetime teaching English, studying the ways in which verbal dialogue, often argumentative, between students in secondary school can contribute to their understanding of school subjects, and arguing that "writing across the curriculum"—the writing that students are required to do in the course of learning things other than how to write—would be more effective if it were conceived of in dialogic terms, as one side of an exchange, often an argumentative one, with a real or imagined interlocutor (Martin et al. 1976[1]; Medway 1980; Torbe and Medway 1982; Martin 1984; Medway 1984). The beginnings of a new insight into the pedagogic fostering of argument came when I found myself spending time in secondary school and college Design and Technology workshops (reconstituted and intellectually beefed-up successors to the old crafts/industrial arts/"shop" classes), where students were more articulate in the defence of their design proposals than I had ever observed them in any mainstream academic class (Medway 1990, 1991). It was a natural progression to studying the role of language in one of the grown-up equivalents of those design courses, in a university school of architecture (Medway 1996, 1999).

So I approached architectural education, starting in 1991, with a primary interest in student-to-student and student-to-teacher argumentative dialogue around the devising of nonverbal physical solutions to a variety of human needs and desires. I have found plenty of that dialogue and have confirmed that many students learn to argue well (though in speech more than in writing) in schools of architecture. What I did not expect to discover was that learning to argue was dynamically interrelated with learning that architectural design is itself a rhetorical and even an argumentative process. In other words, *both* processes—architectural design and the verbal justification of design decisions—essentially involve learning to argue. Establishing that case here will require two moves: demonstrating that architecture is itself a rhetorical activity and defining the relationship of the verbal argumentative structure to that nonverbal activity. I will then be in a position, finally, to make the more speculative or philosophical suggestion (to do with our purposes rather than our methods) that we should, across higher education, be keeping our eye on the broader goal of rationality and reasoned judgment.

The Pedagogy of Schools of Architecture

The Ecole des Beaux Arts of nineteenth-century Paris placed the design *studio* at the core of the architecture curriculum, a tradition that has prevailed in most western countries ever since. Students learn architecture by designing (rather than from lectures and textbooks) and by discussing and defending their designs verbally in a dialogue with their own studio teacher and eventually, at the end of each major project, with a panel or "jury" of "critics," who include practitioners as well as academics (though many of the teachers are themselves also practising architects). These oral events are known as "critiques" ("crits") or "reviews." The ability to explain and justify a design is, of course, professionally valuable, in that architects need to persuade clients, committees, and public meetings of the merits of their work, a process that usually occurs orally (though competitions may call for written and graphical submissions in the first round).

But the professional relevance of the rhetorical skills of oral justification is not the main reason for the prominence of the crit or review in architectural education. Explanation, justification, and defence are valued primarily as contributing to *design* by promoting a metaconsciousness of the choices and decisions involved, which the student may in the first place have made without conscious deliberation or by default, without entertaining a range of alternatives or of implications. Although architectural educators do not say this in so many words, it seems to me, having analyzed a considerable amount of it, that architectural discourse (i.e., architects' ways of talking) embodies conscious and explicit knowledge of, and involves the naming of design moves, architectural elements and effects, grounds of evaluation, design processes, and so on (Medway 1999; Dias et al. 1999, chapter 5; Medway, forthcoming). Thus "translating" one's design efforts into a verbal account framed within the highly specialized discourse that architects use amongst themselves (and sometimes, it must be acknowledged, tactlessly among uncomprehending outsiders) involves *identifying* terms and expressions from the discourse that appropriately refer to what one has done—thereby invoking at the same time, whether one intends to or not, the set of alternative terms (on Jakobson's *paradigmatic* axis[2]) that the discourse makes available to occupy the same structural slot.

To be clear, then: the main rhetoric in which architecture students are involved is the rhetoric of the architecture itself. The verbal rhetoric and argumentation of the crits is a means of becoming more conscious of that primary rhetorical process. So I need now to address that process, though I will return at the end to the verbal discourse that sits on top of the design, and the acquisition of the skills of verbal argumentation.

Architecture as Rhetoric

Architects and students of architecture regularly talk as if buildings and structures speak. A student erecting a column made of logs in the university grounds said, "I don't want it to get to be like a one-liner, where it just becomes like a precarious condition and that's all it is." A one-liner is, of course, a type of utterance. Another student, speaking of two related parts of her construction, said, "They seem to speak of two different conditions," and "This speaks more of frame in space." A third was seeking "to create an object that is going to question its own objectivity." Built constructions, it seems, can *speak, say,* and *question.* Published critical writing often employs the same trope, speaking of buildings that employ a *language, announce* things, and are *read.*

Linguistic analogies for architecture are widespread and come in different forms; the oldest and most significant is based on rhetoric (Bell, forthcoming). The presence of rhetoric in architectural discourse was already evident in the Roman writer Vitruvius, and was revitalized with Renaissance discoveries of previously unknown ancient rhetorical texts (Vickers 1988, 341–2). Since the eighteenth century, however, rhetoric has acquired a bad name ("empty rhetoric") connoting dissembling and empty pomposity. In general, this way of thinking of rhetoric is based on ignorance, an ignorance that within modern architectural discourse is exemplified by Alison and Peter Smithson's 1973 book, *Without Rhetoric: An Architectural Aesthetic 1955–1972.*

The Smithsons were distinguished British architects (Peter Smithson still is[3]). Figures 1 and 2 show an example of their work.

Figure 2-1

Hunstanton School, Norfolk in 1954 (Smithson and Smithson 1982, 36)

Figure 2-2
Hunstanton School (Smithson 1997, 36)

The Smithsons disarmingly name the style that this school exemplifies "the New Brutalism:"

> What is new about the New Brutalism among *Movements* is that it finds its closest affinities not in a past architectural style, but in peasant dwelling forms, which have style and are stylish but were never modish: a poetry without rhetoric. We see architecture as a direct statement of a way of life and in the past ordinary, prosaic life has been most succinctly, economically, tersely expressed in the peasant farms and the impedimenta of Mediterranean rural life that le Corbusier had made respectable. (Smithson and Smithson 1973, 6)

We note immediately that rhetoric for the Smithsons means what is modish, indirect, and the opposite of succinct, economical, and terse. But at the same time, the terms "statement" and "expressed" leave us in no doubt that buildings are in the business of *saying.* In other words, what might be thought the most problematic and implausible leap is made without hesitation: to the assertion that buildings are not just structures that provide shelter and perform useful functions, but are *about* something other than themselves, such as a way of life; that they are in the business of *aboutness*—of reference, symbolization, or semiosis. Once that is admitted, the possibility of a quasi-rhetorical analysis becomes realistic. If you are in the business of *expressing* something through your work, and you are going about that business with any intention of exercising control and making choices consciously, then you are clearly engaging in a rhetoric-like process.

The decision to be terse and economical is a *rhetorical* decision; *style* that is meaningful conveys part of what you want to express and represents a semiotic choice. We might say that the Smithsons are adopting a decorum of terseness, one that appropriately evokes democratic modesty rather than ostentatious power. The Smithsons' real objection is not, in fact, to rhetoric but to the florid and hypocritical rhetorics embodied in so many nineteenth-century buildings. One reason why their buildings have been an inspiration is their deep understanding, in their bones if not their discourse, of the rhetorical nature of their work; it's only the term "rhetoric" that they have misunderstood. Numerous comments reveal how pervasively rhetorical the Smithsons' view actually is. For example, they illustrate a small Japanese storehouse (Figure 3) and comment on its "easily accessible . . . metaphors:"

> For example . . . how the roof is four times thicker at its edges than it needs to be to keep out the weather to indicate *roof* . . . how columns are made to seem to support when they do not do so to indicate *support* . . . how the two crossed gable poles celebrate the once teepee-like crossing of the rafters . . . how those barrel-like logs at Ise and Izumo are there to show that the roof will not be blown off by any typhoon of this world. (Smithson and Smithson 1973, 51)

Figure 2-3
Ise, small storehouse: photographed in 1960 by Peter Smithson
(Smithson and Smithson 1973, 51)

What those logs "show" is so statement-like that it can be formulated in a *that*-clause: "that the roof will not be blown off. . . ." Some architects today would say that this Japanese building is engaging in a work of rhetoric in so far as it doesn't just function but *expresses* its function, through the inclusion of architectural features that are not themselves determined by function. The building tells us about itself. And even in twentieth-century buildings, despite the modernist slogan, form rarely just follows function. The gap between them is the space of rhetoric.

Quite obviously, the presence of such allusive or referential devices contributes a great deal to our experience of the richness of a building. They give us a lot of reading to do. Encompassed in our experience is not just the phenomenal presence of materials and structures, but the semiotically evoked presence of other things, states, and processes. For example, that roof may bring rain to mind when it is not raining, demonstrating that buildings can evoke conditions that do not currently exist—hypothetical or possible conditions. And if buildings can do *that* rhetorically, they can do more, by evoking *imaginary* or *ideal* states. As Barry Bell (1996) points out, implicit in many great buildings is a *utopic* reference to a divine or ideal order, to heaven or a just society or a world of reason. Bell is an architect, teacher, researcher, and critic; his views of how architecture works have, as we shall see, direct implications for pedagogy in schools of architecture. It is to his explicitly rhetorical approach to architectural practice and criticism that I now turn.[4]

Bell's paper (1991) on the Ducal Palace at Urbino takes it for granted that architecture is in the business of "aboutness," of evoking a sense of something beyond its own stones, glass, and timber. The interest in this case is that the "reputation and wealth" of the Duke who ordered the building "were founded on selling violence" as "a successful mercenary soldier" ("the butcher of Volterra"); yet he was also known as an ideal Renaissance prince and humanist patron of the arts. It is clearly, then, an interesting question what his building will endeavor to convey about the nature of the rule exercised from within it over the inhabitants of Urbino. Bell's paper is concerned, in the face of some recent trends in architectural criticism, to emphasize the distinction between what the building *expresses* by its crude presence and what it seeks to present *rhetorically.* The building's *architectural* meaning—an accomplishment of rhetoric—is different from the meaning it derives simply from associated historical circumstances. In the following passage, the italics are mine, emphasizing the communicative function attributed to the building—its "aboutness:"

> In its simple existence the palace *demonstrates* authority. It is large, *expressing* the virtue of magnificence so crucial to Renaissance ideals of princely authority. It also houses a large court (five hundred mouths to feed according to a contemporary observer). Grandeur *demonstrates* personal authority, and generosity inspires awe. Yet beyond this simple existence the building's *expression* of power is a subtle and complex one. It *manifests* a spirit of negotiation and reconciliation, a model of contextual appropriateness, stitching itself into the city in a variety of intriguing ways. This *demonstrates* an idea of authority rather than brute force, supporting an elevated architectural vision rather than *expressing* power solely for its ends. A *symbolic transformation* results, developing from the circumstantial and actual to the intentional and propositional. (Bell 1999, 1)

Specifically, what manifests the "spirit of negotiation" is the manner in which the Palace's edge that separates it from the city (the other side faces a steep drop into the valley) accommodates itself to what is already there, fitting itself into available space and adjusting to local conditions rather than seeking to assert domination by the sort of show of "brute force" that we associate with, say, Norman castles. Note that the building "demonstrates an idea" in so far as the viewer's "reading" of the architectural presence "crosses over" from "circumstantial" interpretation of a phenomenon that indicates a cause (wealth and power) into a *symbolic* understanding of a potential, ideal, or aspirational order. Thus

> [i]t is possible that the building manifests a different society from its historical one, though brings them into a relationship for their mutual benefit. The

> question of the real and the ideal is taken into account: the actual society of the patron, and the propositional society of its architecture. (ibid.)

The ideal is most vividly expressed by a central court which "is perfect in its form and articulate in its language. . . . framing a geometric version of nature within an ideal of architectural expression" (2–3).

Proposition is an important—and unexpected—word in architectural discourse. The building *proposes* . . . What the term implies does not seem to be a quasi-linguistic *predication;* the proposition is less a sentence than a vision that is posited or advanced for contemplation. The effect sought is *belief*—though it is an experiential belief, an experience of some reality, rather than a conclusion drawn from argument.

Beyond whatever direct expression the Palace achieves by its simple presence as an expensive structure on a prime site, the building seems, in Bell's account, to address two essential aspects of rhetorical performance: *ethos* (character) and symbolic *proposition* (Aristotle's *proof*). Bell described in an interview the way in which these two Aristotelian elements, along with that of *pathos,* are applicable to architecture—and to architectural education:

> The emotion [*pathos*], which is the emotional predisposition of the audience, the character [*ethos*], which is the character of the speaker, and then the demonstration proper [*proof*], which is what the actual tenet or persuasion of the speech should be, or in our case of the building.

Pathos is thus equated with essential elements of the situation that are *given* to the orator/designer as preexisting constraints. It is *ethos* and *proof,* however, that are more relevant to the Urbino discussion. The building is a sort of argument, the arrangement of elements in support of a claim; the palace takes you through a sequence, presents you with a particular disposition of conditions, with the result that you draw a particular sort of conclusion from the overall effect and final experience: domestic, functional, and unassuming spaces, and then geometrical order and an idealized version of nature at the center. You experience a clear and special meaning set against more mundane and everyday significances; you gain perhaps a sense of some other criterion for managing one's affairs, other than opportunistic adaptation or the imposition of naked power. We can note in passing that the Smithsons, had they been more rhetorically informed, could easily have given an account of Hunstanton School in terms of an *ethos* of modest and workmanlike seriousness.

It is important to see Barry Bell's espousal of rhetoric as contextualized. It's a polemical position, a counterassertion to fashionable approaches both in architectural criticism and in architectural education. In criticism, the sort of approach to which I take it Bell is opposing his rhetorically informed analysis is represented by this extract from a review of a new art gallery in Barcelona, designed by Richard Meier Architects:

> At this point of arrival, which is articulated with a beautiful, simple curvilinear counter in white marble, it is also possible to see out into the *paseo* and across into the western wing of the museum and vice versa. From the entrance lobby, the abrupt rotation of movement from the rotunda, through the preliminary atrium is again breathtaking—with the prospect of the great linear attenuation of the ramp-hall ahead. As you go up the ramps, an ever-widening panorama of the surrounding medieval city is revealed. . . . The main circulation to the art galleries is in the form of a glass-lensed edge of the main structural floor, a threshold of light, that has to be crossed in order to access the art, in the north-facing, flexible exhibition halls. (Richards 1997, 40)

The writer seems to have some implicit sense of the building as "saying something" or having a symbolic dimension over and above a simple spectacular presence, but he presumably sees this aspect as too speculative or subjective or ineffable to discuss explicitly. The absence, however, of any treatment of the building's "proof" or idea seriously disables the critique, leaving the architectural features described to appear as essentially pointless or arbitrary apart from their inducement of wonder. So at the point of arrival "it is . . . possible to see out into the *paseo*." This is clearly implied to be a good thing—but why is it so? Is seeing *out* of a building—particularly an art gallery, the most obvious point of which is to focus attention on its contents—necessarily or always a good thing? If it's a good thing at this point, the reason presumably goes beyond the consideration that it's nice to have a view—and may well, we might speculate, to have to do with some *idea* about the relationship of the gallery and its contents to the city in which it is located. Similarly, is a "breathtaking" "rotation of movement" with a prospect *always* desirable? If not, why here? And, again, the "panorama of the surrounding medieval city"—to what end? Why is it a point for favorable comment that the viewer has to cross "a threshold of light" to get to the art? Might it not be argued that an imperceptible transition from life to art could be desirable? The *criteria* for these evaluations are missing; and the reason they are missing seems to be because they can only be explicated by taking seriously the building's *idea,* a notion the reviewer seems to find embarrassing.

Architectural Education as Rhetorical Education

In education, Barry Bell's position is against subjectivism and an irrational intuitionist view of design as a mysterious and deeply personal process. While the eventual effect and meaning of a building are neither fully stateable in verbal terms nor fully determinable by the architect, that doesn't mean that rational discussion of either is impossible or futile. Bell and his students are quite clear that "proposition" isn't meant literally: what's meant to be communicated architecturally can't simply be expressed verbally. People's interpretations of what is put in front of them, while never entirely predictable, are nevertheless to some extent so—enough for it to be realistic not to fall back on a hopeless relativism (with everybody seeing what they want in it) but to count on the consideration that the eye of the beholder is to a significant extent socially constructed. Reasonable and informed judgement about the *probable* effects of a building is possible and indeed essential.

> An architectural education, like proper professionalism, should be centered upon the development and practice of a reasoned educated judgement which is true to the discipline itself, in all its confusing breadth. Academic knowledge and technical skill are both crucial components in the foundation of this judgement, but only that. True judgement must be trained and tested in more fluid, chaotic and human settings—ones closer to the world where architecture finds itself; studio remains the best example. (Bell 1993)

It is very much in the spirit of *rhetorical* education to train students to cope with the fluid contingencies of human situations. Quintilian makes it clear that this ability is the most important of all for the orator:

> The practising orator, on his feet in a lawcourt, needs above all a clear grasp of the immediate situation, and lacking this, knowledge of the most elaborate rules is "a dumb science". . . . the ability that matters most is to be able to address the actual situation, with a readiness to abandon fixed ideas and prepared scripts according to the needs of the moment. (quoted in Vickers 1988, 41).

Rhetoric, including argumentation, was at the heart of classic humanist education. But it is worth recalling that it was there as one of the arts of *the practical,* as befitted the education of students whose destiny was to be not cloistered scholars but men of affairs: princes, governors, diplomats, and military leaders. Rhetoric was a training in the practical, a preparation for establishing and maintaining mastery in a world of complexity, indeterminacy and human unpredictability.

Verbal Argument and Design in the School of Architecture

Architectural education, at least in the view I have attempted to represent here, is primarily about producing designs, not verbal arguments. Buildings that lack a "proposition" or idea and that disregard the essential Aristotelian practical attention to situation (ethos and pathos) are ineffective (as is criticism that evades these issues). Yet students are *also* required to argue, in order to make apparent and justify the "logic" of the design—how the means are rationally adapted to the given circumstances and to an aim that may of its nature be hard to express in words.

It is important to be clear about the subtlety and indirectness of the relationship between the architectural proposition and the verbal discourse that seeks to represent and explain it. The student's verbal argument is not a *translation* or *transposition* of the building's argument or meaning. Indeed, as Barry Bell explained to his students, if words could adequately communicate what the building was seeking to express, there would be no point in the building. The student's central aim is often, therefore, and inevitably, conveyed in what sounds like vague and inarticulate language—"I'm dealing with the theme of enigma;" "I'm addressing the condition of the labyrinth." That inarticulacy of aim has simply to be accepted. Where rigor is required, however, is in expressing the rhetorical rationale of the design decisions that followed from the aim: "In order to do X I needed to establish Y;" "This element will appear to be more A if I juxtapose it with this radically contrastive feature B." The student is called on to display that "a reasoned educated judgment" lies behind the design. In articulating this judgment, the student in dialogue with expert architects inescapably engages with the specialized verbal discourse of architecture with its arrays of evaluations, distinctions, and categories, in such a way that this discourse, over the years of education, tends to become internalized as, eventually, integral to spontaneous design thinking.

Concluding Observations

I see at least three broader implications of the above account of rhetoric in architecture and rhetoric in education for architecture. The first is that argumentation is not the preserve solely of the verbal disciplines. Something that is at least analogous—a sequence or configuration of articulated elements that bring one to a "point" or "conclusion" and leave one with the conviction of the reality or truth of some state of affairs—is clearly at the core of architecture, as it probably is of dance, other forms of design, and other art forms (see, for instance, Raney 1997; Mitchell et al. 2000; Mitchell, forthcoming) However, the exigences of both teaching and learning architecture create the necessity for an accompanying verbal argumentation. Teachers need to know their students' thinking, and not just its results as manifested in drawings, so the students are constantly required to elaborate *why, with what considerations in mind, in anticipation of what effects, by the application of what general principle, why in this particular case, as an instance of what category of design move,* and so on. And at least on the evidence of the writing in their notebooks (Medway, forthcoming), which are not assessed or even seen by their teachers, some at least of the students come to think in those terms—as they need to, since internalizing what I have called the discourse of architecture is a large part of learning to think architecturally. It is *because* architecture is itself a sort of argument that argumentative verbalization is possible, useful, and necessary.

The second point to stress is that learning to argue in the school of architecture is very much a social business—much more nakedly so than in, say, geography. Crits can be quite vicious: critics have strong views about what should and should not be done in the name of architecture, and what counts as good work, and they don't hold back in giving voice to these views. The students on the other hand are defending their babies, the products of months of sweat, all-night sessions, angst, and exhaustion, artifacts that reflect, at least in some cases, principles about which the designer cares deeply. Learning to argue is learning to stand your ground; it is as much a training in what is still, in architecture, called "character" (a term that in contemporary life has given way to "personality:" White and Hunt 1999). It's a matter of courage and will as much as of ability to organize argumentative structures (the "dumb science"). In this sense, arguing is a highly *practical* business—a means of addressing a specific situation, opposing or neutralizing specific enemies and bringing specific potential allies alongside. It's akin to the quality that enables effective architects (those who get things built they way they want them) to face down a contractor who is messing them about or doing bad work.

The third implication is a question, whether we ought to think of "learning to argue" in broader terms. In specific contexts, ability to argue is undoubtedly what we need to promote: in academic essay writing, for example, in seminar discussion, in policy making, and in the formulation of legal judgments. But this ability should perhaps be seen as one manifestation of a more general virtue of *rationality,* which would show itself in such qualities as *reasonableness* in decisions about action and in dealings with people. Bell's "reasoned judgment" partakes of that spirit. And it might be salutary to remember that an ability to argue or reason in the absence of an ethic of reasonableness can all too easily give rise not to the rationality we associate with civilized conduct but to the inhuman "instrumental rationality" (lucid rationality about means in the absence of any ethics of ends) that according to Zygmunt Bauman (1989) characterized the planning of the extermination of the Jews in Nazi Europe, that according to Richard Ohmann (1976) led to the barbarities of the Pentagon Papers on the Vietnam War and that today characterizes neoliberal economic thinking.

Notes

1. I take the opportunity to place on record that although I am not listed as an author, I wrote the original version of a substantial amount of the text in this book.

2. Saussure's term was "associative," but "paradigmatic," used by later linguists including Jakobson (1987), is less ambiguous and goes better with Saussure's contrastive term, "syntagmatic." The syntagmatic axis is the linear arrangement of linguis-

tic items sequentially in a sentence; those linguistic items are selected from the repertoire (on the paradigmatic axis) of terms appropriate for that syntactical and semantic "slot."

3. For more on Hunstanton School and the Smithsons' work in general, see Smithson and Smithson 1982, and Smithson 1997.

4. I am grateful to Barry Bell for permission to quote his paper, for the insights I have gained from his chapter on rhetoric in architecture (Bell, in prep.) and for the many explanations of architectural issues that he has given me over eight years.

3

Blinded by the Enlightenment: Epistemological Constraints and Pedagogical Restraints in the Pursuit of "Critical" Thinking

Doug Sweet and Deborah Swanson

Introduction

Our argument follows in the wake of a broad and rippling educational turn toward pedagogy/curricula generically called "critical thinking" or the pursuit thereof. We find it interesting that such a mounting tide for what often gets called critical analysis would appear concomitantly with many universities' rather forced adjustment to a more multiple-cultured student population; institutional seams are bursting with so many different stories, so many different ways of telling, so many different ideologies. Combine this reality with what Isaiah Berlin has noted, that "the view that truth is one and undivided, and the same for all men everywhere at all times, . . . this view, in one form or another, is central to western thought" (1990, 53).

Given this transcendent ideal of a unified and constant "truth," accompanied by an equally unified and transparent concept of reason (logical "rules" that function with the universality of mathematics)—variety, dislocating diversity, or confusing multiplicity must completely disappear when subsumed in the process of teaching students how to "think." It's this erasure we wish to note in relation to critical thinking pedagogy, for as Berlin has noted, "No doctrine that has as its heart a monistic conception of the true . . . can allow variety as an independent value to be pursued for its own sake" (ibid., 57).

Underscoring Berlin's comments, we want to suggest that much current critical thinking pedagogy relies on a severely truncated conception of the suasive nature and use of rhetorical thought, and on a thoroughgoing commitment to Enlightenment epistemologies—all of which rest squarely on notions of argument as reasonableness made clear, and reason itself as essentially ahistorically transparent. Perhaps better put: we are going to explore, both practically and theoretically, how Enlightenment theories of knowledge—concepts of what counts for evidence, for truth—are essentially inert, visual, static, and bipolar. Such theories and the practices that reflect them presuppose what bell hooks calls "the false assumption that education is neutral, that there is some 'even' emotional ground we stand on that enables us to treat everyone dispassionately" (117); they presuppose that "fairness" is an attribute of the search for truth just as objectivity is its form; they presuppose an inherent prioritization of logic over rhetoric; they presuppose western metaphysical dualism as our never-shifting ground of being.

What will drive this discussion is a close analysis of a teacher's beliefs about and approach to critical thinking, and the writing his students produced. Speaking to such matters, our discussion will concentrate on this teacher's way of teaching critical thinking and on what happens when students try to engage in "argument" while operating with proscribed and legitimized rhetorical strategies that presuppose a bipolar approach to persuasion, arguing always either "pro" or "con," arguing from an Enlightenment epistemology of objectivity.

Though many might find this teacher's cries for "clear and distinct" language and "objective" thought to be almost humorous misunderstandings of the nature of symbol systems, a quick look through most department libraries will attest that college writing texts continue to proffer guidelines for teachers and students that base persuasive success on "constructing a well-developed central argument" (only one argument per writer will persuade) with "significant logical or persuasive evidence" (logic as "rules-based" and evidence as "objective"), all of which beg important epistemic questions.

We begin then, where our claims are perhaps most readily observable—a writing classroom devoted to developing critical thinking skills in college freshmen.

A Case Study of Learning to Think Critically

A freshman writing class is underway at Stanford University. The year is 1987, but it could be 1998 if our observation of some of our colleagues in our respective universities is at all representative. John Bale (pseudonym) is introducing his class to the thinking "tools" he believes are not only vital to their survival in college, but more importantly, to their ability to negotiate in a world filled with rationalizations, simplistic reasoning, and opinionated broadsides.

In short, John tells his students that his course is as much a class in social criticism as anything else. He warns them that, "rather than think about our beliefs and actions, most of us simply rationalize the conclusions we hold to others." Unfortunately, such rationalizations have "nothing to do with critical thinking, nothing to do with it at all [since] you've already made up your mind." Moreover, the conclusions we *start with* are rooted in the programming we receive from others, or in the unconscious decisions we have made in the course of living. He tells his students, "When you begin this process of critical thinking, . . . you discover that a lot of what you value, you value for a very simple reason: your parents valued it; your teachers valued it; your priest valued it" (transcript, 12/1/87, 338). At best, he says, our everyday thinking is simplistic, seeking only one argument to bolster our case: "Most cases that we make for most things are . . . one argument, one shot. . . . It's not necessarily a mistake to reason in that simple a way, but you can see it's very risky that the mind is set up to just find one argument to approach a situation that it knows it needs to make a decision on." This is a dramatic claim indeed that the mind, in "everyday thinking" is "set up" to find "one truth." Why are we satisfied with such undernourished thought? Because, John argues, we loathe cognitive dissonance, a natural consequence of looking at the complexity of issues. Instead, we're motivated by a desire for simplicity that in turn prompts us to settle for definite conclusions rather than truth.

> The problem is we can't live with ambiguity. We need answers but we need confidence too. We need simplicity. So the whole reasoning process, the process of critical thinking for most of us is a process of trying to escape cognitive dissonance. We're not going looking for truth—we're looking for simplicity. Now that's the wrong motive for doing your thinking.

But John believes he has an answer to such simplicity—students should examine "the other side" of their beliefs, opinions, values. John admits to his students that he did not always have such attitudes about critical thought.

> I actually came into the critical thinking stuff having spent a lot of time in religious philosophy and meditation. So I was sort of skeptical at one level about how valuable, how far you could go reasoning very carefully about things, how well you can put into words your real feelings about things. All I can say is that over time I'm less impressed with my intuition and my capacity for raw, gut feeling than I was a long time ago. With time, it seems to me most of my intuition is just kind of, what? a summation of my experiences and prejudices and not a particularly good source of knowledge. So I hammer away; I try to put [my intuitions] into words. If I don't have it in words, I'm a little suspicious of it. Sometimes I know there's something there, a belief, so I'm very suspicious about the reasoning that I've done about it.

Intuition is gut-raw, a "summation of experiences," and quite obviously intellectually suspect. A far better method of knowing, he states, is being objective, giving serious consideration to ideas and arguments that oppose his initial conclusions about a subject. To counter the simplistic thinking his students rely on, he wants them to create oppositional structures which are, quite clearly, binary constructs. Hoping his students will benefit from this insight, he tells them that they should not settle for their "first impressions" but rather make themselves "go through the work" of asking "Is that true? What can be said on the other side?"

Indeed, the central mechanism of critical thinking is questioning. At the outset of the term, John tells his students that

> objectivity has nothing to do with the conclusion you draw; it has to do with what you look at before you draw a conclusion and the fact that you look equally and intently on both sides. In fact, if you're predisposed towards one side, what you really have to do is look harder at the other side because your mind is not going to want to do that.

If a basic critical question is the triggering mechanism of critical thought, then arguments are the fundamental building blocks of a case. Technically, he defines the term "argument" as a "statement with at least two parts." The part of the argument that is being supported or backed up is called the "point" or "thesis" or "conclusion." The other part is the "reason" or "evidence" that answers the basic critical question being posed.

Individual arguments are clearly the workhorse of development in John's scheme of writing. He tells his students that the argument is the "key concept" they "absolutely need to know in order to see the structure of a piece of thinking;" they are the "Lincoln logs . . . out of which the whole thing is put together." Beyond this, if students are "to see the structure of what somebody's doing when they're trying to persuade, [they] have to be able to see the difference between the positive arguments [writers] are giving and the negative arguments they're responding to." John calls these negative arguments "arguments on the other side of the question" and their responses "counterarguments" or "responses to arguments on the other side of the question." He tells them that a case is not complete or solid unless it contains arguments and responses on both sides of an issue. If one fails to look at, and respond to, the opposing point of view, one's case is nothing more than a "broadside." (Figure 3-1, p. 44, illustrates this rhetorical scheme as John often illustrated it on the blackboard.)

What we find significant about this particular way of characterizing argument is its equational form, its balance. In the name of being "critical" John has authorized a method of thinking that values the abstraction of "fairness" by imposing the structure of Libra, the blind judge. As John later flatly tells his class: "To think critically about a subject, you don't need to know anything at all about it. You can ask your questions quite apart from understanding the concepts in the field" (transcript, 10/20/87, 10).

For John then, thinking critically is engaging in "pure," "impersonal," and "objective" inquiry. In general, when he discusses the connections between

Figure 3-1
Instructional Vocabulary and Representations of the Structure of Argumentative Texts

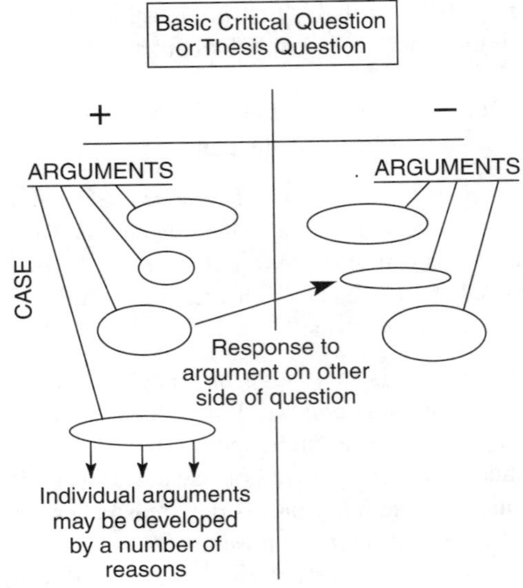

ideas, he typically speaks in abstract terms about arguments and counter-arguments, stressing the need for balanced and objective "structures"—a word he uses liberally throughout his lectures.

Although John states that he doesn't want students to adhere to an explicit structure, he nonetheless gives them a very definite structure to visualize and emulate, one that looks suspiciously like an either/or dichotomy, a dualism, a binary construct.

Balancing Acts

Given the classroom discourse we've just reviewed, and drawing from our own experience as teachers, we suggest that when students are schooled to think "critically" they invariably think they must be "objective," a process requiring them to faithfully "see both sides of something." When they write "on the one hand" we don't have long to wait before "but on the other hand" pops up to neutralize, to balance, to adjudicate. And we believe it's this concept of adjudication, Aristotle's forensic rhetorical form, that seems to have become "the" form for persuasion—taught by relying on bipolar modes: "the cause and effect essay" or "the comparison and contrast essay." Students attempt to create "balanced" arguments, as though argument, by nature, presupposed a leveling, an equilibrium, an evenhandedness. "A good argument is one that can address both the "pro" and the "con" of the issue" we read in text after text. Or, as John's critical thinking class is told, "a case involves two parts. It involves presenting arguments for the conclusion you're trying to persuade someone of. But it also involves responding to the negative arguments, the arguments that are on the other sides of the question." How clear it all seems.

Ramism and Place Logic

To better understand why John stresses the importance of structuring argumentative writing by balancing opposing concepts, we'd like to trace, very briefly, the manner in which classical rhetorical praxis has fallen victim to dualistic views of the world that separate object from subject, knowledge from power, rationality from ideology—worshipping the former as "proof" while denigrating the latter as "contamination".

Walter Ong devotes a considerable portion of his lengthy examination of Ramus to tracing the development, by way of Agricola, of "place logic"—a rephrasing (and reconceptualizing) of Aristotelian *topoi.*[1] And his estimation of Ramus' epistemology describes "building argument."

> Ramus had developed the habit of regarding everything, mental and physical, as composed of little corpuscular units, or "simples." Ramus thus tends to *view all intellectual operations* as a spatial grouping of a number of these corpuscles into a kind of cluster, or as a breaking down of clusters into their corpuscular units. (1958, 203) [our emphasis]

Or, as John's class is explicitly told, "Your task is to differentiate arguments. That's what we're really working on now—how to mentally separate arguments into separate compartments and deal with them one at a time."

Most students of rhetoric are familiar with Ramus' sweeping movement of divorcing "invention" and "arrangement" from the five canons (invention, arrangement, delivery, style, memory), determining these two canons to be matters of reasoning (through a spatial adding and subtracting) and therefore separate and distinct from rhetoric's preoccupation with "striking expression and delivery" (Ong 1958, 280). What we find essential to recognize, however, is that in this separation, not only has *logos* been severed from *ethos* and *pathos,* the very concept of *logos* has been reified into a taxonomic, binary schedule of oppositions which can be plotted, charted, recalled, and ultimately reasoned with (Figure 3-1 illustrates this dynamic clearly).

However, Ramus splits more than the canons, according to Ong. His system is a rhetoric which "has renounced any possibility of invention . . . [since] it protests in principle, if not in actuality, that invention is restricted to a dialectical world where there is no voice but only a kind of vision" (288). Simply put, what Ramus conceives of as "rationality" is demonstrably visible; he *holds* the idea because it is a clear and distinct "thing" which must be "weighed" against other ideas. What gets lost in Ramus' theorizations is the very concept of invention that Aristotle described. Instead, "seen as mere static, stock 'commonplaces', stylized sources for discussion on all kinds of subject-matter, topics have lost the vital, dynamic character given to them by Aristotle, a character extremely fruitful for intelligent, mature discussion of the innumerable significant problems which face man" (Grimaldi 1980, 116). Perhaps now we're getting somewhere. In the context of John's class, *pathos* and *ethos* get in the way of objectivity, and reason persuades precisely because it's free of personal agenda. John's students are told that they can best think critically and persuade effectively by treating their topics as two-sided, by making sure they always argue against themselves in the name of fairness.

We're trying to draw our point this way: Rhetoric—the analysis of persuasion—was drastically disfigured by Ramus-like separations of logic and language; furthermore, we see that subsequent Enlightenment theories separate "reason" and "words," maintaining, legitimating, and strengthening this dualism by clearing off ground for reason to stand as pristine, natural, and observable, while "words" serve generally only to further cloud already muddy waters. In this context, and in the context of John's teaching, being critical is to assume a disinterested stance. Students aren't being told they shouldn't have ideas; they're being told their ideas should always be balanced so as not to give indication of personal preference, which would invalidate their argument.

Undoubted Truths and Precise Language

In the language of John's class, if students must continually be cautioned to be "objective," then there must be an opposing concept of "subjective" which cannot enter into the decision-making process. John Locke's thinking demonstrates this reason/word or objective/subjective division when he "confesses" that

> in discourses where we seek rather pleasure and delight than information and improvement, such ornaments as are borrowed from them [rhetorical models] can scarce pass for faults. But yet if we would speak of things as they are, we must allow that all the art of rhetoric, besides order and clearness: all the artificial and figurative application of words eloquence hath invented, are for nothing else but to insinuate wrong ideas, move the passions, and thereby mislead the judgment: and so are perfect cheats. (1984, 3.10.34)

Certainly, Locke's view of the world is a divided one: truth exists one place—language describes it, if possible, somewhere else. He also describes the essential difference between what he terms "civil" and "philosophical" language, and it's not hard to see which he thinks rests on or refers to truth. The civil concerns communication of "thoughts and ideas by words, as may serve for the upholding of common conversation and commerce," while a "philosophical use of words may serve to convey the precise notion of things, and to express, in general proposition, certain and undoubted truths, which the mind may rest on" (1984, 3.9.3).

So language can "convey the precise notion of things" and can express "certain and undoubted truths." There we have it. Language has two uses, one obviously more acceptable than the other in Enlightenment circles and in the halls of the academy.

But what's at stake with this differentiation runs far deeper than just what one can do with words. What's at stake is a conception of thought that's based on a dualism, on a choice between two opposing possibilities. We shouldn't be surprised at all to see that rhetoric's faults, for Enlightenment thinkers, is that it relies on "artificial" language, language not "clear and distinct," language in which tropes can turn one's head from the truth that reason dictates.

To follow Enlightenment theories, then, is to fall back on the transparent quality of truth as our steadying, centering influence—reasonable language is such because its referent is clearly obvious, observable, "there"—reason is accessible "by nature" as long as we don't use language that smacks in any way of personal contamination, of attitude, of prior interest, of ideology. Or, in John's class, we might hear that critical analysis can only be persuasive when the student has successfully countered every idea with a somehow "equal" idea.

Aristotle Depersonalized

And now we've really come to the matter at hand for us. Classical rhetoric in the Aristotelian tradition acknowledges that humans are social beings, ideologically situated, and that persuading such creatures necessarily entails acknowledging that sociality, that ideological nature. Unfortunately, by the end of the Enlightenment, we find that humans have been subdivided into beings capable of rational understanding—capable of having knowledge of their world—while at the same time languishing in a nether world of emotions, biases, prejudices. The one world is played off against the other, leaving the rational side with all the elements of "proof," but strangely mute when it comes to the messiness of human motivation. Whether we're looking at an empiricist finding sense data or a rationalist finding thought, language can be used legitimately to persuade, according to these theories, only when it gets completely out of the way, when it loses all connection to "passions"—in short, when it doesn't "cheat." We see John's pedagogy firmly rooted in these epistemologies.

According to James Berlin (1996), "one of the supreme conquests of the Enlightenment has been to efface the unique work of language in carrying out the ideological projects of the new dominant group. This victory has been accomplished by denying the inevitable role of signification in affecting communication, insisting instead that signs can and must become neutral transmitters of externally verifiable truths—truths, that is, existing separate from language" (xvii). Certainly, in the class we've used as a model, this denial of the inevitable role of signification underwrites much of what the instructor tells his students about the nature of persuasion.

Fredric Jameson (1981) does a quick job, we think, of bringing us around to the intersection between what we've been talking about theoretically and the directives John actually uses to prompt his students' thinking and writing. When Jameson says that "even the most formalized kinds of literary or textual analysis carry a theoretical charge whose denial unmasks it as ideological", we nod approvingly. But when he offers that "the working theoretical framework or presuppositions of a given method are in general the ideology which that method seeks to perpetuate" (58), we begin to rub our hands together. Here we are! The ideology of our Enlightenment thinkers is that in rationality/empiricism there is no ideology—there is only truth. Truth is beyond ideology. And, strangely enough, these Enlightenment thinkers seem to say, "When you start to talk about truth, you have to be careful to use only that language which will work. That language is, of course, perfectly referential—word for thing, one-to-one correspondence. It has not been filtered or contaminated by having been used by any living being. It's found—much like the truth."

But how are we to know that language is, in Locke's sense, "philosophical" and therefore capable of conveying the "precise" notion of things? Aside from merely believing, won't we be forced to "prove" that it's beyond discussion?

We get the feeling that Ramus is smiling somewhere. The structuring of argument that John's class is being asked to adopt will supposedly be self-evident if students follow his procedural directives. Step one: dump in all data since evidence, example, logical fallacy-vetted point, if processed correctly, are neutral and objective, and if constructed correctly, provide an argument reflecting "both sides" of every key point. Ideally, if fairness and reasoned equanimity inform the enterprise of critical thinking, then we should be home free as writers give their readers clear points in a rationally oiled form. In such a scheme, what, other than a "persuasive" argument, could result?

Language as World View

We'd like to address one more fundamental point: when language is deliberately or inadvertently talked of as existing somehow separate from the beings who use it (as in Enlightenment theories), those who are doing this thinking allow us a quick insight into how they think their world is organized. As Jameson again points out,

> no working model of the functioning of language, the nature of communication or of the speech act, and the dynamics of formal and stylistic change is conceivable which does not imply a whole philosophy of history. (59)

If one's pedagogical model implies one's philosophy, then what particular philosophy have we been examining? What particular philosophy drives a rhetoric that has discredited moving an audience as being nothing but the application of an intellectual theorem? What particular philosophy tells us that the world is locked in a binary code?

Our contention, like that of many others, is that the Enlightenment model of language is woefully simplistic, assuming, as it must, that language is essentially identified or found in the world (if only the world of the mind)—and thus is an artifact of an ideologically neutral, severed subject "seeing" consciousness. We bring up this point because we think teachers, quite clearly, ought to be fearful of notions that accredit or demand that *un*ideological people, unsituated beings, can "critically" find objective arguments.

The Rhetoric of Students' Texts

With these theoretical implications in mind, we return now to John's class, and in particular to an example of writing done by a student which we believe illustrates the Enlightenment epistemology John inadvertently promotes in the name of critical thinking.

Only a few of John's students were able to closely approximate his rhetorical expectations on paper. They often provided only truncated accounts of their thinking while still appropriating the rhetorical elements valued by John. For example, a student named Jim (pseudonym) wrote on the topic of elitism in his hometown of Newport Beach, California. Near the end of his essay Jim writes,

> I'm making Newporters look like really terrible people because I've only shown negative points, but they really can be very nice people. Not all Newporters are elitists and not all of the kids are snobs, but I feel probably other residents would disagree, that enough are for elitism to be considered a problem. From what I have seen, the youth seem to be guiltier of elitism than the adults. I really don't know enough adults to make a good judgement on whether or not the majority of adults are elitist. I know that I consider myself and my parents to be elitists, but we try not to act like them. I can't really stop myself from thinking prejudicial and elitist thoughts, but I try to dismiss them as wrong and try not to act upon them. Youths tend to get caught up in the "I'm better than you" syndrome, and will change if they move away from home. My mother told me many times that she couldn't wait until I moved out of Newport, so I could grow out of my "snotty Newport" attitude and become a real, "down to earth" person.

In this essay, Jim seems to be engaged in a mental ping-pong game, bouncing from side to side on every issue he raises to demonstrate his objectivity, his willingness to look at both sides of the basic critical question he is supposedly asking about elitism in his home town. In the paragraphs preceding this one, he writes in absolutes: "In today's materialistic society, the possession of large quantities of money and material goods are seen as the goal of life and people in Newport have these things." And "Newporters consider themselves to be at the top of the world, everyone else is equal to or below them." As Jim approaches the end of his essay, he counters all of the prior arguments he has offered, signaling that these absolutes don't hold for all people—an illogical stance if he considered the meaning and not just the presentation of his ideas. But again, if he considered the meaning of his ideas, he might slip up and allow *ethos* or *pathos* to be persuasive elements in human interaction.

Jim's problematic logic carries him through a paragraph in which he makes the statement, "I consider myself and my parents to be elitists," then counters with: "but we try not to act like them." What does this concession say about the meaning of elitism? Is it real only in actions and not if it is a perspective one has? Jim neglects the conflict and potential issues he raises as he moves immediately to his next mental balancing act—"I can't really stop myself from thinking prejudicial and elitist thoughts, but I try to dismiss them as wrong and try not to act upon them." Here again, the relationship between an elitist state of mind and behaviors are juxtaposed but not addressed in any kind of analytic way. Clearly Jim is operating within the gap between his own voice and the voice sanctioned by the university, processing his own understanding of elitism according to a schemata of critical thinking John Bale endorses.

In addition to these larger rhetorical codes, Jim appropriates the syntactic forms, phrasing and qualifying terms that John has told his students are important signals of critical thought. At points, for example, Jim asks a question: "Could it be that because minorities are shown in so few television shows and movies that white children would consider them to be inferior or not important?" He then uses a phrase handed to him by his teacher, "From my experiences I have found that . . ." But the discussion ends with an unchecked generality: ". . . Newport Beach youth has negative stereotypes about all minorities." Many of Jim's sentences start with such qualifiers: "From what I have seen . . . ," "I really don't know enough . . .". Like the conceptual balancing act Jim engages in to signal that he has thought critically, these phrases signal his self-conscious awareness of his limitations to speak on the topic.

John has repeatedly told his students that they are limited in their experience and understanding and should signal these limitations if they are going to be honest. The problem is that in the hands of less-skilled writers and thinkers, such caveats enable them to dodge the thought called for by the questions they raise and the commonplaces they cite. Instead, they rest within the closed system of belief their own experiences dictate by speaking of the experiences as abstractions waiting to be attenuated, a system sanctioned by the discourse cues they use to speak with authority about their lack of authority. They've learned to speak about ideology while simultaneously assuring us they don't have any of their own, assuring us they're not tainted by anything that isn't always already "clear and distinct," soothing us with the affirmation that knowledge is "by nature" neutral, fair, and unopinionated. In such a disembodied venture, it's no wonder students see their world as "situations" waiting to happen, see their values as things they can hold, see their beliefs as commodities they possess. Students building arguments with these foundational premises seem to be producing texts which accomplish exactly the opposite of what John claimed his pedagogy would lead them to: instead of moving outside of their own biases and restricted visions, his students write entirely "within" those parameters, claiming an objectivity and reasonableness that essentially erases their own possibility for generative thought.

Reifying Argument / Erasing the Political

We want now to draw this discussion back to its inception. As teachers, we live in a rather swirling montage of writing truisms, pedagogical dogma, rhetorical modes. What we've attempted to do to this point is draw out the epistemological foundations for much so-called "argumentative" writing instruction. We see John Bale's class as fairly representative of the genre as it exists in the academy. At the outset of this analysis, we suggested that most department libraries would have plenty of texts that teach students to "view" argument as an essentially binary construct. We suggest readers verify this claim for themselves.

Our point here is simply to emphasize that "reason" in various forms seems to occupy the epistemological heart of many of the ways we talk about persuasion or argumentation and does so to the exclusion of any thought not purely logical or objective. As Kerry Walters (1994) has noted,

> If good thinking in fact is identical to logical thinking, then it follows that the best way to encourage better thinking in students is to train them in logical analysis: this is the conditional defended by received critical thinking theory and exemplified in its pedagogy. (10)

From this perspective, we argue that much of what then passes as discussion about persuasion is limited to the judicial form—forming judgment after the fact. In this manner, rhetoric seems condemned to be either so personal as to be submerged in subjectivity, unable to reach confidently beyond the self, or it is so luminously "clear" that it couldn't possibly be contaminated by any particular person; this separation seems fundamental to our discussion.

What we've wanted to do here was to suggest how the best-intentioned of teachers often reinforce epistemologies they'd be hard pressed to accept at face value—how the messages we give our students about argument are often predicated on a western metaphysical dualism that implicitly proscribes and delimits the kinds of thinking we accredit or accept as valid. From such positions, students effect their own erasure of the "political" from their thinking under the guise of being "critically" aware: they have, then, no access to matters "of consequence" to them except in a judging capacity, after the fact.

From such a position, we could hardly expect our students to take us seriously when we utter platitudes about empowering their thinking.

Note

1. For a detailed examination of "Class Logic in Space" see Ong, Book 3, Chapter 9.

4

Improving Argument by Parts

Mike Riddle

In this chapter I want to explore the viability of an approach to argumentation that addresses levels of completeness of argumentative structure found in written text. Using examples from students' writing and a three-part core model, I will show how argument can work in discourse either wholly or by parts. The student texts I shall examine have been used in workshops designed for academic teaching staff[1] (and also used with groups of advanced students).

The core model (see Figure 4-1), with its use of the everyday language terms SINCE, THEN, BECAUSE to express the three-part relationship within argument, is motivated by exigencies reflected in current pedagogical debates about argument. There is a need to meet the objections of disciplinary staff who find proliferation of argumentative terminology an unaffordable digression, or in principle obstructive to learning, or judge it to be too analytical and/or beyond the reach of their students. There is a matching need to reiterate the inescapable "connectedness" (Gage 1996) between argument's core elements, when the concept of argument is introduced into discussion in academic situations. From this flows the motivation to choose terms from language use which occurs naturally when discussing relations between parts of argument, such as *since, and so, therefore, because, if,* and *then.* It also seems reasonable to settle on three terms and stick to them, as icons of argument's core meanings[2] (Leech 1981), to provide conceptual stability in the model. Workshop feedback is showing that the adoption of SINCE, THEN, BECAUSE from (for example) their Toulminian equivalents, Grounds, Claim, and Warrant (Toulmin, Rieke, and Janik 1984), is paying off in terms of relative transparency, ease of assimilation, and benefit as an applied model.

The idea of showing how argument can work either wholly or by parts is a matter of facing up to the reality of argumentative situations. Parts of arguments that are self-evident aren't missed when they are dropped; underlying knowledge mutually shared fills the gaps. Such situations are the norm in academic communication between students and tutors, even with written assignments, where the disciplinary content and conventions of study come under severest scrutiny. It is this segment of academic communication that I want to focus on in the first three sections of the chapter, using the three forms of arguing (below) to test how the model works when applied to a familiar but not fully explored aspect of student arguing in text. The term 'Ø' below indicates a "missing" component (to be discussed later).

Arguing, using three parts,
consisting of: SINCE-THEN-BECAUSE, i.e., the core.

Arguing, using two parts,
consisting of: SINCE-THEN- Ø, i.e., the enthymeme.

Arguing, using one part,
consisting of: Ø THEN- Ø, i.e., unsupported assertion.

In the last section I will discuss briefly whether *knowledge of how* arguing works (as represented by the model) can transfer to contexts where levels of completeness are further reduced, and whether it can cross the boundary between (a) deriving argument *from* text and (b) improving the way writers insert argument *into* text.

The Three-Part Argument

Each text in this section illustrates a different strategy for completing the core structure, but together they are typical of the kind of argumentative writing that academic staff reward highly.

> ***Text 1.*** In the normal course of events we experience little difficulty with the question of personal identity over time. The commonplace answer is bodily identity. Although our physical appearance may alter during the course of our lives. . . . it is understood that there is a maturational continuity that identifies the adult with the infant in an uninterrupted progress through time. As the body occupies a spatio-temporal location, empirical individuation is a straightforward matter, for the body cannot occupy two places at the same time.

This is the first paragraph of an essay in answer to the question: IS THERE A SINGLE CRITERION THAT ESTABLISHES A PERSON'S IDENTITY OVER TIME? The student argues from the common person standpoint to assert that "The commonplace answer is bodily identity." The final three-clause sentence is a copybook illustration of the three-part argument. The three propositions can be set out according to the SINCE-THEN-BECAUSE model as below (Figure 4-1). Classical and Toulminian terms are added, and the writer's own connectives appear in square brackets:

Arg 1. SINCE [as] the body occupies a spatio-temporal location
premise 1 grounds
THEN empirical individuation is a straightforward matter
conclusion claim
BECAUSE [for] the body cannot occupy two places at the same time
premise 2 warrant

The writer's choice of connectives is instructive. They are normal substitutes for the logical operators used in the model, and share their semantic features: *as* (like SINCE) introduces "clauses of circumstance," which "express a fulfilled condition or a relation between a premise and a conclusion;" *for* (like BECAUSE) introduces a reason (warrant) which makes rational "what has been said previously" (Quirk and Greenbaum 1973). The formal lexical (and conceptual)[3] repetition across the three parts is characteristic of this style of arguing.

The next example is taken from an exam answer to the question: MUTUALITY OF KNOWLEDGE IN CONVERSATION DEPENDS ON "FAMILIARITY BETWEEN PARTICIPANTS" RATHER THAN ON "CONTEXT OF UTTERANCE."

Text 2. This knowledge becomes mutual once an interaction begins and participants have established what the other knows of their situation and the utterance. This appears to support the claim because the more participants know of each other, the more shared knowledge can become mutual, so that the speaker knows the hearer knows what he knows.

As with most essay titles, this one incorporates a claim, derived from academic positions contested in the disciplinary content of the course studied. The convention is that this particular position has to be addressed by the student with reference to other positions. The mark of a successful answer lies in the way in which the title's challenge is integrated into the essay and how counter-positions are taken up. In this, the third paragraph, the writer is stating the evidence and principle that can support the view expressed in the title. The evidence provides detail of the process of "familiarity" and the principle provides the reason why familiarity is relevant in the construction of "mutual knowledge." The integration of the claim in the title with the body of the text produces an argument of three parts, locking them together across a large span of text, as follows:

Arg. 2. SINCE this knowledge becomes mutual once an interaction begins and participants have established what the other knows of their situation and the utterance.
THEN mutuality of knowledge in conversation depends on "familiarity between participants" rather than on "context of utterance."

BECAUSE the more participants know of each other, the more shared knowledge can become mutual, so that the speaker knows the hearer knows what he knows.

The third text is taken from a coursework essay answering the question: WHAT WERE THE PRIMARY FACTORS UNDERLYING THE OVERSEAS EXPANSION OF SPAIN AND PORTUGAL IN THE 16TH AND 17TH CENTURIES? The student starts by listing popular explanations for European overseas expansion, with the intention of replacing them with expert explanations. He declares his strategy at the end of his first paragraph, where he writes: "What follows is an attempt to discover if any of the above claims [popular explanations] help to explain the process of overseas expansion . . . or if more fundamental factors underlay this process." By paragraph 7 he is able to set out his position on Portugal:

> *Text 3.* Portuguese expansion was the product of clear economic ambitions and necessity. The claims of innate curiosity [one of the popular explanations] are undermined by [a] control which was established over the sea lanes serving the East Indies. This control was achieved by naval might, and, more particularly, military might. The wealth extracted from the spice trade was not simply a fortuitous side effect of exploration. However, a trading relationship based solely on might meant it would only last as long as nobody mightier took control. Thus, Portuguese overseas expansion can be seen to have contained the seeds of its own downfall.

This writer is not content merely to provide the evidence that supports the claim about economic ambitions and necessity which counters the popular explanation of innate curiosity: this would have been sufficient to support his counterarguments. He goes on to reflect upon the link between power, trade relationships, and overseas expansion. He foreshadows his discussion of Spanish overseas expansion (in his paragraph 8) by invoking a principle that explains the transfer of leadership to Spain in matters of trade and expansion. Thus he neatly introduces his next topic and provides the reader with an argument that opens up wider historical perspectives.

> *Arg. 3* SINCE Portuguese expansion was achieved by naval might, and, more particularly, military might THEN Portuguese overseas expansion can be seen to have contained the seeds of its own downfall. BECAUSE A trading relationship based solely on might would only last as long as nobody mightier took control.

It is evident from the text examples above that, though sentence connectives like *as, because, thus,* and *for* occur at transitional points between propositions in argument, the writers do not need lexical links to indicate argumentative relations. Writers can deploy argument and readers can respond to it across wide spans of text irrespective of whether connectives are used or not. However, the use of the icons SINCE, THEN, and BECAUSE to represent explicitly

Figure 4-1
The "Since-Then-Because" Model

The icon **THEN** inherits from the link word ***then*** the *function* of introducing clauses of Consequence, Result, or Conclusion, following on from a circumstance.

It has "roughly the *meaning* 'on that condition' or 'in that event.'" Associated *concepts* are: conclusion, consequence, position arrived at or inferred.

The icon **SINCE** inherits from the link word ***since*** the *function* of introducing clauses of Circumstance "expressing a relation between a premise and a conclusion."

It has roughly the *meaning* of "seeing that" and "that being the case," as in "the weather having improved." Associated *concepts* are: the given circumstances, facts that are accepted or predicted, the data. e.g., "the weather having improved."

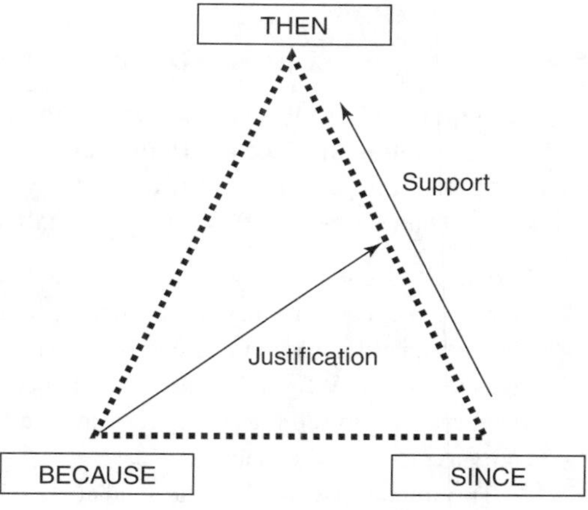

The icon **BECAUSE** inherits from the link word ***because*** the *function* of introducing clauses of Reason when they "concern not the events themselves, but the way a person interprets the events and acts upon [their] interpretation," as in "I thought you liked Peter, because you said how clever he was."

It has roughly the *meaning* of "for this reason." Associated *concepts* are: justification, making rational, legitimating an action, warranting.

Quotations are taken from Leech and Svartvik (1975) and Quirk and Greenbaum (1973, pass.).

the functions within core argumentation adds power[4] and consistency to the diagnosis of the particular kind of cognitive connectedness found in argumentative writing. The triangle shape (in Figure 4-1) is intended to symbolize the three-part interdependency between propositions and the centripetal force that locks them into one inseparable unity (in Figure 4-1). The direction of dependency is shown by the arrows of "support" and "justification."

In the examples studied only the copybook argument compresses the process into a juxtaposition of consecutive sentences. The energy generated by the lexical repetitiveness entailed could, over the span of text, be offset by an effect of torpidity, where it seems that the argument turns in on itself and goes nowhere. However, texts 2 and 3 demonstrate that a disjunctive structure can maintain impetus without loss of completeness. The coherence of argumentative structure allows it to work without all parts set out in sequence. In two-part and one-part "argument," as we shall see, the potential for completeness survives despite the "missing" parts. By virtue of this potential, argument works as an off-the-shelf device[5] for collaborative joined-up thinking (Riddle 1997), in normal exchanges between speaker/writer and audience, and most effectively where the substance of the discourse is shared.

The Two-Part Argument

Two-part arguing has the advantage of being more dynamic than the three-part argument, enabling the pace of argument to traverse large stretches of complex reasoning, without deviating into "taken-for-granted" principles, rules, beliefs, and so on. The text below illustrates this quality:

> *Text 4.* Secondly, television, apart from being a public service, is also a great volume industry that requires funding for its existence. Although in England competition for funding doesn't take place, due to different sources of revenue, both ITV and BBC need to compete for the audience's attention, whether this is to sell it to the advertising market or to show it to the public entity as proof of its efficiency.
>
> This implies having to provide audiences with a "better" product than the competition. In the case of news, this is translated into a race for the inclusion of "the latest" and the better documented, especially visually. These two attributes, though, are a source of internal tension, as they pull in divergent directions, since elaboration requires time, and actuality, especially these days, is often synonymous with immediacy, reducing the possibility of checking and rectifying the information in terms of balance and accuracy.

These two paragraphs are taken from a 3000-word coursework essay in response to the question: TELEVISION'S CONSUMING DEMAND FOR "VOICES" FOR VISUALS AND FOR THE IMPRESSION OF VERISIMILITUDE PUTS ITS QUEST FOR TRUTH PERMANENTLY AT RISK. DISCUSS WITH REFERENCE TO TV NEWS AND/OR OTHER AREAS OF FACTUAL INFORMATION. The writer is acting on the rhetorical principle established as long ago as Aristotle, as follows:

> In this kind of reasoning [the enthymeme] Aristotle says that the links in the chain must be few, for the listener will supply the missing premises that are common knowledge. Thus, Aristotle sees the enthymeme as the appropriate form of discourse when the speaker's concern is human affairs and when the writer's goal is to establish probability, not certainty. (Hairston 1986)

She is arguing towards a position that supports one of her major arguments, namely that, SINCE balance and accuracy is reduced, THEN to that extent "truth" is put "at risk," BECAUSE reduced balance and accuracy entail "truth" being "permanently" partial. Four two-part "arguments" can be derived from the text, as follows:

> ***Arg. 5.*** SINCE both ITV and the BBC are volume industries
> THEN they require funding (to survive).
>
> SINCE both ITV and the BBC have to "sell" themselves (to get their funding)
> THEN they have to compete with each other for the same audience.
>
> SINCE they have to compete successfully for the same audience (to get their funding [to survive])
> THEN each has to provide better products than the other.
>
> SINCE better products imply a race to present the latest and the best documented news
> BECAUSE elaboration requires duration and actuality requires immediacy
> THEN there is pull in divergent directions in TV news production.
>
> SINCE there is this internal tension (pull in divergent directions)
> THEN checking and rectifying news information for balance and accuracy is reduced.

The two-part "argument" is very much the norm in student writing. The reasons for this lie in the communicative situation assessors and students are participants in. In the assessment process, there is shared knowledge of subject material, shared disciplinary expectations, and, usually, a mutual acceptance of academic norms. Students assume that their assessors will know the theories underpinning relevant academic positions. In Text 4, for instance, these could be (a) the economics of the media, (b) the impact of audience preference, and (c) the conditions of TV production. Assessors reciprocate by supplying any "missing premises" needed to explicate the reasoning. Application of the model makes clear how dynamic forward movement in argument[6] draws readers into continuous "conversation" with writers who know how to adjust their argument to its context.

There are benefits for students in this conversational process. They can argue without constant reference to the principles, rules, and beliefs that inform and guide their arguments. They can presume that their assessors will infer their (students') understanding of disciplinary content and theory. Assessors too can exploit the process by gaining a sense of the epistemological "landscape" and internal dialectic of the writer's mind. However, there are disadvantages if it is forgotten that in this simulated conversation, students cannot, as in face-to-face conversations, be challenged to say what justification they have for their arguments. Freeman (1991) in his discussion of the "problematic notion of Warrant" notes that where argument is a written product readers cannot know whether arguers have engaged in dialectic with themselves and made their reasoning explicit to themselves (as a three-part structure). He is rather skeptical about our ability to work backwards from argument as product to reveal the dialectical process of argument construction:

> This [warrant] we must imaginatively reconstruct, to the best of our ability, from the evidence the argument itself provides. Will the argument as product give us unambiguous indications for reconstructing these questions? (Freeman 1991, 51)

Currie (1990) also warns about the disadvantages in reconstructing meaning in students' writing. Writing on the disparity between "initial grading" and the subsequent "more focused and detailed [research] interview," she notes that "The professor is accustomed to seeing arguments in a particular format." And adds that "because of his prior knowledge of the structure of an acceptable argument" he was able to read in the content that accorded with his expectations. I would add, from my point of view of improving the quality of argument, that the benefits and disadvantages lie more in the pedagogical uptake of the clarification that the model brings to the collaborative process that student and marker are involved in. What I would hope for is the reconstruction process being made a conscious part of marking, and the insights derived from it used to inform more explicit and well-articulated guidance for students on the organization of argument, and its expression in discourse.

The One-Part "Argument"

One-part "arguments" have a role to play in student writing because of the intrinsically disputatious nature of academic work. There are points in written assignments where potentially contentious positions have to be inserted into the discourse. Single statements are sufficient to achieve this. They invoke academic debates, rather in the way that single statements in ordinary everyday situations can provoke unsuspected challenge (Shotter 1995). Two places where I have noticed this happening are, firstly, where writers are setting out their stall, and secondly, when they are doing a summary of the relevant literature. In both cases the substance of the propositions is treated as an academic "given," which could be challenged, except that convention or commonsense allow some positions to stand unsupported yet unchallenged. Here follow two examples of writers setting out their stall (taken from the same essays as Text 2 and Text 3 above) and one example of a literature summary taken from an undergraduate dissertation:

> ***Text 5.*** A conversation is a conventional turn-taking structure that is used to affect the beliefs of others. Familiarity between participants is the degree to which each knows the other. . . . The context of utterance is the participants involved, and the time and setting of the utterance.

In Text 5 the writer sets out three definitions of key words in the essay title. Her strategy is to lay the foundation of the arguing to come. Each definition is an explanation of a term, *but also* a conclusion from previous debates in the relevant literature. For this reason the definitions are THEN propositions, the endpoints of arguments accepted as givens in the texts available to the student.[7] They are not at this stage open to challenge, the purpose of this essay being to assess the value of two positions tenable within current theories.

In Text 6 the writer starts with positions, not definitions.

> ***Text 6.*** The popular explanation for European expansion overseas is that it was the result of innate curiosity prompting the irresistible desire to embark on quests for exploration. This is generally supplemented by some more tangible aim such as the search for new fripperies to entertain the Royal court.

He is setting out popular explanations to be argued against. He uses the familiar rhetorical gambit of citing weaker explanations as points of departure for more rigorous academic examination. The structure he uses is a series of unattributed assertions of embedded explanations (THEN [THEN]). This enables him to insinuate evaluations of the explanations, thus setting the tone for the essay, in which a critical approach is expected, and weaker explanations made to concede to stronger ones.

In the next text this strategy of criticism and concession is applied to a short literature review. It is taken from a dissertation entitled A CASE STUDY IN COMMUNITY PLANNING AND URBAN VILLAGES. I am dispensing with the original text because it differs only slightly from the analysis set out below. I am adopting the terms THOUGH and HOWEVER to signify contrastive statuses in a strategy of concession. It is no coincidence that the word *however* occurs twice in the text.

> ***Text 7.*** THOUGH Nineteenth-century projects in social planning were criticized at the time for being unrealistic.
> HOWEVER [They] are now widely considered useful in proving the viability of planned communities.
>
> [THOUGH the previous sentences].
> HOWEVER However, there are various academics who believe that communities cannot be artificially created. They believe that communities can only be formed by natural processes originating from within.
>
> THOUGH The role of planners is theoretically intended to be unbiased and objective.
> HOWEVER However, it is highly probable that the planning process is susceptible to outside influences.
>
> SINCE Peter Ambrise claims that the state and the public are two main factors . . . having significant power to manipulate the planning industry and

SINCE theoretically the entire system is under the control of the State, central and local,
THEN therefore consideration must be given to the philosophies of the State, whose individual beliefs may be incorporated into planning policy.
[BECAUSE the ways of thinking and beliefs of those having power to influence events have to be taken into consideration in planning policy].

The evaluative tone running through the text originates from "voices" in the literature, sometimes hidden by passives, impersonal expressions, or generalities, as in "various academics." The effect of this is to create a series of one-part "arguments" with embedded parentheses, as for example, "Nineteenth-century projects in social planning are now (it is widely considered) useful in proving the viability of planned communities." This supercedes a previous opinion, "Nineteenth-century projects in social planning were (it was thought at the time) too unrealistic." As assessors watch the arguments being batted backwards and forwards, they are aware that evidence is not being cited for and against the impracticality of nineteenth-century planned projects, nor on planning versus natural processes in the development of communities, nor on objectivity versus bias in the attitude of planners. However, the retrospective survey of academic positions provides evidence of a fluid situation into which the writer can insert her view that there is a case to be argued for recognizing the roles of the state and the public in planning policy making. The course of the argumentation in this text (and less obviously in Texts 5 and 6) underlines the value of one-part "argument" as an economic means of preparing the ground for more elaborated arguing historically located in academic debate.

Speculations

To conclude, I want to speculate on the extension of the transfer potential of the model to contexts where levels of completeness are further reduced. To pursue this it might be useful to consider *incompleteness* as the significant entity that needs defining (see "zero" in Crystal 1985). This is because incompleteness of argumentative structure, though correct as a description of absence of the linguistic substance, has been shown to signal the presence of argument in the thinking of users. Language users habitually take account of missing parts of syntactic structure when communicating, because learning a language means learning how to interpret "zero." The question for the "reading in" of argument is how much zero expression of an argument is allowed to be read in, and what degree of linguistic substance has to be present in a text to trigger our "ability" to "imaginatively reconstruct" (Freeman 1991) some relevant but unexpressed argument. It seems that given the right context, very little is needed to bring this about. In the introductory sentences of the three student essays (above) we find such linguistic triggers as follows: "people hold strongly to the belief", "in the normal course of events," "the commonplace answer," and "the popular explanation . . . ." When placed in a rhetorical context familiar to academic writers, they evoke an argument that justifies the "straw-man" strategy referred to earlier. The reasoning might go as follows: SINCE there are unanalyzed opinions about, and BECAUSE a raison d'être of academia is to replace unanalyzed opinion with critical thinking, THEN I will show how critical thinking can be used to replace unanalyzed opinion. The existence of zero prompts us to ask whether transference of the model stops there? For instance, at election time (going on as I write) the act of not voting is often construed as "making a statement of some kind." Is the model robust enough to fill the gap with arguments that lead to that action?

The second issue I want to consider is whether knowledge of how argument works (as represented in the model) can transfer to the improvement of writing arguments in higher education. Though models have been shown to be useful in analyzing argument products, their application to argument processes remains problematic (Fulkerson 1996). The case of disciplinary writing makes the path of transfer more complicated, because unlike compositional writing it cannot draw on the motivation of personal commitment to the argument. Writing in academic contexts involves a social commitment to follow conventional ways of conducting discourse, additionally restricted for students in that they have to show that they *know how* to argue.

For many students, argument does not figure as *the* problem when they face up to their assignments. Information and its organization and expression are their main concerns. These concerns are often met by a cycle of ever more detailed knowledge-telling fixed-format models that transfer readily but superficially to student writing (Riddle 1998). Our concern, in our workshops and elsewhere, is to explore the transfer value of a model that represents a "deeper," more creative level of thinking. The *knowledge of how* to argue cannot be set out like an "Introduction Body Conclusion" sequence, so that the point in the writing process most suitable for its recall cannot be determined by the "what comes next" principle. What is likely to determine transfer effectiveness is the point at which it is recalled, its retrievability and flexibility in use. Matters of cognitive transfer lie beyond the scope of this chapter. However, certain features of the SINCE THEN BECAUSE model, when matched to transfer criteria (Singley and Anderson 1989) give it advantages over "labeled component" models. Further use of the model in workshop and other contexts will test its transfer potential and whether the advantages claimed for the model are justifiable.

Notes

1. The context of my research is the Leverhulme project "Improving the Quality of Argument in Higher Education." I welcome the project's emphasis on improvement and have initiated multidisciplinary staff development workshops as an effective way of implementing this aim. The contents of this chapter owe much to the helpful comments of colleagues who have attended them.

2. In his chapter on "Logic in Everyday Language," Leech introduces the concept logical operators to describe those words that contain both a logical and a content element. The logical element operates as a function within sentences (e.g., negation). The content element carries some generalized meaning (e.g., time). I am using this concept to denote elements (SINCE, THEN, BECAUSE) that function *between* sentences, and enlisting their hybrid function to capture their use as both link words between sentences and labels for generalized meanings (e.g., conclusion, justification). Leech says that logical operators "seem to have a semantic function within the language system itself" and "are defined in terms of their own rules." I suggest that SINCE, THEN, BECAUSE similarly derive restricted definitions from their functions within the argument system. Though they owe their selection to their occurrence in actual argumentative language, they should be kept separate from *since, then,* and *because,* words that enjoy a range of functions and meanings in discourse as a whole.

3. Exact repetition is a characteristic of textbook syllogisms. In the less formal environment of "new rhetoric" argument, it is sufficient that the conceptual connections can be verified by reference to the semantic features of the words used, as for example in Text 3, where "overseas expansion" has been shown (by the writer) to be referentially connected to "trading relationship." In Arg. 1, the semantic features "factual (spatio-temporal) observability", "corporeality," and "indivisibility" come together in the expression "empirical individuation" thus conceptually connecting the three sentences.

4. Leech (ibid.) draws attention to the function of logical operators in the language system: "these elements greatly increase the power of human thinking because they are instruments with which we can explicitly manipulate the categories and relationships of semantic content; . . . they are the controlling elements, as it were, of the semantic system."

5. In "Literacy through Written Argument in HE," I draw attention to research (Banks and Aphothlz 1995) that shows how we have all been building argumentative structure from a very early age. This argumentative competence develops in complexity and remains available for use as an intricate instrument of inquiry, explanation and debate. I question in this article whether so natural an ability has to become transmuted within the educational system into a semblance of its actual potential.

6. The occurrences of significant connectives in the essay as a whole confirm this impression: *since 8, thus 7, while 4, therefore 2, however 8, though 12, on the other hand 4.* Not all signal argumentative moves.

7. W. Downes (1984), who gives lucid accounts of the pioneering studies done by Schegloff (1968) and Sperber and Wilson (1982).

5

A Workable Balance: Self and Sources in Argumentative Writing

Nicholas Groom

Introduction

This chapter pursues a line of inquiry initiated two decades ago, in a now classic analysis of academic discourse by the rhetoric scholar Charles Bazerman (1981). Bazerman's paper proposes that every academic text brings together, and at the same time is shaped by, four distinct yet interrelated contexts: the object of study, the literature of the field, the author's self, and the anticipated audience. From this perspective, judgements about the success or failure of any academic text thus become judgements as to how successfully the writer has managed not only to meet the requirements of each of these contexts, but also to achieve what Bazerman calls "a workable balance" (363) among them. The purpose of this chapter is to explore the complex interrelationship between two of these four contexts—the literature of the field, and the author's self—in relation to the learning and teaching of argumentative writing in higher education. The chapter begins by identifying the particular kind of synthesis of self and sources that argumentative essay writing requires and then describes three common types of difficulty that many students have in achieving this synthesis. Finally, the chapter considers how we as tutors might help student writers of argument to become more adept at negotiating "workable balances" between their own voices and those of the canonical texts of their fields of study.

Balancing Self and Sources: Three Patterns of Difficulty in Student Writing

Understandings of what it means to study at university have been undergoing a radical transformation in recent years, in the wake of an ongoing (and increasingly technologically mediated) pluralization of modes and sites of teaching, learning, evaluation, and assessment. However, the traditional requirement for students to produce written work of various kinds remains, for now at least, a defining characteristic of tertiary study. For many students, then, learning to argue in higher education is still largely a matter of learning to write argumentative essays which will be read and assessed by expert audiences. And learning to write argumentative essays, I would suggest, is in no small measure a matter of learning to reconcile an apparently conflicting set of intellectual demands and possibilities. On the one hand, argumentative assignments provide students with an opportunity to develop, and eventually to display for evaluation, their knowledge and understanding of a given subject area, its canonical works and its key debates. At the same time, however, the defining characteristic of the argumentative essay is precisely that it requires students *to argue;* that is, to make "their own" claims, to make a contribution to current debates by adding their voices to the ongoing academic conversation, and in so doing to claim membership of the discourse communities into which they are being apprenticed (Bartholomae 1985; Berkenkotter and Huckin 1995; Creme and Lea 1997). My own institution's descriptor for A-grade written work at Masters' level, which is quoted in all students' course handbooks, neatly captures this paradox:

> GRADE A is awarded when candidates show evidence of extensive relevant reading and an outstanding grasp of current major issues in the field. This knowledge will have been reviewed critically with insight and independence of thought. Arguments and the presentation of evidence will demonstrate sophisticated reasoning and be exceptionally clear, well-focused and cogent.

The epistemological balancing act that this rubric describes is one that causes problems of various kinds for many students. Consider, by way of example, the following students' comments, taken from a series of insessional academic literacy workshops for students identified as having difficulties in producing work of an acceptable standard at postgraduate level:

> I don't know how to make my own voice clear in the essay.

> If the original author has said it so well already, how can I say it again in my own words?

> My tutor said that my essay was not critical—but I thought I *was* being critical in the essay.

> I find it difficult to be critical in my reading. I seem to agree with everyone I read, even though I recognize that the authors are saying different things.

> I always use "I think" or "In my opinion" when I want to express my point of view. I know this is too simple, but I don't know any other way to highlight my own ideas.

> For me, the big problem is writing argument. If I give my opinion, then the tutor says "where are your references?" But when I use other authors, then the tutor says "I know what X thinks already—what is *your* opinion?"

Of course, there are always dangers inherent in attempting to classify "types of writing problem;" in particular, such classifications overlook the fact that students' needs and difficulties are always situated within individual histories and trajectories and are therefore always contingent and changing (Scott 1994, 1999). Nevertheless, the generic character of argument does make it possible to identify a number of recurring themes in these comments, themes which emerge as recognizable patterns of difficulty in "at-risk" student writing. Here, I shall identify three such patterns, all clearly related to the "self and sources" paradox that forms the central concern of this chapter. I shall refer to the manifestations of these patterns in student writing as *textual voices* (cf. Dowling 1998). The first of these, which I shall call the *solipsistic* voice, takes the readily recognizable form of statements that present the student's own views and experiences without reference to readings in the field literature. Such statements tend to (mis)represent the writer as oblivious to the existence, or even the possibility, of previous work, other voices, or alternative positions. Writing which speaks with the solipsistic voice typically attracts feedback comments from tutors such as "Too partial and anecdotal," "Where is the evidence for any of this?" or "Provide arguments, not opinions."

Another characteristic of the solipsistic voice is that it often tends to be *unhedged* (Hyland 1994, 1996); that is, it often does not make appropriate use of language features which introduce contingency, doubt, or caution into a proposition. Hence, controversial claims are presented as matters of accepted fact, and the student writer is censured for making "Too many sweeping statements of advocacy and opinion." Consider the following sentence, taken from an essay by a Media Studies student:

> Identities, mainly shaped by television, are therefore becoming more and more transnational.

The clausal embedding of one proposition within another certainly makes this sentence hard to unpack. However, the central problem with this sentence, I would suggest, lies not so much in the grammar, or even in the propositions themselves, but in the fact that the academic audience will conventionally expect the student to acknowledge the status of these propositions as *arguable,* by providing some substantiating evidence, by citing recognized authorities, and/or by "hedging" them more fully, as in "Identities, shaped *in part* by television, *may therefore be* becoming more and more transnational." Indeed, the course tutor's extensive and painstaking marginal comments on this piece of work reflected a clear and constant concern with the writer's apparent solipsism: "Are you sure?" "How do you know?" "Another sweeping comment!" and so on. However, the essential point here is that the writer's solipsism *was* only apparent, that is, a textual (mis)representation; in discussion, the student turned out to be well aware of the main lines of debate around identity formation in media studies and in the social sciences more generally, and knew of literature in her field that could be cited as appropriate support for the above proposition. What she was not so aware of was the need to make this engagement with sources an explicit and major feature of her text, or of the need to textualize the more controversial of her claims more cautiously.

If the solipsistic voice is one that denies the existence of other authorial voices, the voice produced by the second pattern of difficulty to be identified here is one that appears to do the reverse; that is, to *deny its own subjectivity.* This voice manifests itself in essays, or sections of essays, which present a patchwork of summaries of other authors' views, usually strung together with simple descriptive or narrative links provided by the student writer. Such writing characteristically fails to make discernible claims of its own, but attempts to mediate arguments exclusively through the words of other authors. That is, where we might expect a claim from the writer herself or himself, we find instead statements such as

> According to Parsons, the growth of citizenship can be a measure of the modernization of society due to the fact that it is based on values of universalism and achievement.

Tutors' comments on such writing may focus directly on the matter in hand ("I know what X thinks already—what is *your* opinion?"), or may come in the form of more generalized remarks about an overall lack of "critical thinking" ("too much description, not enough analysis"). Formal and informal discussions with students themselves reveal a range of possible motivational factors. The student quoted earlier, who "thought [he] *was* being critical" in his writing, had thought that the act of selecting and then quoting or summarizing another author was itself a sufficiently "critical" and "analytical" act, and that his readers would recognize where he was speaking "through" quotations and summaries from source texts. Riddle (1996) usefully describes this as a confusion between *the presence of arguments* and *the activity of arguing.*) Other students cite a lack of confidence in their subject area ("I seem to agree with everyone") or in their own linguistic competencies ("How can I say it again in my own words?"), while still others cite a personal or cultural predisposition towards reticence or deference (cf. Moore 1997).

However, it is also possible that these difficulties may reflect an unfamiliarity with the set of conventions relating to the acknowledgement of sources in (western anglophone) academic texts. The complexities of these conventions have been particularly well elucidated in work by the textlinguist Angela Tadros on the *attribution* and *averral* of propositions in expository prose

(Tadros 1993, 1994). "Attribution" here refers to authorial distancing from a proposition, as in the following:

> According to Parsons, the growth of citizenship can be a measure of the modernization of society.

Here, another author has been identified as the "owner" of the proposition; the statement has been *attributed* to Parsons. Crucially, the act of attribution also removes the textual voice of the student writer from the scene altogether: the reporting clause is to be construed as neutral, giving us no indication in this case as to whether the writer endorses Parsons' view or not. However, this absence of authorial commitment is only a temporary state of affairs: attribution signals not the *denial* of the writer's voice, but only its *deferral.* That is, attribution sets up a kind of contract between writer and reader, wherein the writer must at some subsequent point in the text go on to establish her or his own attitude or position in relation to the attributed proposition. Tadros refers to this as *averral.* In the example above, for example, we assume that we will eventually find out whether the student writer agrees or disagrees with Parsons—or at least we will see why the writer has brought Parsons' proposition into his text at all. Students who do not aver, therefore, are in effect constructing what we may refer to as *unaverred* textual voices for themselves, and will therefore be accused of having offered no argument or critical analysis, or of failing to "answer the question" altogether.

The above discussion also hints at the third and final pattern of difficulty that I want to distinguish here, which, to borrow again from Tadros, I shall refer to as the *unattributed* textual voice. Simply put, the unattributed voice is one that avers propositions which western anglophone academic convention dictates should be attributed to other authorial voices. For example, a student who avers that

> The growth of citizenship can be a measure of the modernization of society

is, wittingly or unwittingly, inviting us to understand that this is his or her *own* idea, when in fact it has been taken from another source. The consequences of this particular misunderstanding or misuse of the attribution/averral system are both clear and serious; as Tadros (1993, 113) points out, students who "do not clearly signal when they have switched from expressing their own views to reporting or vice versa . . . may be accused of at best ambiguity and at worst plagiarism." (For a critical perspective on "plagiarism" see Pennycook 1997a).

Negotiating Workable Balances: Pedagogical Issues

So far, I have argued that the achievement of a workable balance between self and sources is a defining characteristic of successful argumentative writing in higher education, and that a failure to achieve or sustain this balance in a conventionally recognized and recognizable form may have serious and even disastrous consequences for the student writer. The question that arises here, then, is: how are we to help students who are encountering such difficulties? This question becomes all the more urgent if we consider the growing social and cultural diversity of the contemporary student body, a diversity which means that it is no longer possible to take a laissez-faire attitude towards academic literacy issues.

The traditional mode of help, of course, has been in the form of feedback comments, a number of instances of which have already been reproduced in this chapter. More recently this mode has been augmented by the development of criterion-referenced evaluation sheets, and by the introduction of explicit writing guidelines into course handbooks. Certainly, moves towards increasing explicitness in relation to the writing conventions of the academy are to be welcomed, at least insofar as they indicate an awareness of the increasing diversity of the student body as mentioned above. However, research and tutors' own experiences both suggest that these forms of academic literacy support tend to be of least benefit to precisely those students who are in the most urgent need of help (Hounsell 1987). This is because such advice tends to *tell* students that they must, or they have failed to, "construct an argument well supported by evidence," or "avoid plagiarism," when what struggling students are looking for is something that will *show* them what these things mean, how they work, and what they look like in and as text.

That universities have acknowledged the limited nature of these traditional forms of guidance and support is well attested by the growth over the last three decades or so of more formal modes of academic literacy provision of various kinds. This provision is sometimes integrated into mainstream courses of study (see, e.g., Krueger and Ryan 1993), although more frequently it tends to take place in separate programs under various labels (Writing Across the Curriculum, English for Academic Purposes, Freshman Composition, etc.). These programs tend to focus in the main on language issues, typically either within a study skills or "process writing" frame, or through a more textlinguistic focus on the written genres of the academy (e.g., research papers, critical reviews, etc.). Many of the published materials that have been produced by practitioners working on such programs contain valuable insights into the textualization of self and sources in argumentative writing, and describe language features which would appear to be of fundamental importance in helping students to move beyond the solipsistic, unaverred, and unattributed voices identified earlier. Popular coursebooks by Reid (1988) and Jordan (1992), for example, are typical in providing lists of "useful phrases" such as "According to X, . . . ," "A recent study by X shows that . . . ," "X has suggested . . . ," "It is generally accepted that . . . ," "In conclusion, we can say that . . . ," and so on. Another popular coursebook by Swales and Feak (1994) contains exercises on such features as reporting verbs (*claim, state, argue,* etc.) and evaluative adjectives in critical reviews (e.g., "flawed but interesting"), while Weissberg and Buker (1990) apply a similar form of analysis to such issues as citation patterns and their relationship to thematic focus and verb tense choices.

Interestingly, however, books such as these tend not to deal with "Argument" in an explicit or direct manner, but with "argument" as a conceptually undefined adjunct to other issues. The examples mentioned above, for example, are tied to discussions of specific text types, and have to be adapted and recontextualized to various degrees in order to make them relevant to a class dealing explicitly with the representation of self and sources in argument. This inability to come to grips with argument may possibly indicate a reluctance on the part of the language specialist to "get involved in content issues." It is equally likely, however, that approaches that place emphasis on the process of composing a term paper, or on the generic description of the explicit features of specific text types, ultimately offer little purchase on argument at a substantive level at all, given that "Argument" is not a text type, but a fundamental rhetorical mode that operates in and across various types of text. This is a point much better understood within social semiotic conceptions of genre, which construe genres as recurrent social situations in which texts are produced (Kress 1989, 1994; Cope and Kalantzis 1993), but is perhaps most clearly demonstrated in the work of the philosopher Steven Toulmin (Toulmin 1958; Toulmin et al. 1984), who conceptualizes argument as a relatively context-independent logical/rhetorical system of claims, grounds, warrants, and backings.

Indeed, recent and current research and pedagogy using a Toulmin-derived model of argument (e.g., Mitchell 1997; Riddle 1997, see also this volume) has crucially problematized the fundamental assumption of language-focused approaches, that argument can be taught and learned solely by the identification and analysis of a recognizable set of explicit textual features. For example, we cannot recognize whether the proposition,

> the world is all that is the case

is a claim, in Toulmin's terms, or whether it is acting as grounds for another claim, or whether it is an arguable proposition at all, merely by means of an analysis of its linguistic features. Instead, we need to know (1) that this is the first sentence of Ludwig Wittgenstein's *Tractatus Logico-Philosophicus;* (2) that the *Tractatus* participates in the particular social practice of philosophical discourse; and (3) that philosophical discourse, as a variant of academic discourse, construes argument as a form of situated logic which links propositions, evidence, and sources of authority in a complex and recursive rhetorical process. We also need, of course, to make use of our own general knowledge and experience of the world in assessing this proposition; and, if we are to engage with it in an essay, we also need to know something about its epistemological status, about the prestige of its author, and perhaps about the author's own subsequent rejection of the position taken in the book from which this sentence is taken, and so on.

The point is that, from this perspective, argument is a *cognitive* rather than a linguistic phenomenon, and it follows from this that teaching a putative set of "argumentative language features" is likely to be of no more than peripheral value, and at worst may even be counterproductive and misleading to students.

Instead, it is argued, what students need to be shown is an explicit model of argument as a logical and rhetorical process, which can reveal and explain its otherwise textually and contextually embedded operations.

These are certainly powerful arguments, and they echo my own growing perception of the limitations of the language-focused tradition that I have been working within as an academic writing tutor over the last decade or so. Indeed, I have found that the introduction of a Toulmin-derived model of argument into my own writing classes has helped my students to move towards a far deeper understanding of the activity of arguing than that offered by mere considerations of the surface features of texts or text types. However, this does not mean that we should therefore give up language-focused work altogether. On the contrary, the previous discussion of students' difficulties clearly indicates that language issues must remain a central plank of any academic literacy pedagogy focusing on argument. The issue of hedging, discussed earlier, amply demonstrates this. Compare, for example, the unhedged proposition

> There are two kinds of economic growth.

with just three of its many possible hedged reformulations:

> Economic growth can be divided into two kinds.
>
> Broadly speaking, economic growth falls into two main kinds.
>
> For the purposes of this essay, economic growth will be divided into two broad types.

There is no space here to discuss the lexicogrammatical differences between these sentences in detail, but it should already be abundantly clear that these reformulations draw on a complex and subtle system of resources, which "at-risk" student writers in particular need access to, and need to practice using, if they are to learn how to argue with *engaged,* as opposed to solipsistic, voices.

The same is true of the attribution and averral of propositions drawn from secondary sources. Consider, again, the statement that

> The growth of citizenship can be a measure of the modernization of society.

The student writer is perfectly entitled to claim this statement as his own, and as can be seen from the use of the modal construction "can be," he is aware of the need to signal its contestability. However, it will be recalled that the claim comes originally from elsewhere, a fact that needs acknowledgement (which will not only make the claim conform to "academic ethics," but will also indicate the writer's scholarship) through an explicit attribution:

> As Parsons points out, the growth of citizenship can be a measure of the modernization of society.

Classroom instruction also needs to engage here with the difference between this sentence and the unaverred "*Parsons argues that . . . .*" And if the epistemological difference between "As Parsons points out, . . ." and "Parsons argues" is not clear to many students (and it is not), how then are we to account for the difference between "Parsons *argues*" and "Parsons *shows*?" Again, there is not enough space to discuss the complexities on display here in full. However, work in systemic-functional and corpus linguistics is now making strong inroads into the analysis of these resources, and the interested reader is referred to this work (see, e.g., Hunston and Thompson 2000). What I have tried to do here is indicate some of the ways in which language-focused work on academic discourse can benefit from an engagement with cognitivist perspectives on argument and vice versa. However, and to close this discussion, I would like to suggest that the most important potential beneficiaries of such a multidimensional treatment of the relationship between self and sources in argumentative writing, or of argument in general, will not be ourselves as researchers or tutors, but will be our students.

Conclusion

In this chapter, I have argued that there is a clear relationship between the quality of written academic argument and the construction of a "workable balance" between the author's own voice and the voices of the literature of her or his field of study. I have also argued that the complex range of strategies and resources which constructs this balance of textual voices needs to be the focus of explicit pedagogical attention. One final question that arises here, however, concerns whether the explicit teaching of "dominant" academic conventions such as these is in some way "prescriptivist" and "assimilationist," and therefore politically and ethically questionable (Street 1995; Pennycook 1997b). This is a serious issue and deserves a fuller treatment than I can give it here. I shall simply suggest that the dangers of overt prescriptivism can be avoided, or at least mitigated, if academic literacy pedagogy is construed as a *dialogue* between the generic description and the critical deconstruction of the discursive practices of the academy (cf. Brown and Dowling 1998, 162–168). Such a dialogue is, I think, essential for any program or institution which aims to value and build on the social and cultural plurality of its learners (Kress 1994, 1995). Such a dialogue is also desirable inasmuch as it construes a "workable balance" of its own; a workable balance that is also an *ethical* balance, between the need to provide students with a clear account of available resources and existing constraints, and the need to show that these resources and constraints are not normative, but are socially and culturally located, open to challenge, and subject to change.

6

"I Don't Have to Argue My Design—the Visual Speaks for Itself": A Case Study of Mediated Activity in an Introductory Mechanical Engineering Course

Maureen Mathison

In recent years it has become more common to incorporate extended writing assignments into curricula across the university. To that end, we might find instructors in biology lecturing on how to write laboratory reports, just as we might find students in sociology conducting peer-reviews on their final drafts of a book review. Many students, however, find it confusing to enroll in composition courses and at the same time receive instruction in their own discipline about what counts as "good" writing. In their first-year composition courses, they are learning general rhetorical principles that they can apply to many writing situations. In their more specialized courses, they are learning the rhetorical conventions valued in their discipline. At times students find the general rhetorical principles and the rhetorical conventions of their disciplines in tension. They have difficulty in understanding how the two can be complementary rather than at odds.

In my recent work in the discipline of mechanical engineering, I have found that oftentimes students do not recognize the importance of written prose, primarily because of the emphasis on the teaching of the numerical and the visual in their more technically oriented classes. Writing is generally seen by such students as something that is done "over in the Humanities." While arguing is said to play a critical role in the engineering curriculum (and is often mentioned in the syllabus), students receive little or no instruction regarding its relevance and application to the work they will do as professionals. Thus while instructors often think of themselves as teaching argument, they are actually teaching content without the rhetorical strategies through which that content might be given significance. This chapter examines more fully how argument is situated in a technically oriented discipline. Specifically, I examine the teaching and learning of argument in a first-year mechanical engineering course at a public university in the western United States as students are introduced to some of the basic principles of communicating in their discipline, and as they interpret what it means to argue as an engineer.

Argument in Mechanical Engineering

Argument as it is taught in engineering classrooms is distinct from the traditional views of argument often taught in composition courses. In composition courses, what comes to mind when we think of argument is the supporting of claims with reasoned evidence. The discipline has generally adhered to Toulmin's model of "data, claim, and warrant" (1958, 97–99), teaching students that a good argument is one that asserts a claim based on logical reasons that are presented through language.

In engineering, or at least in mechanical engineering, what counts as "data, claim, and warrant" differs, as language is often not considered the primary mode of knowing. An engineer's way of knowing involves multiple symbol systems, some of which are verbal and some of which are numerical and visual. More often than not, they rely on the latter to make a claim persuasive; calculations and schematics often dominate their texts. In addition, the terms under which an argument is judged logical is generally not inferred but is often considered a priori through the knowledge that is applied at particular points in the text. Toulmin (1958) explains, for example, that in his *Philosophical Essay on Probabilities,* La Place draws explicit attention to this class of substantial-yet-conclusive arguments: "In the applications of mathematical analysis to physics," he says, " the results have all the certainty of facts." (137)

In such cases, the writer must contend with the very validity of the theory applied to a problem dealing with, for example, thermodynamics, or with the application of a calculation, such as Ohm's Law, in order to question or dispute the conclusions on which a claim related to them is based.

Many of the more technical disciplines operate out of this argument field, valuing the theoretical and its nonverbal forms of meaning-making as a method to persuade. It is important to examine argument in this context because many of the students who enroll in higher education composition courses are in fields of study that require they learn to argue through multiple means, emphasizing the numerical and visual over the verbal as the primary means of persuasion, without recognizing the importance of the verbal.

The perceived uses of these means of argument lead to different ends, one being more text-based and the other more product-based. In composition courses students learn to understand the rhetorical conventions associated with texts in their disciplines and to present information coherently and logically. The final product is emphasized in written form, whether it be a summary or a research report. In the more technical disciplines, such as mechanical engineering, the pedagogical goal is to teach students to employ the principles of science to technical problems and to solve them. The final outcome is often emphasized as, quite literally, a product or a prototype, a three-dimensional model of an object—a grease trap, ski apparatus designed for paraplegics, or even a device to improve upon cancer radiation treatment.

Working with students in the more technical disciplines can be frustrating for someone like myself whose own discipline tends to value the written over the numerical or visual. A curriculum that supports technical thinking is based on physics and mathematics, courses in which the written is generally considered after the fact. It is common for students to believe that writing is not integral to the design process (in which students conceptualize and build preliminary models of a mechanical device) but is ancillary. Students consider it redundant because after all, the visual itself embodies the underlying principles and illustrates their technical application. Resistance to the written can be heard in such phrases as "I don't have to argue my design—the visual speaks for itself."

Such comments point to what Bucciarelli (1996, 62) has termed the "object world," the conceptual modus operandi through which engineers design and construct products. According to Bucciarelli:

> . . . it is the fixation on the physics of a device that promotes the object as icon in the design process. . . . while different participants in design have different interests, different responsibilities, and different technical specialties, it is the object as they see and work with it that patterns their thought and practice. (4)

Many students learning to become engineers remain fixed on the device itself, ignoring the rich social processes by which its design is influenced. They focus on the inconsistencies and weaknesses of it at the expense of the actual communicative processes that help identify and correct them. Students in the technical disciplines often have a tendency to believe that if they just apply the right scientific principles and technical know-how, they can either create or improve upon a device. Ultimately what is at stake for them is a product that works, not a final research report that describes it.

Unfortunately this belief oversimplifies the everyday communicative conditions in which many engineers work. Mechanical engineering is a discipline that requires interaction among the many people who have a real interest in the

and need to tap into the right brain." He continued by saying that an articulate communicator in mechanical engineering would exhibit the following characteristics:

nonverbal
synthetic
concrete
analogic
nontemporal
nonrational
spatial
intuitive
holistic

Seemingly innocent, the list includes many words that are counter to the nature of writing—nonverbal (versus verbal), nontemporal (versus narrative), nonrational (versus logical), and intuitive (versus purposeful)—and negates the value of argument through the verbal. Students were being taught to reorient their perspectives in order to view the world from an engineer's lens, which drew more from the right brain than the left, the hemisphere of language.

After the third week of the course, the daily lectures were actually not lectures at all but exercises from the textbook that were completed during the class period, with the instructor explaining the particular concept under study. As the class sketched together, the instructor would elaborate the necessary skills to produce it, such as using a grid accurately or constructing appropriate line types for their unique significations. More importantly, students learned to read a pictorial in one form and construct the same object in another. They were becoming adept at translating, moving back and forth among the different views that would provide information about an object. The goal was to articulate a conceptual world through the visual.

The visual began taking on a life of its own, speaking for itself, as witnessed in the following phrases spoken by the instructor throughout the term:

- The dots *aren't part of the communication.*
- You need to *get your point across* and not be artists.
- I do this so people can *see what I'm talking about.*
- If you can *get the information across* in one view.
- People shouldn't have to *assume what we mean.*
- If you're going to learn how to *communicate efficiently,* to convey how something might look like, you have to learn some of the rules.
- You're gonna take a plane and *tell somebody about it.*
- On the back side [of a pictorial] the *same sort of behavior is going on.*

Students learned that they did not need to argue that the design was worth constructing, but rather that the design *must* speak for itself, must communicate its purpose and form. Communication then can best be summed up as it was presented in the lecture by the following statement:

> If there's some way to misinterpret something you've put on paper, they [machinists] will.

Ultimately the instructor was not teaching students about the design process but was providing them a common visual language that would bring a design to fruition as a tangible product. Drawing was about communicating the behavior of an existing device to another, in this case, the machinist. Said the instructor, "In the real world you can pick any view you want, project off of that and present it. If it's not presented accurately, the machinist is gonna want to know what you really want. Think about how it's [product] gonna be made and give the machinist enough information to show them what you want." In other words, it was assumed that students had a viable design and did not need to persuade anyone of their decisions along the way, nor did they need to persuade anyone of the quality of their product. Build a three-dimensional prototype, not an argument.

Students' Understanding of the Written

The survey responses showed that students overwhelmingly believed that the class was about the visual. They claimed that the course was, in the words of one student, ". . . mainly a training class. I have been taught the basics of drawing and communicating strictly through pictures and models. I have also been given a taste of what it is like to be an engineer—i.e., starting with an idea and drawing pictures, presenting the idea and finally constructing a product."

While all of the students who completed the survey emphasized the visual aspects of course content, only four mentioned that writing was part of the design process. That is not to say that students did not think about the role of written prose. It was after all incorporated into the curriculum at various points throughout the term, although it was never explicitly taught. Survey responses to the role of written prose in the design process were varied, as seen by the language students used to describe it. Below are categories of response with the number of student responses in parentheses (38 students responded to the survey but the numbers exceed that because some of them explained that writing played multiple roles). In descending order, writing is used in the design process to:

- Describe (8)
- Gain approval (7)
- Record information for the purpose of a trial (6)
- Revise a design (6)

- Inform (5)
- Understand (4)
- Present a finished product (4)
- Communicate at a distance (3)
- Visualize thinking (1)
- Organize ideas (1)
- Articulate information better (1)

If we examine the language students used to elaborate their responses, we see that most of them view written prose as ancillary, as something done once the design is determined and a potential product exists. Half of the students (nineteen) remarked that writing occurred after the design was decided. These students were apt to claim that it was for purposes of describing, gaining approval, or presenting a finished product. Fourteen of the students claimed it occurred throughout the design process. One student claimed that "writing is important at each stage to help present, remember goals and steps taken, to allow others to sit down and in their own time review your ideas." In this case, the design process becomes more manageable, and the design itself is thought of as something to be revised and improved upon. But the majority of the fourteen students still found written prose to be peripheral to the process remarking, for example, that "written reports must also be given to people in charge on a regular basis [to inform them of progress]." In cases such as this, the design was assumed and writing served to apprise parties involved in its development.

Four students said written prose played a role before the design was decided and after it was decided. These students thought it important to communicate with a client to determine customer needs and then again once the design was determined—to communicate back to the client, as well as to the company. Finally, one student claimed written prose was not important because engineers spent the majority of their time talking.

Incorporating Argument Into the Classroom

As an introduction to engineering practice, students in this classroom were presented with the charge of visually communicating, and more specifically, with communicating a product rather than a process. In this classroom, the product was already presupposed; it was not contested as it would have been in the professional world, where engineers routinely submit written arguments that attest to the quality of their product. These students did not have to engage in argument. In this case, they assumed their designs would result in a quality product, one whose features spoke for themselves. As a result the importance of written prose in the design process became subjugated to the visual. This attitude may have been subtly reinforced throughout the term as the instructor emphasized right-brain activities at the expense of left-brain ones. The idea of argument became associated with the visual rather than the verbal. Earlier I mentioned that engineers use various means to engage each other in thinking about and arguing for particular aspects or features of a design, yet in the classroom they were being trained to focus on only one. As a result their developing sense of what it means to be an engineer, to interact in and produce written documents for an engineering environment, was limited. An analysis of their writing showed, for example, that there was little difference among the different genres they were producing. A laboratory report closely resembled a proposal. They were not learning to differentiate among the various engineering genres and their social actions (Miller 1994).

Clearly, instructors are restricted in the experiences they can provide students about real-world engineering, particularly early on in their education. At the same time students are learning the content and conventions of the discipline, they are also applying them to engineering problems. In short, they are often placed in a dual position, that of student and practitioner (Burnett 1993; MacKay 1997). To expedite the process of transforming engineering students into engineers, however, instructors designing courses can be aware of some of the issues that emerged in this study.

Integrating the various symbol systems throughout the introductory design course might orient students differently toward written prose. I am not suggesting that mechanical engineering courses emphasize the verbal over the visual, but I am suggesting that it is every bit as integral as the visual. While a mechanical engineer's primary way of knowing is often through the visual, his or her communicating of that information to others is often through the written . . . and in the form of an argument. Visuals, like numbers, do not speak for themselves. They must be interpreted and made persuasive to others. Throughout the design process, students do this through e-mail, memos, progress reports, and most explicitly, through proposals. While the theoretical and the mathematical might be foregrounded in their reading of the visual, engineers embed their beliefs about what constitutes a technically sound device within written prose that is meant to be persuasive. From a rhetorical point of view, the theoretical, mathematical, visual, and verbal are interdependent. Each supports the meaning of the other and in the case of engineering, contributes to the overall process of the designing of a device.

If the rhetorical nature of engineering design were made explicit to students, they might begin to understand the mutual, ongoing relationships of the multiple symbol systems that come into play as a design evolves and is refined. Rather than viewing writing as an activity ancillary to the design process, they might see its centrality. As shown in this introductory course, the visual must speak for itself when the audience is the machinist and the process has become a product, ready to be built. But when the audience is not the machinist, and the concept is in progress, the design must be explicated so that aspects of it can be approved, contested, and ultimately, transformed. Engineering is as much about arguing for the technically sound, marketable product as it is about building it.

7

Context Cues Cognition: Writing, Rhetoric, and Legal Argumentation

Paul Maharg

Introduction

The contemporary rhetorical turn in law has developed a diverse and substantial literature, much of it concerned with the critique of law's culture. Stemming from older rhetorical traditions, and more recent seminal work on rhetoric such as Perelman and Olbrechts-Tyteca (1969) it now includes cognitive, sociolegal, semiotic, and sociolinguistic approaches and analyses. This body of research on law's rhetoric is complemented by a substantial corpus of research into the conditions under which communication takes place in the legal arena. Language in the courtroom, for instance, has for some time now been a rich seam for research, as has communications between lawyer and client, both oral and in writing (Alfieri 1990; Dinerstein 1990; Cunningham 1989, 1992; Felstiner and Sarat 1988, 1992; Margulies 1990). In legal education, too, there has been a remarkable growth in the quality and quantity of research on many aspects of the legal curriculum, much of it interdisciplinary (Maughan and Webb 1995, 1996; Le Brun and Johnstone 1994; Twining 1994). However, the extent to which this research is being used with students in legal curricula is uncertain.[1] Most legal curricula in the U.K. contain elements of instruction in writing and argument skills; and in the absence of data on the subject it is rash to generalize. But it would probably be true to say that this research is used most often in specialist clinical legal courses, and that much of it has yet to filter down to any great extent into undergraduate pedagogy, particularly in what might be regarded as the core areas of legal writing and argument.[2] This chapter describes the attempt to take a rhetorical and interdisciplinary approach to writing and argument in the teaching and learning of law. I shall discuss some of the cognitive and contextual issues arising from the integration of rhetoric and argumentation within a law syllabus at Glasgow Caledonian University; illustrate how these issues were dealt with in practice, and draw some conclusions as to the use of rhetorical strategies in the teaching of legal argument.

Some of these issues are generic to the teaching and learning of argument, and are well documented in the literature (Galbraith and Rijlaarsdam 1999). Often they crystallize in the form of apparent aporias: self-expression versus paradigmatic forms of writing and argument (Elbow 1981; Bartholomae 1985); the private domain of the writer versus the disciplined community of readers (Bartholomae 1995a, Bartholomae et al. 1995b; Fish 1989; Bizzell 1982; Goodrich 1986; Kress and Threadgold 1988; Kress 1989; Bazerman and Paradis 1991); process of writing versus product of argument (Scardamalia and Bereiter 1982; Flower and Hayes 1981; Jackson 1995); generic theory of argumentation versus specific and discipline-based implementations in educational and professional practice (Toulmin 1958; Fulkerson 1996a; Fairbanks 1993; Achtenberg 1975; Gale 1980; Boyer 1988; Cox and Ray 1990; Neumann 1990).

All these issues bear directly on the student experience of learning particular forms of argument and writing within a professional discipline. The claim of each item within the contrasting pairs above is a valid one, but each item requires to be balanced not only within its own dyad, but within the dialogue of other dyads, other issues, and many other competing claims to priority within the curriculum and within the profession. In this respect, the resolution of each pair involves a consideration of all: if educational interventions into argument and writing are to be effective, they require integrative strategies which are underpinned by researched and appropriate educational theory, and designed for local programs of study. The literature of curriculum design and cognitive research supports such an approach. Flower and Hayes (1989, 283), for example, join their voices to those of many educationalists such as Eraut (1994) and Barnett (1994) when, with reference to cognitive research into writing, they call for

> a far more integrated theoretical vision which can explain how context cues cognition, which in turn mediates and interprets the particular world that context provides. What we don't know is how cognition and context do in fact interact, in specific but significant situations. We have little precise understanding of how these "different processes" feed on one another.

Genre Research and Learning and Teaching in a Law Syllabus: A Case Study

Glasgow Caledonian University's department of Law and Public Administration hosts two programs of legal study: a B.A. in Law with Administrative Studies, and an undergraduate diploma in Legal Studies. The diploma program entitles students, after a period of traineeship, to practice as a licensed conveyancer or executor in banks, estate agencies (that is, real estate offices), and the like. The typical diploma year group is composed of students in their late teens and mature students, in a ratio of approximately three to one. Students who entered their first year were given a four-day induction course that was discipline-specific in content. It aimed to introduce students to the university and its ways—the social scene, practical advice, ice-breaking activities—and introduced students to legal research and discipline-specific study skills. In their first semester, students took an introductory module designed by me (Legal Skills 1), which aimed to develop students' legal reading, argument, and writing skills.

The Legal Skills module was structured around three units: legal reading, writing, and research. In the reading and writing units a multidisciplinary approach was taken, in which research drawn from rhetorical analysis, genre theory, cognitive, and discourse strategies was applied to legal texts and argument. Students were taught not just to describe the internal and external elements of any argument, but to "'take into account the dialogic principles and methods used to realize a particular genre in the specific situational context'" (Paltridge 1997, 21 quoting Guenthner and Knoblauch 1995, 12). In their own writing in particular, the idea of what one might call "persuasive eloquence" was emphasized, namely that, for any discourse community, there is a persuasive or appropriate body of writing forms and argumentational rules that the writer must be aware of and learn to use in appropriate contexts. In this sense, an important theme in the module was what Lea and Street (1998) call the "academic socialization" model, in which genres are identified, analyzed, reconstructed, and where disciplinary terminology is explored and defined.

Students were inducted into forms of legal argumentation *via* analysis of examples of argumentation in legal texts.[3] In workshops, activities were used to help students construct situational models of the discourse genres they were required to read (case reports and statutes, for example), and those they were expected to produce (seminar papers, problem-solving, and discursive essays). They created these situational models by identifying the rhetorical markers of textual representations of law. This approach led to productive meaning-negotiation discussions in which they began to construct the sense of what it is to have genre expertise. This metacognitive sense of genre was important, for as Zwaan points out, genre expectations "influence the way texts are processed and represented in memory, independent of textual characteristics" (Zwaan 1994, 930). Indeed, as Zwaan claims, "[t]he general notion of 'interpretation' can be specified as a strong situation model, a representation in memory that will tend to dominate incoming information" (ibid., 921).

When learning to read the structure of case reports, for example, it is crucial not only that students learn consciously to recognize the structure of a report but also that they are aware of the complex sets of reading skills they bring to bear on it. A case report is, to a new reader, a confusing mixture of legal exposition and argument, as well as a narrative of facts and incidents. The catchwords at the start of a case summarize the legal points at issue, the headnote provides an abbreviated narrative of relevant points of fact and law, while in the judgements, narrative and argument are frequently juxtaposed. In introductory legal textbooks the difference between *fact* and *law* in cases is analyzed and illustrated, and students are told they ought to practise separating factual and legal issues as a case report-reading skill. However, while this is an important analytical skill in law, it does little to help first-year students read case reports. Really, the problem for students lies not in the formal characteristics of the case report genre but in their understanding of the relationships between these characteristics. As Kress has pointed out, narrative and argument are two quite different modes of communication:

> Narrative . . . is a form whose fundamental characteristic is to produce closure; argument is the form whose fundamental characteristic is to produce difference and hence openness. (Kress 1989, 12, quoted in Baynham 1995, 36)

Students are often baffled by the frequent switch from one mode to another in a case, and by the complexity of the relationship between the two forms, particularly as they seldom have encountered this particular "mixed" genre before in their academic reading. Much of the problem of understanding the genre lies in the fact that, as Einstein, McDaniel, and other researchers into reading processes have pointed out, expository texts stimulate item-specific processing, while narrative texts stimulate relational processing (McDaniel et al. 1986; Einstein et al. 1990). If, however, relational processing is applied to exposition, then readers find it more difficult to organize textual meaning.

The following extract from the headnote of a nineteenth-century case is an example of the difficulties facing students in this regard.

No. 84 - - - - - - Feb. 2, 1872. Wilson v. Dykes	ARCHIBALD WILSON, Complainer.—*Watson—Lang.* JAMES ALSTON DYKES, Respondent.—*Sol. Gen. Clark—Balfour.* *Property—Occupatio—Wild Animals —Summary Conviction.*—A conviction under a summary complaint, charging the theft from a public road of a pheasant, the property or in the lawful possession of A B, but not specifying how it was his property or in his possession, *suspended,* the Court holding that, where theft of an animal *feræ naturæ* is charged, the complaint must specify how the animal became property.
High Court of Justiciary. Justiciary Clerk	This was a suspension of a conviction obtained before one of the Sheriff-substitutes of Lanarkshire (Spens) at Hamilton, on 12th December 1871, by which Archibald Wilson, a miner, was sentenced to twenty-four hours' imprisonment for the alleged theft of a pheasant which had been picked up on the high road between Bothwell and Hamilton by Wilson, as he was returning from his work.

> The complaint against Wilson set forth that he had been guilty of the crime of theft on the date mentioned, in so far that he had, on the turnpike road between Hamilton and Bothwell, wickedly and feloniously stolen, and theftuously taken away, a dead pheasant, or a pheasant totally disabled by shot, the same being the property or in the lawful possession of His Grace the Duke of Hamilton and Brandon. The Sheriff-substitute, in respect of the judicial confession of the accused, found him guilty and sentenced him to be imprisoned for twenty-four hours. [. . .][4]

This brief and fairly typical extract presents considerable difficulties for twenty-first-century first-year law students. In addition to different font sizes and marginal notes students have to cope with lengthy, often periodic syntax, Latin terms of art and latinate diction, and specialized lexis, some of which is largely irrelevant to a student's reading of the case ("Sheriff-substitute," or the names of the advocate and solicitor representing parties in the title of the case), or some of which is crucial to the outcome of the case ("*theftuously* taken away," [my emphasis]). There is the apparent prolixity of the account, which is given in four different versions in this short extract: first the italicized catchwords, summarizing the legal points at issue; next the single-sentence expansion of this, followed by a one paragraph summary of the facts of the case; and finally a résumé of the details of this account, dovetailing fact and law. For a student, one of the main difficulties is maintaining a sense of reading purpose in the apparent confusion of expository and narrative styles and the processing conflicts stimulated by these styles. This continues into the body of the case where judges' judgements often intermingle case facts with legal points.

Several activities were used to familiarize students with this difficult form. The concept of audience was explored: Who was this written for? What could we say about what the reader expected to read about in the case report? Having defined this, a useful genre comparison for students was with newspaper news articles, a text type which, in its introductory paragraphs at least, often adopts a similarly circling style of structure. We explored why this form of introduction was adopted in both sets of writing. Readers also practised identifying legal terms of art important to the case from relatively unimportant ones.

Above all, students practised separating narrative from expository passages. They read photocopies of cases and, using two colors of marker pens, marked up the margins according to the status of the narratives, then compared these to my version. Other activities included think-aloud protocols in which the purpose was not only to identify and define informational features in the text but also to help them identify the different forms of reading they brought to bear on the text. Once they could do this, they were given cloze procedure activities: they read case reports which had the catchwords or the headnote stripped out, so that they had to supply these once they had read the judgements and other materials. To do this, they needed to apply their understanding of the functions of catchwords and headnotes, and the terms of art which report writers use when compiling headnotes from legal judgements, as well as applying skills of reading narrative and expository argument in the case in order to reconstruct these missing parts. While no specific data on reading improvement *per se* was collected, feedback from students confirmed that these approaches helped them to read cases more effectively.[5] Through this and similar activities, particularly on topics of precedent and *ratio decidendi,* students come to a realization of what de Beaugrande and Dressler (1981) have rightly termed the intertextuality of legal cases.

The same approach was taken to the reading of legislation. After introductory classes on statutory writing, which drew not only on well-established texts on legal argumentation such as Twining and Miers (1991) and others, but on genre theorists such as Bhatia (1987, 1993), Bhatia and Swales (1983), and Swales (1990), students were given drafting activities. Thus, after reading Gunnarsson's three types of legislative rules (action, stipulation, and definition rules) they were asked to draft private members' bills on given situations (Gunnarsson 1984). For example, in small groups they were given a scenario in which use of longbows had become popular as a sport, but which was endangering public safety. They were asked to draft a Bill: what would they do to alleviate the situation, and how would they draft the Bill? They then compared their versions to each other's work, and to a real Act of Parliament arising from a similar situation, namely the Crossbows Act, 1987. From this comparison arose issues concerning the invisible rules of reading which are implicit in the structure of the genre, forms of language used in statutes, the points at which deliberate ambiguity is used by draughters, and points at which clarity is paramount, the status of definition, and the language of command and description—in short, the critical features of the argument of a statute.

In the writing skills unit genre analysis was similarly used to identify the structure and audience expectations of academic legal essays. The heuristic of the "writing conference" was employed to enable students to think critically about the argumentative tasks that were set for them. Coursework consisted of two 1,000-word essays, the first being the subject of miniconferences and unassessed, the second being the more formal and assessed task. The point of these conferences was not to discuss essays generally with students, for this discussion could take place to an extent in tutorials where reference was also made to the writing tasks required of students in their other, concurrent modules. Rather, the purpose was to facilitate argumentative structures by helping students, in the words of Scardamalia and Bereiter, to "internalize" these structures. This was done by scaffolding the student's own modelling of the structure:

> A more readily internalizable form [than dialogue] might be the "assisted monologue" . . . where the talking is primarily done by the student, with the teacher inserting prompts rather than conversational turns. (Scardamalia and Bereiter 1986, 797–8, quoted in Matsuhashi 1987, 62)[6]

The argumentational models they structured and the writing heuristics they experimented with in their first essay and which were analyzed in the conference could then be used in the second, assessed essay.[7] Within the miniconferences, students were encouraged to comment on brief prompts I inserted in the margins of their texts. They were asked by me to analyze their work using the conceptual tools discussed in the tutorials. The conferences were taped, and students could keep a copy of the tape if they wished. Attendance at the conference was voluntary, but most students attended.

The conferences were initially run along lines suggested by Scardamalia and Bereiter, with the intention that they would improve students' understanding and production of legal discourse. However, it became clear after the first few conferences and on studying the conference transcripts that, in spite of their familiarity with the genre-based tools of analysis used in the reading unit, it was difficult for students to discuss the structure of their own writing without describing its social and performative aspects. The following extract is a good example of this.[8] The "assisted monologue" began with the topic of clarity of structure. The student, Ian, shifted it to a discussion of how his use of disciplinary terminology, which he felt unsure about, affected the structure of his argument:

Interviewer: [. . .] do you think [. . .] you're unsure about your writing?

Ian: I don't think—not too much. I suppose there is maybe a possibility that I just don't want to be cornered —I don't want when I'm writing the essay to put it as if—I don't want to be cornered, to look as if I haven't got a clue what I'm talking about. So you try and cover as much ground as you can, if you know what I mean, so that you don't, you aren't totally wrong rather than following one chain of thought and then "Oh that's completely wrong." If you try and make it a little bit more broad then you've got a better chance of not being wrong. But it's maybe just a habit I've got into trying to do that because I think in a lot of the exams I did in the Higher there wasn't maths or anything like theory; it was like Modern Studies, Geography, Economics, English. A lot of essays I had to write in the exam. I think that's what's got me into the habit of it, writing like that, so that when the marker comes to mark it, it's not—they can't say "Oh that's right or wrong." I've tried to cover myself.[9]

What was turning into a discussion of surface features suddenly became an exploration of Ian's coping strategies when faced with the task of writing an essay on law. Uncertainty of language, he felt, led to uncertainty of structure, and his strategy of "covering myself" he considered a weakness arising from anxiety about register and legal terms of art. This was a turning point in the conference for Ian. Later on it was possible to show him that, while there could be a causal link between language use and structure in his writing, what he viewed as a mere coping mechanism was one amongst a variety of possible and acceptable rhetorical moves, and one often used by academics and judges alike.

Other students made the same discursive shift from text structure to personal experience and process. One mature student described powerfully her feelings of frustration in struggling to express herself in the constraints of disciplinary argument:

Sarah: So I knew myself it was just absolutely, totally, it's not what I wanted it to say, it's not exactly what I wanted it to say, I mean, Friday afternoon at half past three I was still typing it out and I thought "This is ridiculous, I've usually got everything done by now." I just couldn't for the life of me get what I wanted down on paper, and I thought "There is no point in changing it now, it's too late—it's to be in for four o'clock." Just a fail. I just knew it right away. I was like that "There's no way that's gonny pass."

Interviewer: It's a dreadful feeling that, isn't it?

Sarah: Oh no, I knew myself I even said, I says, the essay is a lot of crap, I says, it's total and utter rubbish that's in it. But now I can see it, I've looked at it at home, I mean I've got a copy in the house, and I have actually sat and read it, I thought, "I should have put that there, and that there and that should have been further on."

Reviewing the transcripts, I found myself in them adopting less of the "prompt" role described by Scardamalia and Bereiter, and more of a collaborative role; one that was more Rogerian in tone.[10] Sarah had already started working on her second essay, and she used taped recordings to help her manage the complex sets of lectures notes, book notes, and essay fragments out of which she assembled her argument. This was a technique I had suggested in class, but it was also one she had used before, at high school 16 years earlier. The particular context of this extract is again a discussion of structure, and Sarah is discussing her second essay:

Sarah: [. . .] In my [second] essay I actually taped it first [. . .]. I sat and I had all my notes down. I just relayed off what I wanted to say and then just took it bit by bit—that's relevant to that and that's relevant to that and then did it. So I took your advice on Wednesday night and I was up to 4 o'clock on Thursday morning doing that essay right enough. I did! I taped it first and then when I sat down with all my notes, bits of paper here, and I went, "Well I'm wanting that in this bit here" so I would have it all and this is to be added in to such and such a bit [. . .]

Interviewer: But did the taping of it work?

Sarah: Yeah. I find it a lot easier, a lot easier, because my brain works faster than my writing so if I've said it all right—I've added that bit and that bit—so that's fine I'll just write it out, what I've said, and then I can add the bits in here, there and everywhere. And I thought well that's it—perfect, got it.

In the second essay Sarah abandons the attempt to write formal English from the start. Instead, she discovers a method of splicing taped speech and notes which works for her. She is learning to control process in order to achieve product, and her method mediates between personal voice and disciplinary argument. It relies heavily on arrangement of blocks of argument and the use of taped voice to review notes and merge the blocks in one meta-argument. The student here is really engaged in learning on a number of levels—how to cope with the demands of disciplinary argument, how to learn the law, how to write using her own past experience and the new genres of text she is encountering at university. Investigating the conflicting demands that take place between these items (and there are many more), we can begin to discover, as teachers, how the "negotiation of inner voices shape[s] the *hidden logic* of the text" (Flower 1994, 55). To an extent this negotiation was aided by what might be thought to be a version of Brandt's (1990) concept of literacy as involvement of reader and writer; but while conducting the miniconferences, and on review of the transcripts, I found that it was characteristic of the discussions to move from analyzing students' arguments solely within the context of their texts, to active collaboration by means of an exploration of the texts' social and personal contexts. Sarah, for example, perceived that the higher grade she achieved in the second essay was the result of the discovery that a way of working she had learned in another part of her life could be a valuable heuristic at university. In this respect the collaboration was a re-membering, a putting together again of forgotten compositional practices, and adaptation of them to the demands of a new discipline.

Conclusion

It is a well-documented tendency for law teachers to focus on the teaching and learning of substantive law, rather than legal skills or the integration of skills and knowledge. Within the last few decades this has been the subject of considerable critique. Kissam (1987, 142), for example, has argued that law schools, by failing "to employ the writing process as an effective learning device," generally encourage legalistic attitudes towards language. The concentration on substantive or "black-letter" law and the finished product, he posits, inculcates formalist views of genre and gives students the illusion that *auctoritas* is to be found in legal terms of art, and not in argumentation or problem-solving analysis.[11] This was the case with Ian, as we saw above.

Legal Skills 1 was an example of a module designed around the rhetorics of legal argument. It alerted students to the choice of strategic alternatives within processes of writing, reading, and legal research, and concurrently, the preexisting genres of legal argumentation relevant to their level of study; and enabled them to integrate one with the other. In this respect the process models of Flower and Hayes and others were useful to first-year students, for the language of student writing process was more available to them than that of generic argument structure, which they found difficult to enact. When argument structures were taught in a localized genre sense, within legal assignments, they became more readily available to students. But as Creme and Lea point out, "writing cannot be regarded as something that exists in a decontextualized vacuum" (1998). It was crucial to take into consideration the situated learning experiences and personal constructions brought by students to the task of learning the law.

Notes

1. The most recent reports into law teaching methods in the U.K. are Leighton, Mortimer, and Whateley (1995) and Grimes, Klaff, and Smith (1996). Neither reported specifically on these issues. Grimes et al. suggest that from the evidence of their survey, "skills are seen by the educators as more than training and properly part of the academic curriculum" (66); but they do note that a follow-up survey is needed to determine quality and quantity of skills teaching and the extent of curricular integration. For a survey of some American Law Schools' basic training in writing and argument, see Silecchia (1996).

2. A notable exception in the U.K. is Maughan, Maughan, and Webb (1995), which describes the educational application of research into professional practice, which was set within a conceptual framework derived from the work of Schön (1987) and Argyris and Schön (1974). In their skills textbook, Maughan and Webb (1995) cite cognitive research on legal writing.

3. While it takes what some legal academics might regard as an overly rhetorical approach to interpretation, this module takes a middle road between a traditional research and writing course, and a more broadly based skills course. See Silecchia (1996) for the differences between these approaches. At 266–8 she outlines a series of questions which in her opinion all such first-year courses must "grapple with;" and these include many of the issues described above.

4. *Wilson* v *Dykes* 1872 SC 444

5. For an approach much more based on logic and founded on the socratic method of American law schools, see White (1989).

6. In their advice here, upon which topic they have conducted much research since then, Scardamalia and Bereiter are of course basing their approach on "procedural fa-

cilitation" rather than "substantive facilitation;" the intent of this being "'to enable students to carry out more complex composing processes by themselves'" (1986, 61). The approach is one variant amongst a number. For a summary of others, see Newell and Swanson-Owens (1994).

7. I use the word "heuristic" here in the same sense that Flower and Hayes used it in their early work which defined writing as predominantly problem-solving, and heuristics as being those routines and subroutines that writers depended upon to produce coherent argument and form. See, for example, Flower and Hayes (1981). In addition, computer-based learning courseware is used to support learning of legal argumentation. *Contracts,* written with Professor Joe Thomson of Glasgow University, introduces students to the skills of legal problem-solving; illustrates the major stages of the writing process; facilitates the analysis of students' own writing processes; and presents good models of legal writing and alternative strategies to enable good practice (Maharg 1996a). *Stylus,* an online style guide to legal essay writing, gives guidance to students on presentation, use of paratactical materials, and legal citation.

8. Students' names have been altered to preserve confidentiality.

9. The "Higher" is the Higher examination which is usually taken in fifth year of high school. The grades obtained are a key determinant of university entrance in Scotland.

10. An important part of this collaboration was empathy with the learners' construction of meaning; and in this respect Rogers' definition of empathy is acute: "[i]t means frequently checking with [the client] as to the accuracy of your sensings, and being guided by the responses you receive. You are a confident companion to the person in his/her inner world." (Rogers 1980, 142)

11. The literature on this is extensive. See, for example, Maughan and Webb (1995), Le Brun and Johnstone (1994), Maughan and Webb (1996), Maharg (1999).

8

Eager Interpreters: Student Writers and the Art of Writing Research

Claire Woods

Introduction

In this chapter, I explore what happens in the first-year writing workshop class of a B.A. with a major in Professional Writing and Communication. What do we, the teaching team, invite first-year students to do as writers and why? How do we help them develop a confidence in themselves as writers who learn to write in the academy, in different disciplines, and for personal and public purposes when they might write to persuade, entertain, or defend an idea or opinion?

Important for us is the way in which we ask students to reconsider what the "essay" form can offer the writer as a mode of exploring, or of arguing a case. At the same time we want them to rethink how written argument might be reconceptualized as not necessarily adversarial but as perhaps personal and exploratory. Our students (as we discover when talking with them) tend not to credit argument with the plurality of functions listed by Richard Andrews—to clarify, persuade, win, entertain, unload, resolve, and find identity (Andrews 1995, 154–5).

In the writing activities we assign, we hope to show students not only such possibilities but also the way in which argument is closely related to form and style. One such activity is an assignment to undertake a project in which the student must be a participant-observer (assuming the role of an ethnographer) in a particular situation. By introducing them to the process and practice of writing as ethnographers, we hope they will understand the rhetorical, including stylistic, considerations of making a case based on evidence and data so that the audience is persuaded of a particular interpretation or conclusion.

We are interested in "ethnographic argumentation and the rhetoric of evidence" (Atkinson and Hammersley 1994, 254). Such issues are of concern to qualitative researchers who are particularly aware of how research data is represented and how the researcher accounts for and makes a case for any interpretation or conclusion drawn from evidence. The rhetorical self-consciousness of the research endeavor can be seen as an exercise in utilizing what Anderson has termed (in relation to nonfiction essays), "style as argument" (Anderson 1987).

The use of "style as argument," says Anderson, is the definitive experience in the reading and writing of contemporary nonfiction essays, including reports and accounts described as new journalism or literary journalism. He comments:

> . . . . nonfiction reportage is more than informative: it is an effort to persuade us to attitudes, interpretations, opinions even actions. The rhetoric of reportage is subtle—it must be interpreted, the texts read carefully for nuances of imagery and tone—but it is there, powerful and persuasive. (1987, 2)

Anderson suggests the work of writers such as Joan Didion, Tom Wolfe, Truman Capote, and Norman Mailer is defined by a rhetorical selfconsciousness—a very particular awareness of the "value of form as form, style as style" and thus of "style as argument" (1987, 6). At issue here, says Anderson, is the reader's experience of style and language:

> We are never able to look completely past the words on the page to the people and events they evoke; we are always aware of the words themselves, of their rhythms and their textures. (1987, 1)

More specifically, as he unpacks the prose of these four writers Anderson reveals how with the use of literary devices such as point of view and symbolism as rhetorical devices for representing experience (content), authors seek to shape "the reader's attitudes and perceptions" (1987, 2).

Such writing, with its often self-conscious manipulation of language, says Van Maanen, in his discussion of the writing of ethnography, has considerable affinities with ethnographic texts. He describes writing of this ilk as "literary:"

> Literary tales offer the fresh perspective of some very talented and insightful self-styled ethnographers who are blissfully unconcerned with and free of the historically routinized formats of cultural story telling. The best literary tales display a fascination with language and language use and make the phrase "active reading" more than a cliché. Such possibilities spill over into academic worlds. (1988, 136)

It is these issues I discuss here in relation to the writing activities in which we involve our first-year writing students.

The "Essay" and Argument: Student Views

Students usually come to this course with a fervent desire to be writers. They see themselves as writers of fiction (perhaps of poetry, scripts, short stories, or the great novel) but certainly as writers of what they would call creative or imaginative writing. They do not think of writing in academic disciplines or business, technical, or other professional writing (such as the range of nonfiction writing) as creative and artisanal activity.

The boundaries between genres (narrative versus essay/argument, fiction versus nonfiction) seem to students to be quite clear cut. They might also speak of narrative and argument as oppositional modes, one seeming to demand the resources of the imagination, the other those of "reason." These are crude distinctions. Yet, our experience is that for first-year students such distinctions seem to hold. That such categorization might be challenged is new to them.

For most of our students, the idea of "the essay" has a strictly limited connotation. It is seen as a response to a set question that involves making a case, perhaps presenting different sides in an argument, and demonstrating what the student knows about something in a discipline area. Given their school experience, they often confuse argument and exposition and thus perceive of the essay as a conventional if not "ritualized form;" a "ritualized form with little expression and thought" (Andrews 1995, 168).

Students tend not to acknowledge the possibility of the essay being a site for discursive experimentation, nor do they see it as being allied in any substantial way with personal, reflective, or imaginative exploration. Thus, they do not regard an essay as a site that enables the writer to walk the fine line between the subjective and objective, between the personal and the public, and, in a dialogic and often playful manner, to reveal his/her thinking for the reader's pleasure if not instruction. They have not experienced the essay as a text written to show "the author's process of discovery" (Owens in Heilker 1996, xii); as "a loose sally of the mind" (Andrews 1995, 10); or as "*essaying*—less a noun than a verb" (Heilker 1996, 180).

We want to provide a process in which they are asked to pay particular attention to the way they write an account—usually in essay form. We intend that they are particularly conscious of how they might describe, present, analyze, and interpret data and evidence in order to convince the reader of their point of view or of their version of a situation, or of their interpretation of an event. We begin this by inviting them to become writer/researchers from an ethnographic perspective in their first class.

We draw their attention to the statement:

> A good writer must be a good ethnographer. He [sic] must carefully observe and record situations, events, behaviors and ideas. Most of all, his [sic] characters and their actions must be believable. They must make sense to the person who knows the culture an author is writing about. A good writer is able to convey to the reader the meaning of all those taken-for-granted aspects of experience. . . . (Spradley and McCurdy 1973, 4)

We intend to lead students into understanding why we have adopted this proposition. As our students experiment with form and style some of the contentious issues pertaining to the writing of research and to the use of style as a means of arguing particularly perhaps to entertain and persuade are debated and scrutinized.

The first piece they write is what we call a "participant observation piece"—a preliminary foray into the realm of the researcher/writer. Their final piece, at the end of the semester, is a longer "ethnographic" essay; that is, an account written after they have spent some time as participant observer in a "cultural scene" (Spradley and McCurdy 1973, 24). It is clear that our first-year students are not in the position to carry out a properly ethnographic study, for this is not a course in which they learn in depth about qualitative research theory, method, and practice. However, on the basis of their involvement in a particular cultural activity, event, or site over some weeks, they write an account in which they attempt to describe, analyze, and interpret what goes on there.

Diana's Poem

In writing the first assignment, Diana took seriously our admonition that students should allow their subject, as well as their interpretive stance in relation to their topic, guide their choice of form and style. In a poem, Diana concentrates on one incident in which passersby ignore a homeless man sleeping in a doorway. (See appendix A for extracts from her poem.) Later, she explained how she had originally written the piece in essay form but decided that rewriting it as a poem and reformatting by taking advantage of left-justified margins and different spacing might allow her to present her case more forcefully.

Diana's piece offers a personal response to the tragedy of one man in the city. She wants to make a case about the hidden face of the poor in society. She uses point of view as well as the judicious choice of image to persuade the reader of the injustice in the situation and to confront the reader's conscience. Her point of view is directly that of the participant observer. The reader sees the scene through her eyes. With her we stand at the bus stop, deserted even within the hectic street scene—peopled, chaotic and a site of madly frenetic activity. The observer is nevertheless, alone. The contrasts are made clear.

She poses questions, inviting the reader to deal with the situation of the homeless derelict who is shunned by passersby— "his silent acquaintances."

She advances the proposition that by deliberately ignoring this man and others like him, those who "have" can continue to live with ease. There is an organized sequence of information, propositions, and assertions with which she builds her case, and with specific selection of details (evidence perhaps) she persuades the reader about the place of poverty in the community. While the poem is relatively unsophisticated, there is a personal poignancy about it, which is effective and persuasive.

For Diana, the essay form constrained her intentions as a close observer and commentator. Yet, the participant observation exercise gave her a chance to consider in a preliminary way the issues of the rhetoric of evidence and more particularly of "style as argument." These are the issues of the writer as researcher and of the researcher as writer with which we confront our student writers.

Blurring Boundaries: Possibilities in Form

With these writing tasks we open for exploration the blurring of the boundaries between fiction and nonfiction, between the ethnographic account and the travel essay, and between narrative and argument in persuasive, explanatory, and interpretive research accounts. How much is the researcher/writer engaged in an artistic and creative endeavor? What role is there for the imagination in the construction of the account? What are the issues of style in nonfiction or ethnographic writing?

For the nonfiction writer, as Anderson notes there is a "rhetorical dilemma"—"the nonfiction author's self conscious and meta-discursive approach to language and form" (1987, 5). This dilemma is shared by qualitative researchers who have become particularly conscious of how they represent data and write their research and acknowledge the possibilities of blurred boundaries between genres.

The "rhetorical turn" among ethnographers, write Atkinson and Hammersley, "is part of a much broader movement of scholarship toward an interest in the rhetoric of inquiry that has been manifested in many of the human and social disciplines" (1994, 254). The issue of the "rhetorical turn" has been and continues to be the focus of scholarly discussion among researchers (Van Maanen 1988, 1995, Clifford and Marcus 1986, Atkinson and Hammersley 1994, Richardson 1994, Agar 1980, Denzin and Lincoln, 1994).

Atkinson and Hammersley note:

> Although the respective disciplines have slightly different emphases, the broad themes have been similar: the conventionality of ethnographic texts, the representation of "Self" and "Other" in such texts, the character of ethnographies as a textual genre, the nature of *ethnographic argumentation and the rhetoric of evidence.* (1994, 254—my emphasis)

This is territory to which Clifford Geertz has made a significant contribution. It is to his work I wish to turn now as a way of highlighting the kinds of issues we ask our students to consider as they observe and write, including the relationship between research, writing, form (specifically, the essay), and argument.

The Ethnographic Essay

I have a particular fondness for the classic ethnographic essay by Clifford Geertz, "Deep Play: Notes on a Balinese Cockfight" (1973). Here are to be found issues of authorial presence; of the relationship between narrative, analysis, and argument; and of the interrelationship between personal and academic discourses. The essay prompts consideration of the rhetorical issues of the researcher's craft in constructing the research account. Further to this, an essay such as "Deep Play" suggests the contiguities between such forms as the qualitative research account, the nonfiction essay, reportage, and literary journalism. The essay is well known. However, let me relive it for you briefly.

Geertz begins his account of the Balinese cockfight with the dramatic subheading "The Raid." The reader's anticipation is immediately aroused. The protagonists, time, and setting are introduced: "Early in April of 1958, my wife and I arrived, malarial and diffident, in a Balinese village we intended, as anthropologists, to study" (1973, 412). Geertz and his wife experience a sense of awkward presence in the village:

> As we wandered around, uncertain, wistful, eager to please, people seemed to look right through us with a gaze focused several yards behind us on some more actual stone and tree.

In fact, Geertz points out they were regarded as being no more than as "a cloud or gust of wind." This changes however with the episode central to the essay: their attendance at a large cockfight. When the local police raid the cockfight (an illegal activity), Geertz and his wife in panic, flee the cockfight ring along with all the other spectators. Then, they are dramatically "rescued" by a man and his wife who pretend to the pursuing police that all of them have been innocently sitting in a courtyard sipping tea. Their host proceeds to offer an impassioned explanation and defense, revealing to Geertz a surprisingly detailed knowledge of his occupation and purpose in the village. Then:

> The policeman retreated in rather total disarray. And after a decent interval, bewildered but relieved to have survived and stayed out of jail, so did we.

Geertz as researcher and writer is particularly aware of his position in the scene and in his text: an essay that involves narrative, argument, and interpretation in a complex and subtle mix as Geertz explicates the Balinese cockfight. At issue is the capacity of the researcher to persuade readers to accept his interpretation on the basis of the data presented and to conclude what he has concluded.

Dell Hymes comments on the relationship between narrative and argument in this essay, seeing both as essential to the task of explication, interpretation, and persuasion about the credibility of the social knowledge presented in the account:

> Through his narrative skill, he is able to convey a sense (mediated by his personal involvement) of the quality and texture of Balinese fascination with cockfighting. Evidence of the fascination is important. It supports taking the activity as a key to something essential about the Balinese: it helps us understand the analytic statements. (1980, 97)

The place of the narrative account as a component of an argument is interesting for students to explore as they write their ethnographic essays. We ask them to develop an account of a particular "cultural scene." We involve them first-hand in the dilemma of "ethnographic argumentation and the rhetoric of evidence." We are well aware of how problematic an activity it is to present information in such a way as to reveal, as Geertz says, "something of something" and persuade the reader of its credibility as an account. Here is how Ynys took on the task.

Ynys Shapes an Ethnographic Account

Twelve weeks after writing her first participant observation account, Ynys deliberately shapes her final piece of work titled, "Local Gods—A study of skate-board riders in the Southern Area". She is more deliberately in researcher mode, and while she situates herself directly in the scene as an observer, she moves readily into description and analysis of the context, the participants, the language, and the patterns of behavior that characterize the skate-boarders' domain.

The title, taken from the lyrics of a song from a current rock group, establishes the metaphor she has chosen to characterize the members of the cultural scene she has studied for some weeks. The reader understands immediately that her piece will argue that in the very male domain of the skate-board rider, there is a sense in which each one seems to "feel like a local god" when he is "with the boys." She wants to persuade the reader that not only was "she there" and understands the substance of the scene and the activities of the skate-boarders, but also that her conclusions about their motives and their values are valid and credible.

She persuades the reader that at the club, where "The ceilings are low, the walls are marked and chipped, the floor is a mass of gouged and blackened linoleum," there are different groups of skaters who have "an air of concentrated mania about them." She asks, "Why is it that skate-boarding is so popular?" and ". . . why skate-boarding as opposed to . . . roller-blading?" She uses such questions to direct the essay while she examines the line drawn by the participants between themselves and those they describe as "town skaters," or between themselves and nonskaters. In particular, she indicates the skill factor that seems to set the boys who skate apart from others and give the participants their sense of belonging:

> . . . skating here allows them to prove to everyone, including themselves, that they have the skills and perseverance to pull off tricks. It means a lot to gain respect from our peers in any field, and this skate club gives them the opportunity to gain that respect.

In a concluding paragraph, she sums up the case she has made and returns to the proposition with which she began. In this paragraph, the scene, the boys, the activities, and Ynys's personal response and embryonic interpretation of a particular cultural scene are neatly captured.

> The skate club is a great place to observe skaters in their natural habitat. Beyond the deafening noise of wheels and bodies landing with a thud, beyond the carefully displayed carelessness, beyond the cool hair and trendy shoes is something I believe to be very important, a place where boys can be united in expending energy in a constructive, fun and cool-looking way. No one is forcing them to try so hard, they push themselves. And it pays off; these boys who fly through the air on their boards look like nothing so much as local gods.

Through the participant observation exercises, what we hope to expose is the self-consciousness of the rhetorical enterprise in research. The writer crafts the account to persuade the reader that the researcher was there and that what is represented matters in some way; and finally that evidence has been marshaled appropriately to sustain the conclusions drawn. Geertz says of this:

> Ethnographers need to convince us . . . not merely that they themselves have truly "been there," but . . . that had we been there we should have seen what they saw, what they felt, concluded what they concluded. (Geertz 1988, 16)

He notes: ". . . persuading us that this offstage miracle has occurred, is where the writing comes in" (1988, 4).

My reader's sense is that Ynys "was there;" that she has tuned into the language and ways of behaving in the skate-boarders' context, and that she has begun to understand what it is to participate as a member of the cultural group of Southern skate-boarders. Here is a piece which has begun to deal with the rhetorical issues of presenting a credible account, of situating the author in relation to the data presented and in relation to the participants, of observing, describing, analyzing, and finally of persuading the reader of a particular interpretation. Here is a piece of "ethnographic argumentation"—not yet as sophisticated as that of the experienced researcher but clearly recognizable as such and certainly persuasive.

Writing the Account—
Artistic and Artisanal Endeavor?

A significant issue for students as they write the ethnographic essay is how they as writers work the rhetorical devices that will shape their accounts. They are aware of the need to stay close to their data. They are also conscious of how they can imaginatively reconstruct the scene, events, language, and behavior. They must confront directly their own position in relation to their data and make a decision about how they will locate themselves within the text. How close indeed will they be to the action in the final account? How central to the account will they be? How will point of view be handled in the piece? How will the piece be framed and organized? What metaphors and images might they employ? What evidence will be used to support the conclusion?

There is an artistic endeavor in the writing of such representations. Spradley and McCurdy's note that "Another potential spin-off for the ethnographer is in writing short stories, themes, and novels" (1973, 4). And indeed the translation of ethnographic and interpretive research into popular fiction or the amusing travel account is a recognized practice (e.g., Barley 1989). Students are particularly conscious of how close they come to stepping into the world of the imaginative re-creation—the world of fiction even—as they develop their pieces. "How easy it would be," one student commented, "to turn the experience into a fiction."

One territory we have not taken them into is that of turning the researcher's interpretive research into an artistic display—although for many this becomes an issue. And perhaps Diana's poem moves into this domain. Van Maanen calls for experimentation in writing the ethnographic account: "we need to shop around more and encourage ingenuity and novel interpretation . . . we need more not fewer ways to tell of culture" (1995, 140). (See, for example, work by Pacanowsky 1983; Grindal and Shepherd 1993; and Glesne 1997.)

Conclusion

The student work referred to here was produced in the first few weeks at university. It is indicative of some of the issues that arise as students become engaged in rethinking what it means to write from experience, persuade a reader, and argue on the basis of observed data and reconsider the form in which an essay might be constructed.

We aim to create a foundation for students majoring in writing and for their development as writers of professional writing of all kinds, whether fiction or nonfiction, technical documents, radio and TV scripts, and so on. We intend them to gain an understanding of how texts are constructed, of the discursive construction of knowledge, of genres, and boundaries between genres.

What we want to make explicit is the idea that each of us is a participant observer in everyday life. We are always engaged in learning ethnographically as Hymes suggests (1980, 98). Thus, students as writers, whether producing a novel, or a business report, will be engaged very particularly with a context and with writing within the social and cultural constraints of that context. As the semester of writing, reading, and group discussion unfolds, each writing activity reinforces our aim of problematizing writing and reading practices as discursively and culturally constrained.

We want students to experience the dialogic impetus of texts and the "very eclectic natures of genres" (Andrews 1992, 9). We want to give them a chance as Elbow says to "render experience" (that is, their personal experience) and "explain it," that is, deliver it for academic purposes (Elbow 1991, 136). We hope that they gain an ethnographic sense of themselves as cultural persons.

We continue to reflect on our own pedagogy as we invite students to attempt the "offstage miracle." Is there room to offer students even bolder options for experimenting with form and style? How specific should we be in developing an awareness of style as cultural capital? Are we ourselves still bound by a normative style simply because we are imbued with academic discourse? Does this prevent us from encouraging different and counter texts by our students?

Are we asking something too sophisticated of our first-year undergraduates; something that is neither fully fledged ethnographic research and writing nor the recognizable academic essay? If so, what are the implications? Is this piece a hybrid which, despite our intention to problematize the issues of text, genre, writer/reader roles, cultural intertext, and so on, does not serve all students usefully as they step into the academic context or step into different places in the world?

The complexity of teaching writing demands that we challenge our practices and assumptions about ways of involving students as writers in the world. From day one and throughout the three-year degree, we foster the idea that the writer is ethnographer, the writer is researcher, and the researcher is writer. Thus it is that we offer our students an induction into the arts of discourse in context. Our intention is to engage them in understanding that we all learn ethnographically and that in this sense we are all researchers; that research is a rhetorical enterprise; and that in one significant sense "style is argument", as the writer works to persuade, inform, clarify, or entertain.

Note

I am grateful to Diana Makoter and Ynys Osman for allowing me to use their work.

Appendix A

Extracts from Diana's Poem

The city street crowded
I watch from my deserted bus stop
the air of madness surrounding me.
People with people to see.
so many different places to be. And yet,
amongst this organized chaos
I feel alone.
. . .

And then across the hectic street
I see a man
in a green overcoat
a beard and long unkempt hair
in search of cigarette butts.
And suddenly I don't feel so alone.
Into the corner
of the building he crawls.
My body senses the harshness of the marble
where he nestles
. . .

The burden of survival
his daily chore
The passers by
his silent acquaintances
. . .

Why do they pretend
this man does not exist?
Ignore it and it will go away!
. . .

Who gave him up first
us or him?
. . .

I am jolted back from a reality
that no one wants to face.
I turn to find a row of people
beside me
and
look up to find my bus
. . .

9

Citation as an Argumentation Strategy in the Reflective Writing of Work-Based Learning Students

Carol Costley and Kathy Doncaster

Introduction: Three Spheres of Knowledge—the Personal, Professional, and Academic

Work-Based Learning is now part of the curriculum offered by many U.K. universities as an acknowledgement of the changing nature of careers and of the relationship between work and education (Brennan and Little 1996). The focus of this chapter is on citation as an argumentation strategy used by students on the Work-Based Learning Studies programs at Middlesex University, England, which currently have over 700 students. The authors draw on their experience of facilitating reflective practice (Schön 1987) on these programs. Carol Costley is Head of Research and Kathy Doncaster is the Curriculum Leader for postgraduate Work-Based Learning Studies programs.

A key feature of Work-Based Learning Studies at Middlesex University is that it is a generic program with generic assessment criteria. At under- and postgraduate level, it offers a set of core modules onto which the four elements of Kolb's experiential learning cycle (Kolb 1984) can be mapped. An initial module (and the one on which we focus in this chapter), involves reflection on existing learning from work and experience, with subsequent modules covering theorizing and planning, and application of theory to problem solving at work. This generic framework enables students from a wide range of work and professional backgrounds to negotiate a program of study which is customized to their own and their organization's needs and interests. Thus, the university works in partnership with both students and organizations to fully integrate their learning and knowledge needs into programs of work-based study (see Doncaster and Garnett 1999, for a review). As a consequence of this partnership between the student, the employer, and the University, another key feature of Work-Based Learning Studies emerges. Students' assignments must integrate knowledge from the three different spheres of knowledge represented in this partnership: the personal, the professional, and the academic.

One of the ways in which knowledge from these three spheres is filtered into assignments is through the use of the argumentation strategy of citation. We are using the term here to mean the direct or indirect quotation of "expert" voices from any of the three spheres of knowledge (the personal, the professional, and the academic) which students draw into their assignments. The reason for focusing on citation in students' first assignments is because the range of voices drawn on is likely to be more apparent here, since students' ability to integrate the knowledge from these three spheres is likely to be less sophisticated at this stage. Our aim as teachers is to help students progress to writing which is more integrated and well analyzed as they move through their programs of study.

What we show in later sections of this chapter is how students use citation in a variety of ways to support lines of argument which they develop in this initial reflective assignment. For students who have past experience of higher education, the use of citation may represent existing knowledge from the academic sphere (that citation is an academic convention used in argument making), while for others it may be a deployment of what other people say in an informal and conversational way (the use of argumentation within the personal sphere).

The topic of these reflective assignments is students' own learning, which requires the deployment of knowledge from all three spheres. One of the ways such knowledge is deployed is through citing the personal sphere "expert" of the self (the student is an expert on her/his own learning). Another is to cite what professional sphere experts may have to say about learning (for example, some, though not all, students may be familiar with concepts of organizational learning from continuing professional development programs in their workplace). We return to this later, but we start by explaining the Work-Based Learning Studies context of knowledge making, in which these reflective assignments are written.

The Work-Based Learning Studies Approach to Knowledge and Argument

The partnership approach to learning in Work-Based Learning Studies means that knowledge from the personal, professional, and academic spheres is all valued. In this section, we discuss several principles concerning knowledge and argumentation that arise from this, and which underpin our teaching, learning, and assessment practices.

Firstly, we acknowledge that what is considered a well-argued piece of writing is as much rooted in the interior features of written form as in epistemology. Bazerman (1988) points out that the ways in which knowledge is organized cannot be separated from the writing of that knowledge. Argument in Work-Based Learning Studies, informed by these three different spheres of knowledge, involves a reconciliation between academic language, the language used in work, and everyday (commonsense) language. The "modes of discourse" (Bahktin 1986) generally considered to best suit academic learning involve abstraction and complexity which is often subject-specific. In contrast, modes of discourse in the workplace are often succinct, technical, serve a practical purpose, and are based on experience, while everyday language may involve colloquialism and address the personal. All three modes of discourse may be apparent in students' assignments, usually in an increasingly well-integrated way as they progress through their studies. The fact that students have the opportunity to make connections between the different spheres of knowledge that they possess tends to enhance their confidence, awareness, and ability to manage their own learning. For example, in the initial reflective essay, students have to bring together spheres of knowledge that, in their minds, they have often kept separate, since the task is to generate a whole picture of their learning, personal, professional, and academic. This helps them to understand their learning and knowledge holistically, but they have to develop argumentation strategies in order to develop such a picture. This initial exercise is crucial in helping students to use existing expertise to create a basis for arguments that they can then refine in later writing on the program.

Secondly, learning which is Work-Based tends towards interdisciplinarity. By this we mean that students often use knowledge from more than one academic discipline area, and also combine academic knowledge with key skills and experiential knowledge, in order to apply it in the workplace. For Work-Based Learning Studies students, valid knowledge is likely to be found not only within the university, but also within work and personal learning, since all three spheres of knowledge must inform and underpin their situated practice as workers. We measure students' success in academic writing by their ability to use "argument as a vehicle to take the whole context of a situation (including expert opinion and commonsense matters) into account. . . ." (Costley 1997a).

In the past, the theoretical, knowledge-based interests of universities and the practical, skills-based concerns of the workplace have been unduly separated. A third characteristic of Work-Based Learning Studies is that these two spheres of knowledge are brought together. Here, it is learning which is gained from practice which is theorized in students' academic writing. The grounded knowledge of Work-Based students contains an awareness of how learning might be applied; of how and when opportunities might be grasped; of the need for forward thinking, planning, self-awareness, communication skills, confidence, and the understanding of how these fit together operationally. By placing experiential learning first, students have a relevant and informed platform with proof and evidence (often in the form of citation) for their arguments.

Work-Based Learning Studies programs allow students to argue through their own epistemological lens (and thus achieve the connections between academic knowledge and the specificity of their professional knowledge described above). As they create syntheses which cut across traditional knowledge boundaries, they are able to question underlying assumptions and look for new possibilities in their work. This approach is supported by theoreticians who are moving towards new ways of not only problem solving but problem making that are grounded in Work-Based activity (Lester 1998; Checkland 1981; Stevenson and Yorke 1998; Portwood 1999). The result of this for students, for example in the initial reflective essay assignment, is that they draw together hitherto separated spheres of their knowledge and understanding and frequently accede for the first time the breadth and connectedness of their knowing. As they draft and redraft, their arguments become synergized, new learning occurs, and there are moments of revelation about themselves personally, in their work, and as knowers/learners within an academic framework.

A fourth aspect of Work-Based Learning Studies which affects argumentation is that it often involves collaborative (team-based) work and learning. Students undertake study within a work organization or community and consequently must engage with the work of others. Students/workers have to argue from their own perspective but also from the perspective of a community or team, where the collective opinion and collective culture has a strong influence. Students often cite the expertise of professional colleagues in their reflective essays. They are used to working collaboratively and, although we are recognizing individual achievement as teachers and assessors, we acknowledge that the ability to communicate effectively for work-related purposes involves cooperation and interpretation of the ideas of others. The importance of collaboration at work is often articulated in students' writing through the use of citation, in recognition of the interdependence of students' knowledge and that of their work organization or community.

In the following section, we detail how students draw on the three spheres of knowledge discussed here through their use of citation in their initial reflective writing assignments.

Citation in Initial Reflective Writing Assignments

Throughout their studies, Work-Based Learning students at all academic levels are positioned at the interface of academia and work in a way not experienced either by full time students, or by students studying "traditional" academic subjects. As has been explained, their assignments, especially the early ones, may reveal the tensions inherent in trying to integrate knowledge from the personal, professional, and academic spheres that they uniquely bridge. In addition, as mature students, many have not written an academic essay for some time and some have never written for academic purposes. Others draw overtly on an understanding of academic conventions from previous exposure to higher education.

At both under- and postgraduate levels, the initial assignment is a piece of personal reflective writing on students' Work-Based and professional learning to date, and its relevance to the program of study being undertaken. Students' uses of several means of citing the voices of "experts" to provide evidence of learning and knowledge in these reflective assignments are discussed below.

Citing own views

We frequently observe that, in writing the reflective assignment, students use the argumentation strategy of posing the question "What is learning and/or knowledge?" and then answering it by explicitly giving their own views. This is a strategy related to the academic convention of using citation, but where the expert quoted is the student themself. The voice of the student (an expert from the personal sphere of knowledge) is being quoted, as it were, though this voice is not separated from the rest of the text by quotation marks and the use of direct speech within them. Since this is an assignment focused on personal reflection about own learning, this is a reasonable strategy to employ, even if it may not always be used consciously as an argumentation strategy.

Assignments sometimes make explicit reference to students' views on or beliefs about learning. These can range from single sentences making a single point, to a couple of paragraphs that elaborate on a personal view. For example, the extract below comes from a longer argument in which the writer views learning within the context of personal choice:

> 1.
>
> I believe that each of us has a pattern of existence that consists of many planned routes. These planned routes pre-exist and are not formed by any individual. . . . Some would regard this as fatalistic. I disagree . . . it is my view that each choice which is made by any one of us at any particular time has a cause and effect relationship to choices we have already made. . . . My contention is that because each one of us can choose the direction in which we wish to go, this does not represent fatalism. . . . I do believe that each of us has control over our individual destiny and that it is the manner in which we approach choice and the choices we make which shapes us and causes each of us to become who we are.

Other views are developed around clichés about learning. Extract two makes use of quite a number of different well-known clichés:

> 2.
>
> Life is a continuous learning experience, it's what you do with what you have learned that counts. . . . I accept that education is never easy and as they say, no gain without pain, and all that is hidden shall be revealed.

In approaching an answer to the self-imposed question "What is learning and/or knowledge?" the student writers of these two extracts must have drawn on a range of sources, though the resultant view is given as the student's own views or beliefs. Extract one above makes this clear in clauses such as "*I* believe . . ." or "It is *my* view that . . .", and extract two does so in the use of "*I* accept that . . .". Alternatively, views about learning are sometimes given as unquestioned fact—and therefore inevitably the student's view. Extract three, below, shows the student stating unquestioningly that things are a certain way—"advanced knowledge . . . *is* built upon some simpler basic knowledge"—rather than acknowledging this view as the student's own.

3.
Advanced knowledge in any given area is based and built upon some simpler, basic knowledge that may or may not be directly related to that area.

Extract four below similarly gives a statement purported to be fact and therefore not needing to be questioned or argued over or discussed:

4.
As wisdom is not provided for us, we have to discover it for ourselves.

The dialogic and argumentative aspects of these student views about learning and knowledge are interesting. Students' initial reflective assignments reveal both explicit and implicit understandings that to write an essay requires a juxtaposing of views. At least two dialogues tend to be revealed. Firstly, there are the dialogues students may establish between views on learning *within* their essays. For example, in extract one, the writer acknowledges that the view he expresses as his own may be contentious ("some would regard this as fatalistic"). Secondly, where views held to be universally accepted are stated, a dialogue *between* writer and reader is established. Here, the writer may be understood to be calling the reader's attention to a certain view and/or justifying her own position to the reader by calling upon something assumed to be universally agreed. Extracts three and four could be understood in this way. A view expressed as universally true is also interesting insofar as it absolves the student from arguing over it or discussing it. It acts as a shared assumption between reader and writer which can be used as a foundation on which to build other things the writer wishes to talk about in the essay.

This raises the question of how far back students feel they should go in explaining their assumptions. What should they take to be shared knowledge between themselves and the reader/assessor of their assignments, and what should they unpack? While there is no specified requirement in the essay guidelines for the writers to make clear what they understand by learning, it may be that those who do so have been revealing a knowledge of academic conventions in essay writing, where students learn that to unpack the title is likely to increase their grade. Being able to gauge what can be used as shared assumptions and what should be discussed or should form the basis of an argument in an assignment is likely to be the result of an understanding of what an academic essay should look like. This is discussed further below.

A more sophisticated (because more consciously deployed) use of argumentation strategies in the assignments comes in the traditionally accepted use of citations.

Citing the views of others

The initial reflective assignment is cast as a "personal reflection" on students' own learning, not an academic essay on a traditional academic topic. Consequently, there are no specified requirements for students to use academic conventions in the writing of these reflective assignments, for example, to quote texts by experts or to append a bibliography.

Given this lack of foregrounding of academic requirements, it is interesting to note that some students do make reference to views about learning by citing those they deem to be experts on the topic from the professional and academic spheres of their own knowledge. It is relevant to this discussion to note that citations may be in direct speech and within quotation marks (Leech and Short 1981). Alternatively, they may be in indirect speech, where the student writer paraphrases what the expert says. The student's choice of direct or indirect speech can be interesting with regard to what level of sophistication citation is being used, that is, the extent to which the student writer takes charge of the voice inserted into the essay text and uses it within his own argument. It can reveal the extent to which the student writer has understood what the "expert" quotation says, and/or understands the usefulness of using citations at all. In these reflective assignments, citations of an "expert's" view of learning are used in a variety of ways.

Sometimes students make explicit references to "experts" on learning using direct speech. These reveal a range of levels of sophistication in the way they are represented in the text. The use of quotations may be an indication by the writer of a knowledge of academic expectations in writing essays—a recognition that to use quotations and references is an academic convention. However, not all who use quotations go on to relate the view presented in the quotation to their own text—which is a more highly developed way of using quotations.

At the least sophisticated level, there is simple insertion of an "expert's" voice, with no explication of the quotation by the writer, and where the quotation seems to be considered self explanatory as a consequence. This is the case in the following extract, which is the first paragraph of an essay:

5.

I have now completed the compilation of my portfolio. Therefore it is now the ideal opportunity for me to reflect upon the process of developing my claim. To reflect upon this process I will be looking at how I went about putting my

> claim together and how this process developed . . . Firstly, it is important that I clarify what I understand by the term "learning." The definition of learning which I have used during the compilation of my portfolio is, "learning is the process of acquiring knowledge through experience which leads to a change in behavior" (Huczynski and Buchanan 1991).

Though the writer's quotation by an expert is given as "what I understand by the term learning" this is not directly referred to again. Only in the final sentence of the essay is it retrospectively made clear that this quotation has been intended to underpin the whole text. Here the quotation is slightly modified in verb tense and person to match the writer's use of the past and first person pronouns throughout her text and is not given within quotation marks. The citation has thus been integrated into the student's text in a way it was not in the opening paragraph:

> 6.
> . . . I conclude that by completing this module I have acquired knowledge through experience which has led to a change in my behavior. Thus, according to the definition I have used in the opening paragraph, learning has taken place.

However, this quotation is not explicitly used to argue, through juxtaposition, the merits of one view of learning as against another. Nor is it referred to during the essay as a view against which other views are compared (the student's own views, based on the experience of learning on the module, for example). The citation thus has the appearance of being inserted because quoting is what students ought to do, without taking advantage of how quotation allows writers to argue the merits and flaws in contrasting positions.

Expert voices are also drawn upon in a more sophisticated/more highly academically trained way in these initial assignments, but this is less common. The following extract is an example:

> 7.
> My professional institution requires a record to be maintained of continuous professional development. This record follows the experiential learning cycle as described by Kolb (1974)—have an experience, review the experience, conclude from the experience . . . and plan the next steps. Therefore, without review and reflection it is impossible to fully complete the learning process. By completing this essay, therefore, it is a way of formalizing the affective stage of the learning cycle and will ensure maximum learning is attained from completing the accreditation of prior learning.

Here, the writer has summarized the Kolb cycle in her own words. This is a practice that at least suggests that the student understands what the "expert" says, since she is able to assimilate the "expert's" voice to her own text, that is, make it her own by putting it into her own words. The student also makes clear the citation's connection to her own text: "By completing this essay, therefore, it is a way of formalizing the affective stage of the learning cycle". The student links her own experience on the module with a phase of Kolb's learning cycle, thus creating an explicit dialogue between her own voice and that of the "expert."

In contrast, in the following extract the writer puts into his own words the voice of the expert he was quoting, but with a different effect:

> 8.
>
> I would like to refer to something I learnt from my Yoga Diploma . . . It is suggested that reviewing past experience or skills or knowledge is something that Sages/Yogis do to cleanse the mind and prepare for new ways of thinking. I feel that doing this part of the course has given me a "breathing space" where I can take stock of myself and prepare for new ways of thinking.

This seems much less academically sophisticated because, though the writer has paraphrased the words of the "expert," the "experts" appealed to have little academic validity. In addition, the paraphrase does not appear to be of a particular text (there are no publication details) but appears to encapsulate a general view held by Sages/Yogis.

While it is the case that the student writers who explicitly draw on the voices of "experts" from whom they have developed an understanding of what learning means to them, *are* using the academically valued convention of citation, extract eight leads to the following point. The use of citation is an academically valued convention, particularly effective when used as discussed in extract seven above. However, what extract eight illustrates is that the use of the linguistic device of reported speech, which often indicates the presence of citations, is also common in more informal types of text, particularly in the reporting of personal experience (see Doncaster 1995).

The guidelines for the reflective assignment are that it should be a "personal reflection." This results in texts that have many features associated with informal texts, and fewer features of student academic texts. For example, the texts all use the first-person pronoun and dwell extensively on personal experience. Within this context, the use of citations and students' own explicit views about learning can be understood in a different way. Instead of trying to see these features of the essays as attempts to meet academic criteria, some use of other voices could be understood as devices for dramatizing or enlivening personal experience (Tannen 1989). A link can be made between the formal developing of argument and the informal dramatizing of experience, insofar as argument draws onto the stage of a text a range of players (own and other's views), each with a voice that the writer must relate to the others. Consequently, extract eight could be understood as making use of other voices in order to give an enhanced view of the student's own experience—showing how he has a multifaceted life, aspects of which can relevantly be drawn on to support his understanding of what learning is.

Conclusion

In undertaking the initial reflective piece of writing, students evaluate and analyze the wholeness of their learning by drawing on the academic, professional, and personal spheres of knowledge, often in the form of citation, as has been shown. We have focused on citation as an argumentation strategy because, as teachers and assessors, we have repeatedly noted how students use it to filter knowledge from these three spheres of their experience into their assignments. In quoting "experts" in the ways described in this chapter, students create dialogic spaces in their assignments where different voices can be presented, juxtaposed, and, importantly, students' own views refined and elaborated in the process. Thus, the use of citation in students' initial reflective assignments has a developmental function as well as revealing students' assumptions about academic argumentation when they start their programs of study.

As teachers, we assume that these students are already able, knowledgeable adults when they begin their studies. Consequently, we allow them the epistemological freedom to construct their own "truths" about their learning and knowledge in this first assignment, and use the assumptions revealed in them as the basis for helping students to enhance their academic skills. However, giving students this epistemological freedom may test our abilities as assessors, since this assignment may deploy more knowledge from the personal or the professional spheres than from the academic—for example, in the form of a highly personal style of writing or a turn of phrase that may not be generally used in academic writing. Our experience is that sometimes our own critical sensibilities (Lea and Street 1995) as assessors can be obstructed by biases. We have had to revisit our own assumptions about what is acceptable academic argumentation when faced by students who produce work such as the following (real examples are used here): a police officer who only wrote briefly and factually; a tax inspector who stuck rigidly to a guideline instead of interpreting it; someone working in the domestic sphere who was in a context that some do not think belongs in higher education; a voluntary worker who couched the assignment in a moral/spiritual tone.

In dealing with such issues, which arise from students' attempts to integrate knowledge from the spheres of academic, personal, and professional knowledge and create arguments, we return to the fundamental principle that, as assessors, we must be able to discern a reasoned argument which leads from work-based practice through reflection on that practice, analysis of one's own learning, and a return to the particular work context with a more developed and useful insight. It is possible to evaluate the work of students from a wide range of work areas because the criteria for assessment are generic and focus on identification of sources of knowledge, analysis, synthesis, and evaluation of information and ideas, selection, and justification of approaches to tasks, and most significantly, the ability to reflect on one's own practice. Throughout a program of study, students develop their ability to meet these criteria through increasingly incisive arguments about the contribution of professional, personal, and academic knowledge to their work-based practice.

10

Teaching Writing Theory as Liberatory Practice: Helping Students Chart the Dangerous Waters of Academic Discourse Across the Disciplines in Higher Education

Catherine Davidson

> I came to theory desperate, wanting to comprehend—to grasp what was happening around and within me . . . I saw in theory then a location for healing. (hooks 1996, 59)

> Writing . . . is not an innocent attempt at communication or at learning a discipline or at socialisation into a community—although it clearly has elements of all of these—but rather is a dominant sign of authority and power, a marker of difference, a sustainer of boundaries. (Lea and Street 1997, 15)[1]

While I love my job, teaching first-year international students to write academic argument, I have found over the years that students do not always feel the same way. The course, titled "Principles of Writing," is also known as POW. Indeed some of the students may feel like prisoners, in a war they do not understand, but which is described so menacingly by Lea and Street: an academic universe where writing is used not simply as a tool for learning and analysis, but to maintain hierarchies that mask the power not only of tutor over student, but of western, middle-class and even patriarchal culture over mediating outsider voices which might seek to enter into the discourse. There is a gap between our expectations as those teaching argument that our students will learn a useful, transferable intellectual skill, and the students' own experience of academic life as a bewildering and ever changing set of expectations which differ not only subject by subject but indeed tutor by tutor. If thought bubbles could be placed above the heads of instructor and student they might read very differently. The thoughts of the instructor might read: "Oh joy, here I am unmasking hidden expectations about writing, sparing my students the painful trial and error I experienced as an apprentice writer". The student's shows: "What does she want from me, how can I give it to her, how do I get an A and get out of here?"

This gap between expectations is not the only disjuncture in the writing classroom. We encourage our students to think about their process but evaluate them on their product; we teach argument as a genre while we learn that genre itself may be a fractured and mercurial concept; we teach successful academic writing as if it were a fixed target, while outside our classroom students encounter varying, often conflicting definitions of what that means. It is impossible to help our students prepare for every gap they may encounter, but a starting point is to acknowledge and address the idea of gaps. How can an already overworked practitioner do this while at the same time trying to teach an already complex form of academic discourse?

This paper will suggest a way to bring attention to gaps in the curriculum, to help students analyze the multiple positions from which they must approach academic argument, and suggest that making space for students to theorize as well as practice argument is vital as we ourselves begin to examine the complex nature of academic literacies. It will attempt to explore some of the disjunctures I have encountered in teaching academic literacy and how they led me to change my own curriculum to help my students become writing theorists as well as writing practitioners. Those students have helped to persuade me that theory can be liberating.

By "theory" I do not necessarily mean a particular ideology or analysis—reader response or rhetoric, construction or cognition—but a space for reflection, where what we are doing can be problematized, examined, and analyzed by the students we ask to share our classrooms. Theory can be both a product—a particular type of theory, and a process—a way of thinking, and the latter interests me more. The American writer and educator bell hooks argues that "theory" takes place in the gap between expectation and experience. In her definition, theory is a resource, a process, where critical analysis can be applied to the "common sense" that does not make sense. For many of our students, writing argument is one of the most difficult tasks they encounter; resistance may come from complex feelings about not only the work itself but students' perceptions of the university community, its social structure and values, and their relationship to it.[2] My desire to understand and explore that resistance led me to invite my students to theorize the argumentative research paper; their responses over several semesters led me to write this paper. I am grateful for what they have taught me.[3]

Mind the Gap: Theory as Practice

> It remains possible to observe elements involved in the process of academic writing from an external and detached position . . . to produce theories that seek to answer the many questions that plague the academic writer. (Yemi Babington-Ashaye, student: *Principles of Writing II,* 1998)

Many people who find themselves teaching academic argument in writing classrooms are busy, overworked and underpaid professionals, who may feel far removed from the theoretical debates flung across the pages of journals like *College Composition and Communication.* As the director of one writing program put it, in reality, many do not have either access to research or time to read it (Marius 1992, 467). Grappling with the very practical task of helping our students engage the academic environment, we may even be suspicious of theory as something vaguely unhealthy, emanating from the effete upper reaches of English or Linguistics departments far removed from the day to day difficulties of those on the ground.

In fact, there may be a tension between those who approach teaching academic writing from a practical, front-line perspective and those who write and think about it. In his 1996 article, "After Theory: from Textuality to Attunement with the World," Kurt Spellmeyer, a professor of English, critiques the kind of theory many practitioners may suspect, a theory which has grown detached from everyday life and is very much a part of the hierarchies of power identified by Lea and Street. As academics, we work in a culture of knowledge production that privileges the idea of an elite audience, one where that which is "too accessible" is given low status (897). While those working in academia write for a narrower and narrower audience, their ability to address issues which matter to a wider community, to their students, lessens. By this definition, which is certainly recognizable, theory would be the last thing to interest students and to liberate them. Can the narrow frame of theory written for specialists by specialists, even writing theory, widen the discourse of the writing classroom?

There is, however, another way to look at theory: not as a product which has value in the academic marketplace, but as a process, a way of thinking. By this definition, theory can be profoundly liberating, even life-changing. Spellmeyer maintains that the practice of theory can contribute to a more equitable distribution of cultural power, if it can help students confront the hidden structures, sometimes dangerous, which lurk beneath the placid surface of academic life. Spellmeyer harkens back to Horkeimer and Adorno and the Frankfurt School, for a model of theory engaged with a passionate debate about a changing world. He closes with a definition of theory which is worth quoting: "a practice of immanent critique launched at institutions like the university with their tendency to reproduce the status quo in supposedly objective and enabling routines" (896).

This idea of theory as active practice arises out of a willingness to question whenever there is a gap which does not make sense, when what we know does not measure evenly with what we are told we should think. Alice Miller's *The Drama of the Gifted Child* developed as the psychoanalyst measured the theories offered by Freud and Jung against the gap provided by her own lived experience. bell hooks reinforces this definition when she calls theorizing "a 'lived' experience of critical thinking, of reflection" that can overcome pain. She celebrates theory as a healing act, where explanation releases the frustration and fear that arise when a gap exists between what passes as an agreed upon truth and personal experience (hooks 1994, 61).

The Gap Between What We Know and What We Teach

> Academic writing to me is like a language of its own. One with its own rules and expectations. Like any other language, students are expected to recognize the tenses (past, present and future) and conjugate its verbs correctly with ease because there is a pattern that exists. (Josephine Ndunge, student: *Principles of Writing II,* 1998)

> If you have chosen your subject carefully and given sufficient thought to your audience and its concerns (paying particular attention to any objections that could be raised against whatever you wish to advocate), then it should not be difficult to organize an argumentative essay. (Miller 1989, 12)

Students may have to wait a long time before they can engage in this kind of active theorizing about their role in the academic community and their own writing. In the way we structure academic discourse, at least in the American model, students often learn the "basics"—the vocabulary of their chosen field, their genres—before they can begin to question what they are learning. While we often teach critical reading as an important component of writing arguments, we rarely engage in a self-critical analysis of what we are doing in the writing classroom, to critically read the text of ourselves.

Texts like Lankshear's *Changing Literacies,* directed at practitioners and theorists, point out the way discourses in the classroom reflect hierarchies and values of a global multinational economy. We are urged to "[create] a new Discourse, with a new community of human elements . . . in the name of social justice." (1997, xviii) While this sounds like an exciting goal as theory, how can we fit new forms of discourse into our practice when we are well aware that part of our role is to help students take on "skills" in a system that will indeed penalize them for not conforming? We teach them a language, as Josephine Nduge points out, giving a false impression, perhaps, that all they need to do is learn the "genre". The texts we offer reinforce this impression. For example, in classic rhetorics like *The Informed Argument* or Clark's *The Genre of Argument* theory might appear in the form of Toulmin's model of reasoning or classical forms of argumentation but there is no room to look at how argumentation itself is a cultural artifact.[4] These texts provide important tools, and I do not wish to denigrate them. The problem is the gap between Gee's (1999) call for new forms of writing, new ways of thinking about writing, and our need to guide students through a system they rightly suspect is out to force them to fit in.

Unless we begin to probematize what we do, to question and allow our students to question the forms of discourse we teach, we are in danger of increasing the unease that comes with gaps we do not address. We must provide opportunities for students to critically examine the world that they know and begin to critique it, as Spellmeyer suggests. By becoming academic ethnographers, and examining the details of their own experience in order to begin to theorize about gaps they may recognize, students begin the dangerous and exciting path of asking the question *why*. This process may be as important as the answers they achieve.

The Gap Between Private and Public Writing

> The ultimate goal of academic writing is objectivity. This suggests that personal voice is eclipsed for it is usually linked with the notion of subjectivity . . . We are inevitably subjective in our decisions and choices. Our personality is directly or indirectly incorporated in our writing: in our style, tone, use and choice of words, through the significant effect of our social environment and our personal background . . . The academic essay is actually a personal essay that has an objective aim, style, structure, appearance and tone. (Nadine Shirawi, student: *Principles of Writing II,* 1998)

By the time they reach the end of their second semester in an academic writing environment, I consider my students experts in students' experience of academic argument. I then give them an assignment which asks them to become academic ethnographers, to look at academic argument and their own attitudes towards it. The assignment also encourages them to critically examine the landscape in which they are writing, developing their own theories of academic argument. Abbs (1996, 114) has written about the vital role of autobiography as a way for students to position themselves within a new culture, the culture of the university. This is particularly true for students who come from backgrounds where they may not be naturally steeped in genres which form part of the "hidden curriculum" of the classroom (Berkenkotter and Huckin 1995, 155). The paper therefore begins with some autobiographical writing, which becomes part of their later analysis. Often a strong pattern emerges of remembered pleasure in private, creative writing. This contrasts with fear, nervousness, and resistance around public, academic writing.

This gap between private and public writing is the starting point of the assignment. Students are then asked to discuss why public writing may be so painful.[5] They are able to draw on research and expert opinion. One essay I have used, by Lynn Bloom (1996), points out that expectations about academic writing are rooted in the system of education that turned unruly American immigrants into scrubbed and clean middle-class graduates, where writing becomes the stamp that certifies the product safe and fully tested. I have also given them Bartholomae's 1986 classic essay discussing the idea of discourse and contrasting our expectations as faculty with our students' often bewildering experiences on the receiving end. The text used itself seems to matter less than the process of stepping back and using a wider frame to analyze their private experience. Feminists describe an active theorizing that allows us to see our own individual struggles as part of a wider pattern, the "click" moment. As students begin to discuss their experiences and readings, they begin to have their own "click" moments. These often take place online, during class discussion. Following one thread of argument, I could watch students move from a vague feeling of complaint and unhappiness to beginning to help each other think about *why* those feelings arise.

Ask the Experts: Students Theorize the Gaps

> Educational institutions take full interest in teaching the students skills and information that will be needed later in life. Yet, it seems that for the most part, they leave out the important task of teaching students why they are being taught such things. (Stephanie Bogin, student: *Principles of Writing II,* 1997)

The pre-writing work that goes into the assignment leads inevitably, of course, to an argumentative research paper. In the case of this assignment, students are asked to use their own reflective essays, the class discussions, the reading, and any outside research they have as sources. They are also told they can redesign the shape of the academic argument if it helps persuade the reader to see the point they want to make. Although all semester long they have been learning about conventional structure, thesis, and organization, for the final assignment, I ask them to design their own structure if it is useful to them.

Student theorists have written about many of the same issues we confront when we analyze our own discourse. They have written about the role of objectivity and subjectivity; about the nature of audience and how academic argument changes across disciplines; about evidence and source citation, and the way plagiarism itself can be seen as a cultural artifact. Their own positions, their own arguments, arise primarily from their reflection and class discussion. They use fewer sources for this assignment than any other (usually no more than three as opposed to seven or eight for a typical 2000-word research paper).

Some of their most convincing, imaginative, engaging, and thought-provoking arguments come from this assignment.

Without examining every theory or thread developed, it might be useful to look at one in particular which reflects the responses to the academic argument as a particularly problematic form of public writing: the question of audience. As Yemi Babinginton-Ashaye put it: "The academic writer comes into any discipline in the same way that humans come to the world; born into an already established system." Whereas students may use journal writing, poetry, letter-writing, song-writing as places where they can feel secure in their identity, expressing the world as they see it, when they confront the audience of the academy, they find themselves weighed and measured. They fear they will be found lacking.

They are also aware that this measurement takes place in a system in which the stakes are quite high. Many students make a high personal and economic investment in their education. They feel a great deal rests on their ability to meet the standards of the community. Yet, they resist this process of socialization. They want to maintain their own identity within the community, to learn the language but to remain bilingual. This is made worse by their awareness that as the audience changes from discipline to discipline so to some extent do the expectations about the nature of argument. As Neeta Maini, a first-year student in 1996, wrote:

> Coming to college is in itself a frightening experience, but when a student is faced with five solid courses in five different foreign languages, and no dictionary, independent life at a university suddenly takes a new twist in the path of fear.

This is echoed by an analysis which comes from Muge Dolun's reflection on her own experience:

> Academic writing is designed and formulated to give power to a certain group who can follow the logic of the argument in a given discourse. . . . [S]cientific papers . . . are more open to first person speech . . . However, even this luxury is provided to a senior elite rather than students of the discourse. On the other hand, even in a paper for Anthropology where you narrate participant observation, we are advised to refrain from using first person, and published ethnographers who use many "my village" or "my observations" are criticized for being biased.

To have students articulate these insights in their work is much more valuable in terms of pedagogical goals than to have me tell them the same thing in a form of a lecture or through reading. Yet in many cases, the argument paper also allows students to find a new way of claiming their role in the community, of developing ownership over their work. A shift seems to occur in their essays when they begin to see "standards" and "style" in academic writing as useful for their own purposes, not as something strictly imposed from the outside. The theory paper allows them an opportunity to discover, and therefore to own, their academic voice. Almost in response to the previous student, Dikko Abdurrahman, an engineering major, wrote a paper in 1998 describing the standards of academic writing as a kind of universal mathematics which helps ease communication across boundaries. He articulates both his classmates' sense of conspiracy and his own acceptance of logic as an element of academic discourse.

> Who dictates the laws of academic writing? Why must we conform to such rigid and unpleasant rules of academic writing or be penalised? Such questions give the impression of a few old men in dark suits lurking in the shadows dictating the rules of academic writing as a means of maintaining "power" . . . I would not insult your intelligence by informing you these men do not exist. However if a person picks up an academic paper, regardless of . . . culture . . . he/she would expect some sort of logical arrangement of information.

The conclusion drawn here echoes the quotation from Nadine Shirawi which began the previous section. While initial discussions were often negative in tone regarding academic argument, the papers themselves often took a measured stand in which the positions were more balanced, insightful, and mature. Not that every student completed the assignment a happy foot soldier in the academic ranks. In fact, the strength and confidence in their voices had an interesting parallel in the leaps some of them took in discovering new forms of argumentation.

Writing as Design

> Broaden the definition of academic writing so it is more inclusive. Bore a hole in the center, fill it with yeast and warm water. See what ferments. (Elizabeth Bochtler, student: *Principles of Writing,* 1998)

> For those students who argue that there is not enough room for creativity in writing research papers, there is a solution. What I suggest . . . is to look at writing itself as an art form. (Heather Harrison, student: *Principles of Writing,* 1998)

In *How We Write: Writing as Design* (1999), Sharples points out that we can reconcile some of the perceived conflict between creative and academic genres of writing by seeing all writing as design. The writer designs a response to a problem and creates the format needed to solve it. This concept returns some of the ownership back to the writer, and may help our students see the way they can choose things like an objective voice or researched evidence to solve their own needs, out of their own desire to persuade. Some of them, given a choice, may find ways to redesign the argument. Their creative approaches have helped me rethink the design of persuasion.

Students have used a variety of new forms. One used dialogue as a way to make an argument; the writer argued that personifying and presenting two sides to a controversy may be a more effective form of critical thinking than our rather artificial development of a single thesis (even with polite acknowledgement of the "other side"). One student argued that "Academic writing might become more believable, acceptable and understandable if writers did more collaborative writing" and then designed her paper to include the voices of her family members, whom she canvassed by email to ask them about their own experiences of academic writing. Another used boxes and footnotes as an imaginative way to create a feeling of heteroglossia in a paper in which she critiqued our expectation that academic writing should or could be a unified discourse. Others who wanted to see more of their private writing included in their public expressions leavened their papers with journal writing, song lyrics, letters, and e-mails.

Do these experiments have any impact after the students leave the relatively safe space of the writing classroom?[6] One example does suggest it might. Stephanie Bogin is an American who had experienced a wide variety of both public and private educational systems. She wrote two papers in response to the assignment and formatted them into columns to be read side by side. The first was traditional, using research, evidence, and a clear thesis to persuade the reader that there needed to be more room made for reflection and theory in the academic classroom. The second column was a creative memoir in which she narrated her own development as a writer, moving from the bliss of a sixth-grade creative writing class to mastering critical essays that nevertheless alienated her from her peers. Reading both essays side by side did in fact prove Stephanie's point that more room can be made for reflection. Her design became a piece of evidence in her argument.

The following semester she went to Florence to study literature and art history. When she returned, she showed me a paper which had received an excellent mark. In the paper, she analyzed the role of Dante's Paradiso as a way to understand the geography of Florence; in her design, she used personal reflection and narrative, literary analysis, and historical biography all mixed into a very powerful piece of writing. According to Stephanie, she has since discovered that not every reader is willing to entertain new forms of discourse. As she put it, even postmodernists can be traditionalists when it comes to writing. Whether or not the discourse community in which she writes is willing to listen to her, Stephanie has found both a personal and persuasive voice in which to write academic argument.

Conclusion

An author's ability to display a grasp for discovering and developing theory and to present a coherent argument that engages the audience must be evident in any form of written or spoken rhetoric—academic papers, speeches

> and prose. When Sojourner Truth's words "and ain't I a woman" were proclaimed, her theory echoed the strife of gender inequality and unleashed the motto of egalitarian black feminist sentiment. (Tina Gaye-Bernard, student)

The academic argument is not a neutral testing ground. It is a genre which arises from our culture, one which may even reflect the gender of the academy through most of its long history. In her book, *The Argument Culture,* Deborah Tannen (1998) suggests that our own competitive and perhaps to some extent destructive emphasis on argument as a form of public discourse reflects masculine as well as Western norms. Argument has value, but it should not be treated as stationary or inevitable. For those of us who want to teach argument, allowing a space for our students to argue about argument is a starting point. Perhaps the writers we help to train today will become more engaged, powerful agents of change and persuasion in the public domain. If they can see themselves linked in history to a tradition of rhetoric and persuasive oratory, as designers of texts rather than passive victims of rules, they may indeed help us change our own discourse into something more vibrant and engaging. Certainly, the student theorists who have worked with me have helped me see academic writing in new ways.

Notes

1. From an unpublished article with permission of the author. In the published version (Lea and Street 1998), the quotation reads: "It appears, then, that written feedback on student work, is not merely an attempt at communication, or at learning a 'discipline,' or at socialisation into a community—although it clearly has elements of all of these—but is also embedded in relationships of authority as a marker of difference and sustainer of boundaries."

2. A good deal of research being done under the rubric of "Academic Literacies" points to the complexities of this relationship and the role that writing plays in reinforcing and shaping the social universe of the academic community. See for example Brian Street (1996), "Academic Literacies."

3. I would like to thank particularly the students in the English 102A and Honors groups in 1996–99 who helped with the evolution of this paper. I quote them extensively throughout to acknowledge their contribution to my own thinking about the complexity of academic literacy.

4. Theory filters into student texts. For example, Swales' *Genre Analysis* has had enormous influence; see Clark (1998) and also Bjork and Raisanen (1997) for new books using genre as a way to teach argument. The problem is that the dialectic of theory has already moved on. Experts question genre even as student textbooks reify it. Active theorizing, as I describe here, can be a more flexible way to bring in critical thinking about argument.

5. This is not the only way to approach this assignment. A colleague has instead given students a series of expert writing about academic discourse and asked students to answer the question: Why is Academic Writing so complex? The emphasis in my

assignment comes from my own experience as a writer and what students have identified in their reflections.

6. I say relatively safe, because the paper still counts as part of their assessment. To try to make even this part of the assignment an opportunity for reflection, I ask students to design their own criteria for evaluation and to submit a grade recommendation based on their own assessment.

11

"Argument" as a Term in Talk About Student Writing

Janet Giltrow

Recent thinking about argument notices the situatedness of this form of expression: its different appearances in different cultural or educational locations. Although most seem to agree that the text type we are calling "argument" is recognizable by the presence of backed-up statements, many researchers in this area are now telling us to expect diversity—"evidence," for example, in one discipline would not necessarily count as "evidence" in another discipline, or in another social situation. This chapter takes into consideration the situatedness of argument by reflecting on pedagogical consequences of the use of the term "argument" itself. It deliberates on the utility or outcomes of ways of naming text types and their associated features, and it reflects on the way the term "argument" participates in institutional systems—including traditions of composition instruction.

It seems useful and sensible to propose "argument" as a text type—as distinct from, say, "narrative"—and then be aware of situational differences. But I will offer here evidence of occasions where this terminology, in its working semiotics, can have consequences which well-meaning people may not intend. While "argument" in its colloquial life, as a name for a variety of speech acts, and "argument" in its technical life, as an object of researchers' inquiry, function without dire consequences, "argument" in its in-between life, as a term circulating among the professoriate, in classrooms, and institutional corridors, saturated with ideologies of those places, can mystify and confound writers, and put them at a disadvantage.

Some have criticized argument for being masculinist, eurocentric, and middle-class, or hierarchical and linear. I am not concerned here with such criticisms, for I am more interested in the behavior of "argument" as a term in the discourse on student writing than in argument as something students might do. In accounting for my interest in "argument" as a term or concept, I will mention some of its collocates—words like "logic," "evidence," "thesis," "audience," "voice," which co-occur with "argument" in talk about student writing. And, although I concentrate on "argument" and its collocates, my broader concern is with systems of naming writing—or perhaps any social behavior—at levels so high as to be universalizing. We are all aware of the circumstances Kenneth Burke observed when he said that terminologies "direct the attention:" "Even if any given terminology is a *reflection* of reality, by its very nature as a terminology it must be a *selection* of reality; and to this extent it must function also as a *deflection* of reality" (1966, 45 "Terministic Screens" *Language as Symbolic Action*). But there may be a special effect when the terminology is peculiarly "high," so as to command many significantly different particulars, and when the terminology is involved in the management of language and learning.

Genre Theory in a "Writing Center"

I advance these speculations from an identifiable theoretical position—that of the "new genre theory"—and a particular institutional position—a "writing centre" in the English department of a Canadian university. From other positions, "argument" may have a different profile, and claims I make may not be widely applicable. Conceding the limitations of my perspective, I will say nevertheless that through the lens of the new genre theory—proposed by Carolyn Miller in the early 1980s and elaborated by others since then—"argument" is out of focus. While the new genre theory itself does not dictate any names for types of writing, or prescribe the level of categorization at which naming of text types should go on, it has tended to encourage work at lower levels of categorization. (So, informed by the new genre theory, we are likely to use local names for types of writing, such as "abstract proposal," or "essay for first-year literature course," or "M.A. thesis prospectus.") The new genre theory defines *genre* as *typifiable social situations*—recognizable to members of a community—and *typifiable forms of expression*—also recognizable to members of a community and available to them—which address and maintain those situations.[1] Leaving the set of genres "open," and focusing on situation rather than taxonomy, the new genre theory neglects the project of ordering the world in timeless patterns and, instead, prepares to meet the everyday, variable, and contingent contexts in which language is used.

An example of the level of inquiry encouraged by the new genre theory is Aviva Freedman's study of "an introductory undergraduate course in law" (1996, 97), which required students to write "800-word essays, each in response to a precisely worded prompt" (98). Freedman reports that students' writing developed context-specific features, in response to the particular kinds of reasoning which informed language itself in the course: "the kind of complexly interwoven strands of discoursal instantiations (in lecture, seminar, and text) of stance presented in content-area courses" (111)—rather than in response to instruction in forms of argument. Freedman suggests educational implications: "We must not feel that our goal in the writing class is to teach some form of "all-purpose argument" in order to prepare students to write effectively elsewhere in the curriculum; they acquire the genres of argument far more efficiently and effectively within the contexts of discipline-specific courses" (112).

This kind of research endorses our work at lower levels of definition of text types. But our work is just as much a realization of our own institutional position—and a particular political understanding of this position—as it is a commitment to a theory and its research outcomes. We have *practical* reasons for avoiding "argument" as a research and instructional concept. I am going to concentrate on accounting for these practical and political reasons. In practice, what people *say* about writing matters, the words they use to name text types have consequences, and when they say "argument" in their references to student writing, the practical results are not what we are looking for.

In the Writing Centre, we work at the intersection of disciplines: writers and their writings arrive from many points on the disciplinary map. The first need for our students—and for us—is to understand the research genres as distinct from the genres with which writers might confuse them—the informational or feature article, for example, or the schoolroom essay, or types of polemic. We help writers attend to salient features which research genres share: techniques for summoning published voices that recognize a topic and the knowledge that has accumulated around it so far; techniques for identifying a deficit in that knowledge, or an instability; manners of reasoning that modalize statements and register their limits. The second need for us and for writers we work with is to understand differences among the disciplines. We have found academic readers to be sensitive not only to the incursion of nonscholarly styles into student writing but also to discipline-specific features of writing.

Talk About Writing

So we aim to acclimatize writers to differences—differences between the research genres and other types of writing, and differences amongst the disciplines. Part of this effort involves tuning our ears to the information coded in characteristic styles of writing in the disciplines, and letting these styles act as incentives to students to participate in the discipline that is calling for their contribution. But at the same time we aim to cultivate a discourse on writing—a kind of *talk* about writing—that is an *inducement to write,* and an inducement to participate in scholarly activities. Especially, this talk about writing is meant to reveal writing as something that is *read.* We coach readers to voice their experience for writers: say out loud when they stop and reread, when they stumble or stall, or have second thoughts, or when they begin to look for a citation, or when they find themselves rewording a troubling sentence.

Hearing readers read, writers are motivated to anticipate the reception of their writing.[2]

In this project, we set aside traditional wordings of response to student writing; "argument" is one of these words. When we investigated students' interpretation of marking commentary (Giltrow, Johanson, and Valiquette 1994), we found that they read traditional remarks on their writing as predictable and uninformative. They experience this kind of talk about writing as expression of authority rather than as inducement to write—partly because of the institutional context. Accompanying an evaluation and its consequences, this commentary expresses to them a marker's power rather than a reader's experience. But, equally important, traditional commentary generalizes the criteria for success (or the signs of failure), referring to all-purpose principles which are insensitive to the particularities of context and the materiality of language in use: principles like "logic," "organization," "evidence," "argument." When "argument" shows up in marking commentary, students draw few inferences from it about their own work as writers and tend instead to interpret the term as instance of the inscrutability of professors' tastes. Especially they regard notations about features like "argument" as expressions of typical professorial attitudes towards student writing: lofty, evasive, never satisfied.

What People Say About Writing

Besides cultivating an alternative kind of talk about writing amongst ourselves and our students and our colleagues, we also record other talk about writing at the university, looking to find out what people are likely to *say* about writing, as well as to correlate these sayings with the characteristics of what they read. We ask writers and readers—from graduate teaching assistants to senior professors in a range of disciplines—to read out loud and comment on examples of scholarly writing: sometimes their own work which has been evaluated by others but most often student writing which they have evaluated. We also gather other kinds of commentary on scholarly writing: notations on papers, for example, or handouts giving advice on writing assignments. I reviewed material we have collected[3] in the interests of finding out how the word "argument" *behaves.*

I anticipated occasions like the ones Sharon Stockton describes in her study of writing in History. She found that "[a]ll faculty agreed . . . that *argument* is the key word for good writing and that the absence of argument constitutes the central problem in students' written work" (1995, 50), but that expectations differed depending on students' level, and "[i]n fact, faculty assignments, grades, and comments on student papers seem to imply that explicit argument as such was not the central issue of concern" (51). Despite professors' calls for *argument,* "[u]ltimately, assignments and evaluations show that written sophistication in student writing was in this department a function of *narrative* complexity . . ."—"a certain specialized form of narrative" (52). When professors said "argument," they had a variety of other things in mind.

Like Stockton, I found that readers used the word "argue" and its derivations, or at least its collocates: *thesis, evidence,* and in one case *critical thinking.* Most would probably have agreed with this Literature professor's matter-of-fact way of putting the case: ". . . I am looking for evidence to back up points of arguments. . . ." He looks for students "presenting an argument in which . . . each sentence makes its own sense and the sentence that follows shows a coherency in the argument and as the argument proceeds, as they move to levels of particularization and away from generalization, that's where you start looking for support and evidence." Similarly a handout on evaluation criteria, adapted by a Political Science professor from a rubric prepared by a college instructor of English, takes an argumentational view in distinguishing "A," "B," and "C" papers. An "A" paper has "a perceptive and incisive thesis, richly developed, and an organization to match;" a "B" paper "has a clearly presented and conceptually defensible argument. . . . The body of the essay is well organized and provides adequate support for the elaboration of the argument"; the "C" paper's "thesis is correct and adequately expressed, while the development of the argument and presentation of evidence is sufficient to support the claims being made." A handout for students in History recommends similar structure, advising that writers begin with "the thesis you will be arguing towards" and "indication of the specific arguments you will be making." "Argument" and its collocates appear in our records of commentary from these three disciplines—Literary Studies, Political Science, History—and in commentary from readers in other disciplines, too.

From one point of view—maybe the professorial one—this consensus confirms "argument" as an instructional goal: everyone agrees on the aims of student writing. But from another point of view—maybe the student one—"argument" is not a steady goal but a moving target, one that transforms itself wherever it appears. From our point of view, in the Writing Center, the recurrence of the term under diverse and even conflicting circumstances obscures rather than illuminates the actual conditions to which readers respond.

Talk About "Argument" in History, Literary Studies, and Sociology

I will try to expose some of the diversity obscured by the structural figure so common to statements about "argument:" something more general on top—a "thesis" or equivalent—is supported by more specific things underneath. We find that the thing on top changes according to the discipline. So, the handout offered History students, for example, goes on to warn writers *not* to claim that any historical event was inevitable: that kind of top for an argument is not right for History, although the existence of the caution suggests that writers are tempted by it. Writers are also advised against making broad statements about human nature.[4] But a first-year Literature student refers in an opening paragraph to "the sense of mental anguish and confusion that are felt when we are forced to suddenly change in order to adapt to difficult, unfamiliar, unpredictable situations" and her reader has no objection.

In Sociology, however, statements about humans generally are again risky, for this discipline investigates not the human nature of people but their social nature and its constructs. So when a student in an upper-division course in "The Sociology of the Environment" establishes in her first paragraph that technical culture has "disconnected [North Americans'] relationship with nature," and then writes "It becomes very difficult to realize or empathize with what harm we are doing to the ecosystem when we have become so separated from it" the reader comments, "Now on this I have bracketed "we" and said "who" with a question mark because one of the issues of the course . . . we spent a lot of time talking about is humanity. In what sense is humanity a unity that we can talk about in relationship to nature like this? From some points of view it is; from others, questions of class difference, gender difference, regional difference and all of this override the unity of humanity. So it's a kind of cautionary note. . . ." The reader has spotted something persistent in the writer's approach to her highest claims, for, six pages later, when the student remarks that "the blame [for environmental problems] cannot be placed specifically on systems. After all, what or who is the system anyway? Is the system not made up of people like ourselves?", the reader comments: "This is bourgeois to put it in a nutshell. The system is more than . . . the people that make it up and that is what Sociology is about. This is very problematic when they start talking that way in a third-year Sociology course. I should perhaps write that down there but it seems so basic. . . . I would have to write down a long page about the difference between the individual and the social system." The reader didn't write the long page; in the interview he reported what he did instead. He offered a general comment about argumentative strategy: "I have said at the side: 'Watch these rhetorical questions. They only work if the reader agrees with you.'" He then interpreted the marking notation for the interviewer: "As a reader myself who doesn't agree with any of this, the argument in so far as it exists up to here is completely destroyed at this point and they tend to write out of their own mind rather than explain it to someone else." Both the notation and its interpretation take an argumentational view of the passage, but it is hard to imagine how the student would make useful inferences from them about her own writing. The more useful point here seems to be not about general strategies for argument—"rhetorical questions"—or observations on students' tendencies to neglect the generalized "someone else" who is their audience, but about doing Sociology: using particular interpretations of the world established by sociological thought and recognizing the reader as habituated to these particular interpretations. Remarks about argument conceal these local contingencies.

The Sociology essay incites the reader's reaction not because it is missing the top levels of the ideal structure of argument but, rather, because those higher claims are the wrong kind. And just as the highest claims of "argument" can trigger local, disciplinary cautions, so can the lower, "supporting" structures. The Literature professor looks for "evidence"—just as other readers do. But their expectations are very different. When the Literature professor reads "In the absence of the romantic bond, Othello's life would lose much of its meaning, and he would revert to his role as a 'soldier for pay'", he says, "There are a number of problems there; I asked for evidence. I am asking for evidence as to whether [Othello] was ever spoken of in those terms by anyone including himself as a 'soldier for pay' because that has certain connotations to it and he is a general after all. Is 'soldier for pay' a formulation which matches someone's view of Othello in the play? Is there any evidence that he loses the romantic bond? That this would happen? That he would go back to being a general?" What makes the reader call for "evidence" at this point? Inspecting my own reaction to this idea about Othello, I suspect that the professor has encountered a reading of the play that is generated not by current literary-critical practice (that is, a reading he might imagine as possibly producing himself) but by values associated with other uses of drama in our culture—values associated with television and popular cinema and inspiring a view of the world in which a life dominated by a souless career can be transformed by a surprising but satisfactory heterosexual relationship. The call for "evidence" marks this point where the writer has betrayed his practices as a reader as belonging to the discipline of TV-watching rather than the discipline of literary criticism.

Hearing the Talk About "Argument"

How will the writer interpret this call for evidence? In the first place, he cannot reasonably question the need for evidence in general, for evidence is highly regarded (no one ever says "do not provide evidence"). In the second place, he cannot hear the reader's elaborations on the notation—let alone its unspoken motivations, which involve the defining values of the discipline. Finally, he could confuse the call for "evidence" here with those he has likely heard in other disciplines. How should he *act* in order to correct this deficiency? Where will the writer find evidence to support his claim? Or, rather, how should he have derived the claim in the first place? If he received the handout for evaluation criteria in Political Science (which shares argumentational terms with the Literature professor's talk about writing), he might go to the library, for the "A" paper uses "many sources . . . in developing the key argument" and "[compares and contrasts] the views of several major authors." But the Literature professor's call for evidence should not send the writer to the library but to the text of the play—a single text rather than "many." This is a difference in the material practices of the disciplines, a difference which impinges on what people have in mind when they say "evidence."

The next example illustrates a successful exchange between a writer and reader—one which generates the specifics or "evidence" acceptable to a disciplinary community but without ever using the term "evidence." Reading an M.A. thesis prospectus which begins "Until recently the written history of Palestinian Arabs under the British Mandate (1920–1948) concentrated on the traditional élite who formed and led the explicitly political movements of the period. In the past few years historians and social scientists have begun to explore the lives of villagers and, even more recently, of employees, from casual laborers on rural public works to dock workers in the ports of Jaffa and Haifa, to civil servants in the British administration", a History professor rewords the student's sentences, talks historiographically about ideological "nuances" of arguments in history, and then makes the telling comment: "What I told her was I thought if she went to England to the Public Records Office at Kew Gardens (. . .), she'll find files in English, she doesn't read Arabic, which is the problem, which will be reports, someone reporting on labour affairs. . . . Part of her problem here is she really has just read secondary sources, she hasn't figured out a research technique. . . ." This instruction about how to act in the world, about what to do rather than how to argue, has good results in the opening to the writer's revised prospectus (even though she hadn't yet made the trip). In the revision, specifics, or evidence, peculiar to *historical* writing—dates, numbers, particular actors—appear: "In April 1946 some 15,000 public employees, Arabs and Jews, railway labourers, postal workers, and government clerks, sustained a six-day strike against the British Mandate Administration." Now it is *as if* she had been to the archive, had begun the material work of the historian, and her action is figured in a style she will have encountered many times before in her own readings in the discipline. Her reader is satisfied: the discussion which follows the narrative beginning is, he says, "assertive and clear." (We might speculate here that, if the writer had simply been told to be "assertive and clear"—as many writers are in our collection of discourse on student writing—the result would not have been so distinctively successful.)

When the call for specifics is explicit—as it is in the next example—it conceals rather than reveals the disciplinary values which motivate the reader's evaluation of the passage. Even after the writer in the Sociology course has mentioned what might seem to her to be specifics: "our water comes from a metal tap and flows down a metal drain, we flick a switch and we have light, and we drive over land on concrete roads and highways. A view from inside one's house generally consists of streets and manicured lawns," the reader says in the interview: "This is the point at which I start to wonder when it's going to get more specific; at what point we're going to get real content." While these specifics about taps and lawns could support "argument" in other zones of environmental discussion, they don't constitute specifics in Sociology. Sociological work requires that the writer look in other places for her evidence of technological disconnection from "nature."[5] Were the writer to overhear this talk about specifics, she could be baffled, figuring that she *had* been specific. Or she might accept the comment as another instance of the inscrutability of hard-to-please professors' remarks about student writing.

"Audience" "Voice"

Maybe these differences are simply a matter of "audience," and refinements to ideals of argument would easily accommodate ideas of audience.[6] But when our readers volunteer notions of audience these ideas tend to be as general—and misleading—as their broad statements about what makes an argument. A teaching assistant in Canadian Studies says a "good essay" is one you should "be able to give to someone who doesn't know anything about the topic and they [should be able] to make some sense of it." The Sociology professor expresses similar ideas of audience: "Essays should be written to someone else in this class or someone else in some other class, your parents or your friends, not to me." When something is not right, for a highly defined and particular audience, readers' comments generalize and elevate the issue, beyond the local particularities of the discipline. In an earlier study (Giltrow and Valiquette 1994), we also found readers consulting broad or unrefined conceptions of audience. When readers in Criminology and Psychology encountered statements in which students' faulty estimates of common knowledge of discipline-specific terms betrayed their status as newcomers, the readers—paradoxically—invoked ideas not of local disciplinary audiences but of general audiences—"outsiders."

And while the question "Who reads?" is answered in these broad—and misleading—generalities, the "Who writes?" question can also excite some generalized—and misleading—claims about the preferred stance of the writer. The Teaching Assistant in Canadian Studies reports receiving a four-page paper with "64 citations": "I wrote in the comments 'Where is your voice in all this?'" The handout on criteria for evaluating essays in Political Science prizes a "writing style" that is "individualized" and discounts one that is not so. It may be mean-spirited or bad-tempered to question these assumptions about the value of the unique self, or any of the other sentiments which urge on students the opportunity to find themselves in their writing, but I will do it anyway: what *is* an "individualized" style? Who is to judge the authentic voice or preside over its emergence? How are students to know if they are writing with their "own" voice—or someone else's? While students are urged to speak to a broad, unmarked audience, to take, as the discourse on argument often insists, responsibility for their opinions by constructing well-supported claims, they are also enjoined to speak in their own voices. Uninterpretable as these injunctions can be to student writers, there may be a pattern to urgings towards the authentic voice: they appear to accompany judgements about the writer's capacity to, as Lave and Wenger say, "[become] a full participant, a member, a *kind* of person" (1991, 53, emphasis added). So, reading the successful revision of the M.A. thesis proposal, the History professor remarked, "I think she has found her own voice." I interpreted this to say that I heard her style as "very much an historian's voice," and, although the professor countered by saying that the writer was now "authoritative", I am satisfied that the historian's voice *was* the writer's "own" for this occasion. The episodes of exchange between writer and teacher had resulted in "the development of [a] knowledgeably skilled [identity] in practice" (Lave and Wenger 1991, 55). Had the writer been simply told—as the Canadian Studies and Political Science students were—to use her "own voice," she would have been confounded if not misled, for her success comes from writing as an historian and for other historians: not as her unique or unprecedented self, and not for her friends, or for people who know nothing.

"Argument" Patrolling and Mystifying the Borders of the Disciplines

As readers talked about reading and writing, they did use "argument" to describe the main-claim + supporting-evidence structure. They also used it to refer to other things: to report on the gist of other writers' work, for example (first-year history; third-year sociology); or to the literary-critical practice of "close reading"; or to what we might call a "discourse"—a set of connected interpretations of the world. But especially "argument" and its collocates come up at normative moments—on the one hand, when the ideal is invoked or the successful product is imagined, or, on the other hand, when deviance is encountered. This is how the term behaved as an assistant professor in Fine Arts read reviews of her book manuscript. Some of the numerous reviews of this manuscript were favorable, but some were not, and unfavorable ones remarked on "argument:" "the book suffered from a lack of an overarching coherence and structure, which ultimately reinforced the unease about the coherence of the arguments being made, many of which seemed to be advanced without supporting evidence." The writer, a professional scholar, finds these remarks about argument as baffling as undergraduate writers do: "I find that a really strange comment. I mean, I can imagine, some historians would want a kind of intricate and detailed support for the reading of certain paintings and certain texts. That's fine when it comes to canonical culture, you have everyone writing in response to that culture. But when it comes to aspects of culture that were suppressed or censored . . . how are you going to, I mean there were no reviews. . . , or very few . . ." Struggling to negotiate with these readings of her work, the writer also turns to the concept of "argument", but it is finally not "argument" or its ideals that contribute to her understanding of her predicament. For one thing, there is no ideal that answers readers' criticism: "Everyone," she says, "seems to have an opinion on the order of the chapters." And she is suspicious of the gender identities of her audience: "men," she says, "don't read women's work"—an aspect of the situation not easily captured by "argument." Finally the dilemma for revision concerns her sense of which discipline she will address with her work: art history, feminist history, or semiotics. What matters is differences amongst the disciplines, rather than conformity to an ideal we might call argument. And it is the differences amongst the disciplines' routines for making knowledge, and the discursive representation of those routines, that matter, rather than estimates of weak or strong arguments. Accordingly, the writer summarizes advice from a senior colleague, who told her "not to sort of bond to readers' reports, that you have to understand where the reader is coming from, try to figure out their academic practices or the research practices from what they are saying about your work." In this episode in the life of a professional scholar, and in the episodes of undergraduate and graduate writing reported here, "argument" is a concept that patrols the borders of the disciplines, registering incursion or outbreaks, and in the generality or universality of its authority it can leave tacit and undisclosed the actual, local conditions that give newcomers license to participate.

I would not want to say that there is nothing in the writing in question that would qualify as an "argument" under general applications of the term, but rather that the use of the term is mystifying rather than informative. Hearing the word "argument" repeatedly in contexts the variety of which defies the deduction of any practical principles, students can only infer that there is something they should know that they don't know. So widespread does this understanding of the desired thing seem to be that it appears to be almost a natural condition of being human and to be missing it is unnatural. But "argument," in its actual manifestations, is not natural but social and cultural, contingent on circumstances that are local but *still typifiable* at lower levels of analysis—circumstances like those for example in a first-year course in poetry or a graduate course in historiography.

"Argument" Participating in Institutional Systems

Connected to this mystification are official and bureaucratized procedures: "argument" has an affinity with testing. Perhaps the term's decontextualized generality suits it for these purposes. Discussions of "argument" and its performance often mention testing, leading one to suspect its collusion in large-scale screening procedures.[7] Unsituated and unparticularized, "argument" (or its cognate "expository essay") becomes an occasion for writing out of the blue. And students tend to do poorly, whether in classroom or test situations. So a discussion which suggests new approaches to responding to student writing begins with an account of student argument that presumes failure:

> [students] rarely argue well or even adequately. Each paper seems only one more failed attempt to persuade, and teachers wince at the yearly return of the same faults: poor arrangement of arguments, contradictory arguments, and little elaboration by explanation or illustration. Recent national assessment

> tests likewise reveal the inability of students at elementary and secondary levels to write adequate argumentation (Nelms 1990). (Lynch 1996, 35–6)

Aviva Freedman has explained such results by suggesting that these failures to conform to an ideal of argument are a consequence of students "[selecting] their own contexts to respond to in their writing because they were not being constrained or enabled by what had been transpiring to that point in their classroom" (1996, 112). But this explanation is likely to be drowned out by other interpretations of student writing: results from tests or assignments that call for decontextualized argument are easily converted to materials of what Milroy and Milroy (1985, 1991) call the "complaint tradition"—the cultural practice of disparaging youth and contemporary schooling, deploring the decline in language itself, and linking this linguistic decadence with social disorder. Today, in our country, these attitudes are associated with but not exclusive to neoconservative interests.

When criteria for evaluation are so high-level, so generalized as to envelop and thereby obscure difference, we should expect such political outcomes. As Kenneth Burke observed, higher order terms—"titles" and "ultimate terms"—occlude difference by establishing a "'guiding idea' or 'unitary principle' behind the diversity of voices" (1969, 184, 186). Under the auspices of the "'unitary principle,'" "the voices," he says, "would not confront one another . . ." (187). These conditions, falling along "the wavering line between identification and division"—between shared interests and conflicting ones—render themselves "in stylistic subterfuges for presenting real divisions in terms that deny division" (45). And Bakhtin describes just this circumstance particularly in matters of language when he refers to the "myth of a language that presumes to be the only language, and the myth of a language that presumes to be completely unified" (68), or when he talks about unitary ideologies of language which go with the "current of centralizing tendences in the life of language" and "[ignore the] dialogized heteroglossia" (1981, 273), or when he observes that "'general literariness'" of a unitary view of language goes towards "[preserving] the socially sealed-off quality of a privileged community" (382).

Categories of text type, so high as to unify rather than diversify concepts of language, and effortlessly agreed-upon by members of the professoriate, can have these political consequences, and institutional ones as well. So, while we avoid resorting to ideas of "argument" in our instructional activities, we also avoid ideas of "argument" in representing our work to the institution of which we are part. We don't say that we teach the principles of "sound argument"—although there are those who might say this on our behalf, or would be comforted if we said it for ourselves. By seeming to unify the values and practices of the university population and the respectable public generally, promises to teach argument mobilize the hegemonic forces that Bakhtin recognized in unitary views of language.

"Argument" and the Traditions of Composition Instruction

From a distance, it could seem that we are overdoing our resistance to "argument." It is after all a word frequently and harmlessly at work in everyday talk, and a concept useful to the organization of scholarly inquiry into knowledge, language, and cognition. But between these two domains of usage—the everyday domain, in which speakers resort to the word to describe a variety of speech acts, and the research domain, in which scholars technicalize the everyday, commonsense word—"argument" becomes complicit with interests and attitudes which both confound and disadvantage the student writer. In the milieu in which I work, this in-between use of the term finds its authority in North American traditions of "composition" teaching: an activity carried on by Literature specialists, guided by handbooks composed by other Literature specialists with a belle lettristic and haute bourgeois interest in language and learning, and indemnified by class identifications—carried on, as Linda Brodkey says, by "all those people who teach composition but study only literature" (1996, 89). Use of a term like "argument"—or "thesis statement" or "expository essay" or "narrative"—attempts to professionalize what is an essentially amateur activity. The lords of the disciplines bless this professionalist pretense, for it cooperates, as Bourdieu observes, in producing first the "system of norms regulating linguistic practices" (1991, 45) and then in the outcome of these regulatory norms—the "[re-translation of] social distinction into the specifically symbolic logic of differential deviations . . ." (1991, 55). In the disciplinary constellation, the core work of producing and maintaining categories of distinction seems best left to the housekeeping department of literary studies, where, generation after generation, the handbook tradition repeats but does not examine (having no methodological apparatus for examining) advice on thesis statement and argument, on clarity and vagueness, on logic and organization. Once the work of distinction is assigned to this reliably amateur tradition, the other disciplines can concentrate on their professional knowledge-making enterprises.[8]

I have said that "composition" teaching belongs to "North America." This is not quite right, and as I peel back the layers of political attitude which motivate my resistance to "argument", I will acknowledge a final one: an anticontinentalist impulse, which rejects U.S. influence (usually unsuccessfully) and attempts a nationalist stand. To me, "argument" is metonymic of the "freshman comp" classroom, a U.S. phenomenon. It is an artifact of social and historical or cultural conditions which Susan Miller brilliantly accounts for in *Textual Carnivals* (1991): trepidations of the social order in late nineteenth-century America, the emergence of "English studies" in the context of these trepidations, the realignment of the "modes of discourse"—description, narration, exposition, argumentation—to name disembodied ideals rather than rhetorical purposes, and the relocation of writing studies at the "freshman" or entry portal of higher education to construct a "site for winnowing and indoctrination" (1991, 63).

The classification of discourse that includes "argumentation" has a slightly foreign sound to me, for the sociohistorical conditions Miller describes are not indigenous to Canada (although they are not unrecognizable, and U.S.-originating textbooks have made them somewhat familiar). The flurry of disturbance that arises around students' execution of the "argument" essay—or any product that requires a "thesis" and "support"—the campaigns that seek to rescue failing or stumbling writers and set them on their feet—these disturbances and campaigns address an artifact of the U.S. "composition" classroom—one which is *not* equivalent to scholarly or academic expression, although many commentators presume it to be so.[9] Problems that Dorothy Thompson (1996), writing about "argument," describes in advising a student whose professor in her freshman composition course "labeled her draft [of an 'essay on religion'] 'vague'" and who, according to Thompson, would have been better off using examples from her own neighborhood, and in calming African American students who have so much "trouble as soon as they hear the word [thesis]" that Thompson calls it "the monster"—these are problems created by the "'all-purpose argument'" taught in the composition class. The composition class may be an instance of the "sequestration" of learners from what Lave and Wenger call legitimate peripheral participation. Lave and Wenger observe that sequestration leads to problems of "access" and "the transparency of the meaning of what is being learned" (1991, 104). While the freshman composition class, where "argument" is taught, can seem like an hospitable welcome to all comers, in its undertaking to get basics and fundamentals in place,[10] in fact it may only cultivate aptitudes for success or failure in sequestered activities which have little to do with performance in the target "community of practice"—the knowledge-making activities of research institutions.

Since Canadian nationalist stands are rarely successful in warding off U.S. cultural artifacts, we may not be able to maintain a trade barrier here, and it is probably too late anyway. In any case, my hostility to "argument" as a concept on these grounds has much more to do with my nationality than with fair-minded or "logical" analysis of the classification. I admit this, and at the same time suggest that others' rejection or embrace of any system of classifying student writing will have political motivations, too.

Systems of classification are not neutral but complicit in the interests of those who design or use them. Yet, even if we agree on this, we might still be tempted to argue for or against "argument" on its systematic merits. I would not be a reliable contributor to such a discussion, for I am more impressed by the political consequences of selecting one system of classification over another, and my impressions are nationalist and institutionalist: hardly reputable. But they are also teacherly. From my position—in a particular school of thought carried on at a particular institutional location in a particular country—"argument" looks like too high a term, entailing too many hazards for writers learning to participate in the scholarly disciplines.

Notes

1. Genre theory current in North America should be distinguished from the genre taxonomies of the "Sydney School" and its educational linguistics. While the two schools of thought share an emphasis on the "functional" dimension of language forms, the genre model of the Sydney School has named a set of genres—exposition, explanation, description, recount—at a high level of classification.

2. Karen Schriver's work (1992) with the techniques of "usability testing" as an instructional strategy offers empirical confirmation of this goal of ours to develop *talk* about writing that induces writing. Schriver's study revealed that students provided with transcripts of readers thinking aloud as they used documents improved in their ability to predict actual readers' response to texts. In addition, genre theory supports this practice, for it locates discursive regularities or conventions in the know-how that language users bring to texts and situations.

3. We work as a research consortium, gathering data according to principles and methods we share and regularly discuss and refine, and depositing transcripts and documents in an archive available to all researchers in the group (and to interested students). This consortium includes regular and contract faculty and graduate and undergraduate research assistants. So some of the data I will report here I gathered myself, but much of it was gathered by my colleagues: Elaine Dornan, Reg Johanson, Shurli Makmillen, Marlene Sawatsky, Wendy Strachan, Michele Valiquette, and Bonnie Waterstone.

4. And, even while the History advice calls for a "thesis," students may run a risk in making the broad statements that approach or comprise "thesis"-type wordings, for we have found that readers in History are acutely sensitive to general, opening claims, tending to think of exceptions or limits to the generality rather than welcoming a statement of position. So, when a student writes, "When Jane Austen first started writing, women's position had changed very little in the last five hundred years", the marker responds, "*Well, that is a little worrisome to me because I had made a point in lecture that there had been changes. But I'm assuming that she's going to be focusing on such matters as the access to the intellectual life, and there had not been much in the way of change, I suppose one could argue, there.*" When a student claims that "if [a woman] remained unmarried, she would devote her life to religion", the marker second-guesses her: *"I'm getting nervous because while that is an alternative, it is also true that there is an alternative to be your brother's housekeeper or your father's housekeeper. This I think might be more common in Protestant countries."*

5. An "A" paper in this class gives an idea of where sociological specifics can come from. This paper described controversy surrounding a project in British Columbia known as the "Kemano Completion"—a hydroelectric project designed to provide additional power to an important aluminium smelter. The writer described this project (and its cancellation) and interpreted it in terms supplied by theoretical readings in the course. In a sense, then, "evidence" *can* be found in the writer's backyard—if not on her

"manicured lawn." But the professor's commentary also revealed that "specifics" could come from other sources—from attentive, contrastive reading of assigned texts: distinguished and widely recognized interpretations of society and environment.

6. In an account of an innovative first-year composition course at The University of Texas, Linda Brodkey (1996) describes the application of Toulmin's techniques for analyzing argument. While many other commentators on the teaching of argument recognize the potential contribution of Toulmin's thought, Brodkey's account is distinctive in its focus on the rhetorical *relevance* or *appropriateness* of warrants for claims: on, that is, the situated dispositions of audiences and, espcially, those of academic audiences. This is a promising approach and compatible with pedagogies based in the new genre theory. But Susan Miller's discussion (1997) confirms my suspicion that even careful and systematically repeated acknowledgement in composition class of the situatedness of arguments will not necessarily produce know-how transferrable to writing for audiences in scholarly disciplines. Schooled in principle to differences amongst audiences, students may still not be prepared in practice to encounter the material differences in expression which represent reasoning in the disciplines.

7. In British Columbia, the provincial examination in English at the end of secondary schooling has induced intense preparatory teaching focusing on the production of a "thesis" supported by "evidence" paragraphs.

8. Although the partnership of literature and composition in North American secondary and post-secondary institutions is so longstanding as to seem natural to most people, many in the field do question its legitimacy. Susan Miller (1991), however, has argued historically and semiotically that the affinity of literature and composition is original and enduring—the proximity of the "low" form of students' perversely faulty compositions providing a thrilling measure of the elevation of the "high" ideals of literary form. Tony Crowley (1989) offers a different but still compatible account of the role of literary ideals in constructing language "standards" in Britain. To these distinguished analyses, I add my own speculations that literary studies are a setting in which students either get it or they don't, and getting it is mostly a matter of intuiting when to assume interpretive attitudes current to urban middle-class political conscience (so current literary-critical discourse privileges feminist, post-colonial and queer theory). Without this social intuition—something like what Bourdieu calls "habitus"—students have no recourse, for literary-critical methods of argument and inquiry—unlike those for the social or hard sciences—are not open to explication. (See Susan Peck MacDonald (1994) for a convincing demonstration of professional literary-critical publications as primarily "epideictic" rather than investigative, and the discipline generally as having few explicit standards of adjudication.) This intellectual milieu is hospitable to the unsecured, decontextualized writing of the "composition" class, where writers either get it or they don't, and when they don't, their only recourse is to generalizations about "argument," "evidence," "logic," "clarity," and so on. Students seem to sense this original affinity between literary studies and composition, for they often do not distinguish between the writing called for in literature class and that called for in composition class: both types of writing are "English essays."

9. For example, Watson-Gegeo, developing a post-colonial perspective on argument, says that the model of the "clear thesis" and "a substantiating set of logically developed points and/or illustrations attempting to prove this thesis" (Freedman and Pringle 1984) "finds its fullest expression in academic writing" (1996, 192); looking to

"[rescue]" African-American writers, Thompson conflates "academic discourse" with argument when she says that the former "[privileges] argument as its highest form" (1996, 222); preliminary to examining the "rhetorical strategies" in "Native Americans" writing for assignments that call for argument, Redfield identifies "mainstream academic discourse" as a *target language* (1996, 252).

10. Linda Brodkey refers to "composition courses" as "middle-class holding pens populated by students from all classes who for one reason or another do not produce fluent, thesis-driven essays of around five hundred words for standardized tests or assignments developed by classroom teachers" (1996, 135).

12

Putting Argument into the Mainstream

Sally Mitchell

The ability to argue is generally regarded amongst academics as a defining characteristic of a good student at undergraduate level. Particularly when they talk about student writing, staff tend to claim that a well-developed argument is what they primarily hope for. Nonetheless, the apparent consensus over the value of argument in what academics expect of students is undermined by the range of ways in which they use the term. A number of commentators have noted this (see, for example, Lea and Street 1998; Stockton, 1995). As Giltrow argues (chapter eleven), whilst argument is, as an institutional goal, a clear fixed target, when one tries to fix on its meaning, it becomes a moving one, "one that transforms itself wherever it appears." For students, the amorphousness of argument is obviously a problem as they negotiate the expectations of different lecturers and courses. But it is also a problem for anyone seeking to pursue with staff a common goal of improvement in argument, since it begs the question: improvement of *what* exactly?

It is this problem and this question that I have been confronted with over the last few years whilst working on a funded research project entitled precisely "Improving the Quality of Argument in Higher Education."[1] As the title implies, practical outcomes for teaching and learning were among the objectives for the project, which was not confined to any particular discipline but covered, potentially at least, the broad spectrum that makes up higher education. It is on this project that I wish to reflect in this concluding chapter. Doing so offers me the chance to draw together some of the book's other contributions and to set them against the practical problems of bringing about improvement in students' learning to argue.

The target for inclusion in the project was mainstream staff in mainstream teaching contexts, university-wide, and from the outset I believed that the goals could not be met without their co-operation. I therefore formed collaborative "mini-projects" led to a considerable extent by staff's own understandings of argument and its place in their students' learning. The collaborations had an initial investigative phase and carried with them the promise of consequent changes in practice. Each one cut through the complexity of teaching and learning situations in different ways, opening up different facets to scrutiny. In Geography, for instance, we were to look for evidence of argument in finished written products (dissertations); in Visual Design, at processes of student/tutor interaction; in Nursing, at the notion of students as critical reflective practitioners with consequent implications for personal and professional identity; in Dance, at how students themselves experienced critical, creative, and reflective processes as kinds of argument (see Mitchell 1996). The variety of mini-projects made for cross-project discussions on the nature of disciplines, the experience of students, the vehicles of assessment, the relation of teacher to learner, and so on. These were stimulating and of value in themselves, but they were also, I came to feel, limited in terms of the overall goal of improvement across the sector. An effort of translation was required to make each mini-project into a satellite of a unified central enterprise.

Problems and Potentials of Argument

Three problems emerged from the initial work of the mini-projects. First there was, as I've mentioned, a problem of staff talking to each other about argument. Second, perhaps as an expected consequence of, or just as plausibly the cause of the first, scope for developing argument in the curricula of mainstream subjects was severely limited. Mathison's case study (chapter six) provides an instance of this problem: whilst argument was said to be valued in the engineering course she observed, it received no attention in the delivery of the curriculum which was dominated instead by content and the acquisition of technical skills. Situations of this kind made envisaged changes resulting from the mini-projects very hard to achieve: curricular frameworks could rarely accommodate any significant work on argument and so innovation was squeezed by more explicitly recognized priorities.[2] As a result of the lack of a shared usage of "argument" and of its invisibility in the curriculum, the third problem was the lack of a basis for deducing practical principles for our goal of improving the quality of argument. In so far as these three problems hang together, the third, developing pedagogical approaches, perhaps comes logically last, when it is (a) clear what it is we might expect to teach and learn and (b) when the value we want to place on that is formally recognized by its articulation, alongside content and research methods, in mainstream curricula. Thus whilst the goal of designing pedagogy remained for the project, at the same time the task became more clearly embedded in a broader institutional and therefore political context, which concerned the overall purposes and goals of higher education and its ability to communicate these at every level: amongst staff, to students, to the employers of students, to funders, to government.

As several authors in this book have noted, higher education, certainly in Britain, is currently undergoing rapid expansion and change. Such a situation opens up competing agendas for how its purposes should be defined. A recent major report on the future of higher education in Britain (NCIHE 1997, 216), for example, outlined four aims: to develop the individual, personally and intellectually, to be equipped for work and to contribute to society; to increase knowledge and encourage its application; to serve the needs of the economy; to contribute to a democratic, civilized, inclusive society. Many of the proposals to meet these aims can be perceived as instrumental "top down" and/or low level: the initiative to define and develop programs for the delivery of "core skills," such as communication, numeracy, and information technology, for example (see Drew 1998).

The consensus of academic staff around the term "argument"—however patchy it appears when viewed close-up—could be, it seems to me, a strong alternative place to start defining the goals and purposes of a higher education. Argument has the advantage of being something that academics themselves value highly as a goal in teaching and learning: they do not need to be convinced that it matters or that it is a goal worthy of pursuit. Interestingly, this is the case whichever of the current purposes for higher education outlined above one ascribes to; argument can be valued as much for its practical vocational uses as for its intellectual properties or its associations with high civilized goals. In this book there are a number of strong expressions of commitment to argument. Eisenschitz (chapter one), for example, claims that argument is "a force for democratic social change," and "a means of expanding human choices and enhancing individual development." Medway (chapter two) values argument for the part it plays in the promotion of "a more general virtue of rationality," as long as it is accompanied by "an ethic of reasonableness." In a different way Mathison (chapter six) points to the ability to argue as one of the ways in which a student is prepared to operate successfully in the working world.

In her chapter, Janet Giltrow concludes that the problems associated with talking about argument are grounds for deciding not to talk about the term at all. But the effect of Giltrow's decision to opt for the local as the arena in which you can most usefully locate knowledge could be to leave academic staff without a unified voice and sense of purpose at the political and institutional level. In my view when it comes to articulating high-level goals for education we need high-level terms like argument. However, as is clear, there are problems as well as potentials in argument. Whilst higher education might benefit by adopting it as an aspirational goal, the problems it presents in practice, i.e., at the level of conceptualization, curriculum, and pedagogy, are often more easily evaded than confronted. Foertsch (1995, 378; see Riddle 1997), for example, describes the different ways in which staff deflect responsibility for facing the problems their students have with disciplinary writing: lack of time, reluctance to be explicit possibly motivated by (racial, class) prejudice against students, wish to encourage personal expressiveness, worry that "rules" will be off-putting, desire to be student-centered, rather than teacher-led, a belief that general rules don't exist.

The avoidance phenomenon—a kind of institutionalized inertia—is seen in the way the task becomes that not of all academic staff but of those who specialize in writing: in North America, composition teachers, in Britain, academic literacy tutors and writing/study support staff. The number of contributors to this book who write from such a context is testimony to the association of argument with specialization in writing and to its disassociation from mainstream curricula and mainstream responsibility for its teaching and learning.[3] The irony here is that whilst argument is declared as the pinnacle of achievement in a discipline, to learn it by anything other than a form of acculturation, the student must go outside the discipline. A circular elitism underpins this state of affairs, suggesting a higher value being placed on acculturation than acquisition (Gee 1991) as learning: "we don't need to teach it or change the way we think about what we do, because the good students always manage to meet our expectations."

With the profile of students entering higher education changing so rapidly, this kind of thinking begins to seem increasingly unacceptable—not least to the students themselves (see Jacobs in this book). I think it is important, therefore, to recognize that making argument the concern of writing/language specialists may allow mainstream staff to shrug off responsibility for addressing it in their teaching, to hold an apparently exclusive concern with content and thereby collude in maintaining what Eisenschitz (chapter one) describes as "the hierarchical social relations involved in gaining knowledge". Characterizing argument as a writing, and before this a language issue runs the risk of making it either too basic a task or too specialized: either "it's not my job to teach students how to write" or "you have to be a linguist to be able to do that; it's not my specialism."

A further problem though is that argument isn't always very clearly dealt with by language specialists.[4] As Groom points out (chapter five) the way argument is dealt with in writing textbooks is often "conceptually undefined." He speculates: "This inability to come to grips with argument may possibly indicate a reluctance on the part of the language specialist 'to get involved with content issues.'" From the disciplines' point of view argument is about writing; from the writing specialists' it's about content—no one it seems wants argument! And yet everyone wants it from their students.

Let me take this point a little further by looking at a recent guide for students written from a learning support and academic literacy perspective (Creme and Lea 1997). In the book staff from a variety of disciplines are quoted talking about their expectations of student writing. Each of these quotations contains reference to argument and I've picked these parts out and reproduced them here because they're a useful reminder of what academic staff are commonly heard to say:

> ". . . I'm concerned with getting students to tease out the logic of an argument and look at the relationship between premises and conclusions." (politics tutor);
> [social science students] "are better at developing an argument and using data to illustrate the argument" (social anthropology tutor);
> ". . . difficulties with using their legal knowledge to work through the argument to a legal solution" (law tutor);
> ". . . too much description, rather than the development of a structured argument" (psychology tutor);
> ". . . dump everything on the page that they have heard about it instead of developing a logical argument around it" (management science tutor);
> "They need to be able to organize an argument" (English tutor);
> "It has to have some structure and content and be well laid out and argued"(biology tutor) (29–32)

Here as one might expect is the unmissable consensus over the importance of argument in student writing, the term being used as Giltrow notes (chapter eleven), either to invoke an ideal, or more often, to describe deviance from the ideal. The writers of the handbook are wary of tackling that ideal, however. Instead they invoke the voice of another lecturer to affirm their own conclusion that argument [and structure] are not tangible concepts; we cannot break them down and describe the constituent parts. As this lecturer says:

> I can recognize a good piece of student writing when I see it. I know when it is well structured and has a well-developed argument but it is difficult to say exactly what I am looking for, let alone describe a good argument more fully. (36–37)

Although the book does go on to offer very general advice on developing an argument under the heading of "Constructing your 'story,'" the authors are content at this point to share the mystificatory tone of the lecturer who is in possession of powerful understanding but eschews the responsibility of communicating it. It seems to me a significant omission, and a striking testimony to the valency of the term "argument," that a handbook written to help students seems unwilling to go further than the lecturer.

A Proposed Model of Argument

The "Improving the Quality of Argument" project started with the view that the task of helping students learn to argue better would need to be targeted at staff teaching in the disciplines. As the difficulties of this became clear, but no better alternative presented itself, I concluded, with my colleague Mike Riddle, that if we were to proceed we would need to propose an explicit model of argument that could be widely accepted and could act as a restraint on the proliferation of meanings and challenge obfuscatory uses of the term. It should not be acceptable, we believed, to *expect* argument but not to be able or willing to say more about what that expectation comprises.

In his chapter, Riddle describes the model of argument he is developing (in collaboration with me) to meet the need for a common basic understanding of argument amongst mainstream disciplinary staff. Briefly, it comprises the three-part relationship between data, claims, and warrants (from Toulmin 1958 and Toulmin, Rieke, and Janik 1984) which make up the core structure of a single argument. The relationship is expressed by the iconic linking words SINCE, THEN, and BECAUSE. When thinking through an argument, or analyzing or evaluating one, the parts that comprise it can be slotted into the SINCE, THEN, BECAUSE formula as a way of elucidating the reasoning and checking that it makes sense. Since the relationships expressed by the formula are conceptual rather than linguistic, the formula can be applied to a microargument as expressed within a few sentences or it can be used to try and grasp the macroargument(s) being proposed across a much larger text. When we put this model across to staff it is not in the formal way it appears in this book, but through interactive and adaptive workshop sessions, which we are gradually offering to more and more staff and, by invitation, their students. With their help we are refining our understanding of and ways of communicating it. Feedback so far has been very encouraging.[5]

Aside from the details of the particular model,[6] let me say why the principles that underpin it seem to me appropriate to the task of "improving the quality of argument in higher education." The model offers a definition of argument that is sufficiently stable at a conceptual level to be generally applicable across disciplinary contexts and yet is abstract enough to allow it to be manifested in different ways. That is, it proposes that all arguments share a common structure of relational reasoning (it is this that allows the reasoning to be identified as argument) but makes no claims about (a) what the content of the related elements should be; (b) how the relations should be expressed in language (e.g., what order they should appear in); (c) whether the relations need to be explicitly expressed at all by a single speaker/writer in order for an argument to be understood to be taking place. Unlike, therefore, a proposal for argument as a certain text-type or form of linguistic usage, an abstract conceptual model allows for staff in different disciplinary areas to identify the existence or absence of argument in existing practices. These will include formal written essays, but also informal discussion in seminars, oral presentations of various kinds, the wide range of written forms that Woods encourages in the course she describes (chapter eight) and that Davidson (chapter ten) notes her students are keen to explore. Such a model common across the university need not, that is, lead to uniformity of practices. Its emphasis, more towards the cognitive than the linguistic, makes it the legitimate and unavoidable concern of disciplinary specialists.

On its own an abstract conceptual model does not offer criteria for judging the effectiveness of arguments in actual situations—in effect it says that "all arguments are equal." But we know that as manifested within particular disciplinary fields "some arguments are more equal than others:" an argument can be internally "valid" but externally ineffective or unacceptable—the criteria for judging will be generated by the situation in which the argument is mobilized.[7] Understanding the components within the model can help to bring this fact of disciplinary life to the surface for both staff and students. In particular the "warrant" component (represented by the BECAUSE icon in Riddle's model) goes beyond a commonsense understanding of argument as "point of view plus reasons." It indicates that legitimation for or acceptance of a claim lies not in facts but in assumptions, ways in which the speaker and/or listener has *already been* claimed (Meiland 1989). This element of the model makes it entirely appropriate for use in the many disciplinary communities that make up a university. In a multifield discipline like Design, for example, it can help to clarify whether a student is working to satisfy the demands of the market place or to advance the boundaries of design theory. Or in the work-based learning assignments that Costley and Doncaster (chapter nine) describe it can help to make sense of the different spheres of personal, professional, and academic knowledge that students work within. Awareness of how claims and data are made to "make sense" is also a way to become "critical"—another highly valued goal for higher education. It is this that motivates Eisenschitz (chapter one) in developing a paradigmatic approach to argument. For his students, recognizing the assumptions upon which the claims of the dominant paradigm are based was a way to recognize their ideological nature and begin to develop alternatives.

If the model does not judge what kind of argument might be appropriate to mount when, it also leaves open the different ways in which argument might be given form, the rhetorical strategies that can be deployed in the making of an argument, the arrangement of its parts to conventional or surprising effect. As a generic model for use in local situations this is an advantage. Additionally, the application of the abstract model can elucidate rhetorical choices and the ways in which acts of communication work. For example, it can account for how a literary text such as a narrative or poem can be taken to be arguing a point. Whilst the text itself may supply only part of the argument the interpretative action of the reader supplies the rest. This relationship between text and reader is sanctioned within the study of literature where interpretation—"the making of a text upon a text" (Scholes 1985)—is a recognized dominant practice. Thus the model is mobilized by its rhetorical instantiation in particular forms and by the engagement of a reader or listener who brings to it what Bakhtin (1981, 281) calls "his apperceptive background, pregnant with response and objections." It is—as Wood's examples of ethnographic argument (chapter eight) help to suggest—the discipline's practices, forms, rhetorical strategies, and genres as well as its content that determine what works as argument or does not.

Developing Curricula

This chapter has not been directly about students learning to argue, but about staff learning to say what argument means. The two are connected because staff are hampered in helping students learn to argue better if they are not clear what they are asking for and cannot express it. Without a "discursive consciousness" of argument staff are not able to say much more to students than "you must learn to second-guess your teachers." Helping staff to develop their "practical consciousness" of what makes a good argument in their discipline into a "discursive consciousness" (Giddens, quoted in Giltrow and Valiquette 1994) is a radical, and indeed problematic proposal. It involves, as I've suggested, rethinking current assumptions and practices—about what is teachable and where responsibility lies, and about how curricula are drawn up, described, and implemented.

Knowing *how students learn* to argue makes the link between staff learning to say what argument means and students learning to argue better. The need to develop a curriculum and pedagogy which addresses the rhetorical and cognitive demands of disciplinary study is located here. As Maharg (chapter seven) and others (for example, Foertsch 1995) make clear, the considerations entailed in such an enterprise are complex. They include the issue of how cognition is carried over into writing, how general rules are manifested locally, and how linguistic expression carries an argument's force and nuance (Groom, chapter five). In addition they include recognition of what Jacobs points out is "the personal and emotional commitment" involved in argument and what Medway (chapter two) describes as matters of "courage and will." If these considerations are complex, they are also rich and potentially highly rewarding to students, staff, and institutions of higher education as a whole.

The full development of rhetorical and cognitive curricula has yet to be widely recognized as the responsibility of mainstream disciplines. If it is to be, institutional support will be crucial to help staff acquire new knowledge, adapt and transform it to their disciplines, and develop curricula accordingly. The "Improving the Quality of Argument" project has gone a small way to laying the foundations of such development, but, as the metaphor suggests, this is just a beginning. Nor is its future guaranteed. At the end of his book *The Rhetoric of Reason* James Crosswhite (1996, 298), writing about the underdeveloped place of rhetoric and reason in the undergraduate curriculum, is on the verge of concluding that "the situation is beyond redemption." He draws back from such a position, however, by reflecting on the immense transformative influence individual teachers can have on the students they encounter. I share both Crosswhite's pessimism and his optimism. The imperative to value the quality of argument must come from the "top down." But it is also true—as my experience working with staff on the project and as many of the chapters in this book testify—that commitment to such a goal is engendered in very particular moments of learning.

Notes

1. The project was funded from 1995–1999 by the Leverhulme Trust and was based at Middlesex University, London. Two reports are available: Mitchell (1996) and Mitchell and Riddle (2000).

2. Ongoing collaboration in the Design area is an exception, because here the staff member concerned has been determined to make the development of abilities in argument an explicit component in the curriculum. From this commitment follows the need to develop coherent pedagogical approaches and assessment procedures (see Maharg, chapter seven). The task of making argument a part of an existing Design curriculum is not achieved rapidly, however. There are many inhibiting factors, not least, the need to ensure that all staff teaching on the program share an idea of what is meant by argument.

3. The law course described by Maharg (chapter seven) is a notable exception.

4. My comment here refers to the British context in particular. I recognize that within the North American tradition of composition studies there are numerous textbooks and readers that deal directly with argument. It's less common that they deal with disciplinary-based argument however.

5. An example of the collaborative approach was a member of staff seeking to explain the argumentative structure of an essay on Columbus, by giving students a number of "points in argument" all of which were factual events. In discussion, it became clear that she was expecting students to make interpretations of these events according to commonsense and historical principles, but she was unable to articulate this clearly. The SINCE, THEN, BECAUSE model was a way to make her expectations of reasoning explicit. Each "point" was made into a SINCE from which a THEN and BECAUSE then followed. The formula was also used to elucidate the range of overall arguments that the students were likely to be able to make in their essays.

6. See Mitchell and Riddle (2000) for further details of the model and examples of its use.

7. One of the weaknesses of the approach Sweet and Swanson critique (chapter three) is that it does not recognize the shaping power of discourse or situation on the effectiveness of any argument one might make.

Bibliography

Abbs, P. 1996. *The Polemics of Imagination.* London: Skoob.

Acthenberg, B. 1975. "Legal Writing and Research: The Neglected Orphan of the First Year." *University of Miami Law Review* 87: 218–43.

Agar, M. H. 1980. *The Professional Stranger: An Informal Introduction to Ethnography.* New York: Academic Press.

Alfieri, A. 1990. "The Politics of Clinical Knowledge." *New York Law School Law Review* 35: 7–27.

Alfieri, A. 1991. "Reconstructive poverty law practice: learning lessons of client narrative." *The Yale Law Journal* 100: 2107–2147.

Anderson, C. 1987. *Style as Argument.* Carbondale and Edwardsville, Ill.: Southern Illinois Press.

Andrews, R., ed. 1989. *Narrative and Argument.* Milton Keynes: Open University Press.

Andrews, R. 1992. *Rebirth of Rhetoric—Essays in Language, Culture and Education.* London: Routledge.

Andrews, R. 1995. *Teaching and Learning Argument.* London: Cassell.

Andrews, R. 1999. "Lessons from Ten Years of Research in Argument: implications for higher education." Paper given at Ontario Society for the Study of Argumentation Conference, 13–15 May 1999, at Brock University, St Catherine's.

Andrews, R., P. Costello, and S. Clarke. 1993. Improving the Quality of Argument, 5–16: Final Report. Hull: University of Hull, Centre for Studies in Rhetoric, School of Education.

Argyris, C. and D. A. Schön. 1974. *Theory in Practice: Increasing Professional Effectiveness.* San Francisco: Jossey-Bass.

Atkinson, R. and M. Hammersley. 1994. *Ethnography and Participant Observation,* edited by N. K. Denzin and Y. S. Lincoln. *Handbook of Qualitative Research.* Thousand Oaks: Sage Publications.

Axelrod, R. and C. Cooper. 1985. *The St. Martin's Guide to Writing.* New York: St Martin's Press.

Bakhtin, M. 1981. *The Dialogic Imagination.* Austin, Tex.: University of Texas Press.

Bakhtin, M. M. 1986. *Speech Genres and Other Late Essays.* Austin, Tex.: University of Texas Press.

Banks, L., and D. Aphothlz. 1995. "Argumentation in Pre-School Children: A Study About Topoi and Topic Forms." Paper read at the Symposium on Argumentation, at Utrecht.

Barley, N. 1989. *Not a Hazardous Sport.* Harmondsworth: Penguin.

Barnett, R. 1994. *The Limits of Competence: Knowledge, Higher Education and Society.* Philadelphia: Society for Research into Higher Education and Open University Press.

Barnett, R. 1997. *Higher Education: A Critical Business.* Buckingham: Open University Press.

Bartholomae, D. 1985. "Inventing the University." In *When a Writer Can't Write,* edited by M. Rose. New York: Guilford Press.

Bartholomae, D. 1986. "Inventing the University." *Journal of Basic Writing* 5 (1): 4–22.

Bartholomae, D. 1995a. "Writing with teachers: a conversation with Peter Elbow." *College Composition and Communication* 46, 62–71.

Bartholomae, D. et al. 1995b. "Interchanges: responses to Bartholomae and Elbow." *College Composition and Communication* 46, 84–107.

Bauman, Z. 1989. *Modernity and the Holocaust.* Cambridge: Polity Press.

Baynham, M. 1995. "Narrative in Argument, Argument in Narrative." In *Competing and Consensual Voices: The Theory and Practice of Argument,* edited by P. Costello and S. Mitchell. Clevedon: Multilingual Matters Ltd.

Bazerman, C. 1981. "What Written Knowledge Does: Three Examples of Academic Discourse." *Philosophy of the Social Sciences* 11: 361–87.

Bazerman, C. 1988. *Shaping Written Knowledge: The Genre and Activity of the Experimental Article in Science.* Madison, Wis.: University of Wisconsin Press.

Bazerman, C. 1994a. *Constructing Experience.* Carbondale and Edwardsville: Southern Illinois University Press.

Bazerman, C. 1994b. "Where is the Classroom?" In *Learning and Teaching Genre,* edited by A. Freedman and P. Medway. Portsmouth, NH: Heinemann-Boynton/Cook.

Bazerman, C. 1995. *The Informed Writer: Using Sources in the Disciplines.* 5th ed. Boston: Houghton Mifflin.

Bazerman, C., and J. Paradis. 1991. *Textual Dynamics and the Professions: Historical and Contemporary Writing in Professional Communities.* Madison, Wis.: University of Wisconsin Press.

Beauregard, R. 1993. *Voices of Decline: The Postwar Fate of U.S. Cities.* Oxford: Blackwell.

Becher, T. 1994. "The Significance of Disciplinary Differences." *Studies in Higher Education* 19 (2): 151–61.

Beene, L. and W. Vande Kopple. 1992. *The Riverside Handbook.* Boston: Houghton Mifflin.

Belenky, M. F., B. M. Clinchy, N. R. Godberger, J. M. Tarule. 1986. *Women's Ways of Knowing.* USA: Basic Books.

Bell, B. 1993. "The Assumption of Subjectivity in Design." *Canadian Architect* 38 (4): 31.

Bell, B. 1999. "The Role of Political Power in Architecture: The Real and the Ideal at the Ducal Palace of Urbino." Proceedings of the ACSA Iinternational Conference, Architecture as a Political Act. Washington: ACSA Press.

Bell, B. In preparation. *Rhetoric.* Chapter in Architecture and the seven liberal arts, unpublished manuscript.

Benson, P. 1993. *Anthropology and Literature.* Urbana and Chicago: University of Illinois Press.

Bereiter, C. and M. Scardamalia. 1987. *The Psychology of Written Composition.* Hillsdale, N.J.: Erlbaum.

Berger, J. 1972. *Ways of Seeing.* London: BBC.

Berkenkotter, C., and T. N. Huckin. 1995. *Genre Knowledge in Disciplinary Communication: Cognition/Culture/Power.* Hillsdale, N.J.: Lawrence Erlbaum Associates.

Berlin, I. 1990. *The Crooked Timber of Humanity.* New York: Knopf.

Berlin, James A. *Rhetorics, Poetics, and Cultures.* Urbana, IL: NCTE, 1996, xvii.

Berrill, D. 1999. Response to paper by Andrews, R. 1999. "Lessons from Ten Years of Research in Argument: Implications for higher education." Paper given at Ontario Society for the Study of Argumentation Conference, May 13–15, 1999, at Brock University, St. Catherine's.

Bhatia, V. K. 1987. "Textual-mapping in British legislative writing." *World Englishes* 6 (1): 1–10.

Bhatia, V. K. 1993. *Analysing Genre: Language Use in Professional Settings.* London: Longman.

Bhatia, V. K., and J.M. Swales. 1983. "An Approach to the Linguistic Study of Legal Documents." *Fachsprache* 5 (3): 98–108.

Bizzell, P. 1982. "Cognition, Convention, and Certainty: What We Need to Know About Writing." *Pre/Text* 3, 213–43.

Bjork, L., and C. Raisanen. 1997. *Academic Writing: A University Writing Course.* Sweden: Studentlitteratur.

Bloom, L. 1996. "Freshman Composition as a Middle Class Enterprise." *College English* 58 (6): 654–75.

Bourdieu, P. 1991. *Language and Symbolic Power.* Cambridge, Mass.: Harvard University Press.

Boyer, A. 1988. "Legal Writing Programes Reviewed: Merits, Flaws, Costs and Essentials." *Chicago-Kent Law Review* 62: 23–51.

Brandt, D. 1990. *Literacy as Involvement: The Acts of Writers, Reader and Texts.* Carbondale, Ill.: Southern Illinois University Press.

Brennan, J., and B. Little. 1996. *A Review of Work Based Learning in Higher Education.* Quality Support Center, Department for Education and Employment.

Brodkey, L. 1996. *Writing Permitted in Designated Areas Only.* Minneapolis: University of Minnesota Press.

Brown, A. and P. Dowling. 1998. *Doing Research/Reading Research: A Mode of Interrogation for Education.* London and Washington, D.C.: Falmer Press.

Brun, M. L. and Johnstone, R. 1994. *The Quiet (R)evolution: Improving Student Learning in Law.* Melbourne: The Law Book Company.

Bucciarelii, L. L. 1996. *Designing Engineers.* Cambridge, Mass.: The MIT Press.

Burke, K. 1966. "Terministic screens." In *Language as Symbolic Action: Essays on Life, Literature and the Mind.* Berkeley: University of California Press.

Burke, K. 1969. *A Rhetoric of Motives.* Berkeley: University of California Press.

Burnett, R. 1993. "Some People Weren't Able to Contribute Anything But Their Technical Knowledge: The Anatomy of a Dysfunctional Team," in *Nonacademic Writing: Social Theory and Technology,* ed. A. H. Duin and C. J. Hansen, 123–156. Mahwah, NJ: Lawrence Erlbaum.

Center, Learning Research and Development. *Advanced Cognitive Tools for Learning.* University of Pittsburgh, 1999. Available from http://advlearn.lrdc.pitt.edu/belvedere.

Chaffee, J. 1990. *Thinking Critically.* 3rd ed. Boston: Houghton Mifflin & Co.

Checkland, P. B. 1981. *Systems Thinking, Systems Practice.* Chichester: John Wiley.

Clark, I. 1998. *The Genre of Argument.* Florida: Harcourt, Brace & Company.

Clark, R. 1992. "Principles and Practice of CLA in the Classroom." In *Critical Language Awareness,* edited by N. Fairclough. London and New York: Longman.

Clarke, S. 1988. "Another Look at the Degree Results of Men and Women." *Studies in Higher Education* 13 (3): 315–331.

Clifford, J. 1991. "The Subject in Discourse." In *Contending with Words,* edited by P. Harkin, J. Schilb. New York: M.L.A.

Clifford, J. 1998. *The Predicament of Culture: Twentieth Century Ethnography, Literature and Art.* Cambridge, MA: Harvard University Press.

Clifford, J., and G. E. Marcus, ed. 1986. *Writing Culture: The Poetics and Politics of Ethnography.* Berkeley: University of California Press.

Cockroft, R. and S. M. Cockroft. 1992. *Persuading People: An Introduction to Rhetoric.* Basingstoke: Macmillan.

Cope, B. and M. Kalanzis, ed. 1993. *The Powers of Literacy: A Genre Approach to Teaching Writing.* London: Falmer Press.

Corbett, Edward P. J. 1965. *Classical Rhetoric for the Modern Student.* New York: Oxford University Press.

Costello, P. J. M. and S. Mitchell. 1995. *Competing and Consensual Voices: The Theory and Practice of Argument.* Clevedon: Multilingual Matters.

Costley, C. 1997a. "How Argument Relates to Graduates in their Work and Lives." In *The Quality of Argument: A Colloquium on Issues of Teaching and Learning in Higher Education,* edited by M. Riddle. London: Middlesex University Press.

Cox, B. J., and M. B. Ray. 1990. "Getting Dorothy out of Kansas: The Importance of an Advanced Component to Legal Writing Programs." *Journal of Legal Education* 40 (Summer): 351–61.

Creme, P., and M. Lea. 1997. *Writing at University: A Guide for Students.* Buckingham and Philadelphia: Open University Press.

Creme, P., and M. Lea. 1998. "Student Writing: Challenging the Myths." Paper read at 5th Annual Writing Development in Higher Education Conference, at University of Reading.

Crosswhite, J. 1996. *The Rhetoric of Reason: Writing and the Attractions of Argument.* Madison, Wis.: University of Wisconsin Press.

Crowley, T. 1989. *The Politics of Discourse: The Standard Language Question in British Cultural Debates.* Basingstoke: Macmillan.

Crystal, D. 1985. *A Dictionary of Linguistics and Phonetics.* Oxford/London: Basil Blackwell/Andre Deutsch.

Cunningham, C. D. 1989. "A Tale of Two Clients: Thinking About Law as Language." *Michigan Law Review* 87, 2459–94.

Cunningham, C. D. 1992. "The Lawyer as Translator, Representation as Text: Towards an Ethnography of Legal Discourse." *Cornell Law Review* 77: 1298–1387.

Currie, P. 1990. "Argument and Evaluation in Organizational Behavior: Student Writing in an Introductory Course." In *Language Methodology for the Nineties,* edited by S. Anivan. South East Asian Ministers of Education Organisation (Singapore). Regional Language Centre.

de Beaugrande, R., and W. Dressler. 1981. *Introduction to Text Linguistics.* London: Longman.

Denzin, N. K., and Y. S. Lincoln. 1994. *Handbook of Qualitative Research.* Thousand Oaks: Sage Publications.

Dias, P., A. Freedman, P. Medway, and A. Pare. 1999. *Worlds Apart: Acting and Writing in Academic Workplace Contexts.* Hillsdale, N.J.: Lawrence Erlbaum.

Dinerstein, R. 1990. "Client-Centered Counseling: Reappraisal and Refinement." *Arizona Law Review* 32: 501–604.

Dixon, J. and L. Stratta. 1982. "Argument: What Does It Mean to Teachers of English?" *English in Education* 16 (1): 41–54.

Doncaster, K. 1995. "Making Meaning in Research Interviews: Discursive Practices in Interviews with Mature Students," Ph.D. thesis, Lancaster University.

Doncaster, K., and J. Garnett. 1999. "Effective Work-Based Learning Partnerships: Two Case Studies from Middlesex University. unpublished.

Dowling, P. 1995. "Discipline and Mathematise: The Myth of Relevance in Education." *Perspectives in Education* 16 (2): 209–226.

Dowling, P. 1998. *The Sociology of Mathematics Education: Mathematical Myth/Pedagogic Texts.* London and Washington, D.C.: Falmer Press.

Downes, W. 1984. *Language and Society.* London: Fontana.

Drew, S. 1998. *Key Skills in Higher Education: Background and Rationale.* Birmingham: Seda Publications.

Einstein, G. O., M. A. McDaniel, P. D. Owen, and N. Cote. 1990. "Encoding and Recall of Texts: The Importance of Material Appropriate Processing." *Journal of Memory and Language* 29: 566–81.

Education, National Committee of Inquiry into Higher. 1997. *Higher Education in the Learning Society: Summary Report.* London: National Committee of Inquiry into Higher Education.

Elbow, P. 1981. *Writing with Power.* Oxford: Oxford University Press.

Elbow, P. 1991. "Reflections on Academic Discourse: How it Relates to Freshman and Colleagues." *College English* 53: 135–55.

Emmel, B., P. Resch, D. Tenney. 1996. *Argument Revisited: Argument Redefined.* London: Sage Publications.

Ennis, R. H. 1987. "A taxonomy of critical thinking dispositions and abilities." In *Teaching Thinking Skills: Theory and Practice,* edited by J. Baron, R. Sternberg. New York: W.H. Freeman and Co.

Fairbanks, A. H. 1993. "The Pedagogical Failure of Toulmin's Logic." *The Writing Instructor* 12: 103–104.

Felstiner, W. L. F., and A. Sarat. 1988. "Law and Social Relations: Vocabularies of Motive in Lawyer/Client Interaction." *Law and Society Review* 22:737–57.

Felstiner, W. L. F., and A. Sarat. 1992. "Enactments of Power: Negotiating Reality and Responsibility in Lawyer-Client Interaction." *Cornell Law Review* 77: 1447–98.

Fish, S. 1989. *Doing What Comes Naturally: Change, Rhetoric, and the Practice of Theory in Literacy and Legal Studies.* Oxford: Clarendon Press.

Flannery, K. 1995. *The Emperor's New Clothes: Literature, Literacy and the Ideology of Style.* Pittsburgh: University of Pittsburgh Press.

Flower, L. 1994. *The Construction of Negotiated Meaning: A Social Cognitive Theory of Writing.* Carbondale: Southern Illinois University Press.

Flower, L. and J. Hayes. 1981. "Plans that Guide the Composing Process." In *Writing: The Nature, Development and Teaching of Written Communication. Writing: Process, Development and Communication,* edited by C. H. Frederiksen, Dominic and J. F. Hillsdale, N.J.: Lawrence Erlbaum Associates.

Flower, L. and Hayes, J. 1989. "Cognition, context, and theory building." *College Composition and Communication* 40, 3, 282–311.

Foertsch, J. 1995. "Where Cognitive Psychology Applies: How Theories About Memory and Transfer Can Influence Composition Pedagogy." *Written Communication* 12 (3): 360–83.

France, A. 1994. *Composition as Cultural Practice.* Westport, CT: Bergin and Garvey.

Freedman, A., I. Pringle, and J. Yalden. 1983. *Learning to Write: first language/second language.* London: Longman.

Freeman, J. B. 1991. *Dialectics and the Macro-Structure of Arguments: A theory of argument structure.* New York: Foris Publications.

Freedman, A. 1996. "Genres of argument and arguments as genres." In *Perspectives on Written Argument,* edited by D. Berrill. Cresskill, N.J.: Hampton Press.

Freedman, A. and I. Pringle. 1980. *Reinventing the Rhetorical Tradition.* Conway, Ark.: L & S Books for The Canadian Council of Teachers of English.

Freedman, A. and P. Medway. 1994. *Teaching and Learning Genre.* Portsmouth, NH: Heinemann/Boynton-Cook.

Freedman, S.W. and A. M. Katz. 1987. "Pedagogical interaction during the composing process: the writing conference." In *Writing in Real Time: Modelling Production Processes,* edited by A. Matsuhashi. Norwood, NJ: Ablex Publishing Corp.

Fulkerson, R. 1996a. *Teaching the Argument in Writing.* Urbana, Ill.: National Council of Teachers of English.

Fulkerson, R. 1996b. "The Toulmin model of argument and the teaching of composition." In *Argument Revisited; Argument Redefined: Negotiating Meaning in the Composition Classroom,* edited by B. Emmel, P. Resch, D. Tenney. Thousand Oaks, Sage.

Gage, J. T. 1996. "The Reasoned Thesis." In *Argument Revisited; Argument Redefined,* edited by B. Emmel, P. Resch, and D. Tenney. Thousand Oaks: Sage.

Galbraith, D. and G. Rijlaarsdam. 1999. "Effective strategies for the teaching and learning of writing." *Learning and Instruction.* 9, 2, 93–109.

Gale, R. 1980. "Legal Writing: The Impossible Take a Little Longer." *Alabama Law Review* 298: 317–18.

Gans, H. 1990. "Deconstructing the Underclass: The Term's Dangers as a Planning Concept." *APA Journal:* 271–77.

Gee, J. 1991. *Social Linguisitics and Literacies: Ideology in Discourses.* London: Falmer Press.

Gee, J. P. 1997. "Forward: A Discourse Approach to Language and Literacy" in *Changing Literacies,* ed. C. Lankshear. Buckingham: Open University Press.

Geertz, C. 1973. *The Interpretation of Cultures.* New York: Basic Books.

Geertz, C. 1983. *Local Knowledge.* New York: Basic Books.

Geertz, C. 1988. *Works and Lives: The Anthropologist as Author.* Stanford: Stanford University Press.

Geisler, C. 1993. "The Relationship Between Language and Design in Mechanical Engineering: Some Preliminary Observations." *Technical Communication* 40: 173–76.

George, S. 1976. *How the Poor Die.* Harmondsworth: London.

Gere, A. R. 1988. *Writing and Learning.* 2nd ed. New York: Macmillan.

Gibson, W. 1980. "Authors, Speakers, Readers, and Mock Readers." In *Reader Response Criticism,* edited by J. Tompkins. Baltimore: John Hopkins University Press.

Giddens, A. 1986. *The Constitution of Society.* Berkeley & Los Angeles, CA: University of California Press.

Giltrow, J., and M. Valiquette. 1994. "Genres and Knowledge: Students Writing in the Disciplines." In *Learning and Teaching Genre,* edited by A. Freedman and P. Medway. Portsmouth, NH: Heinemann-Boynton/Cook.

Giltrow, J., R. Johanson, and M. Valiquette. 1994. "Student Writers and Their Readers: The Conventions of Commentary." Paper read at College Composition and Communications Conference, at Nashville, Tenn.

Glendinning, E. H. and B. Holmstrom. 1992. *Study Reading: A Course in Reading Skills for Academic Purposes.* Cambridge: Cambridge University Press.

Glesne, C. 1997. "That Rare Feeling: Re-Presenting Research Through Poetic Transcription." *Qualitative Inquiry* 3 (2): 202–21.

Goodrich, P. 1986. *Reading the Law: A Critical Introduction to Legal Method and Techniques.* Oxford: Basil Blackwell.

Grassi, E. 1980. *Rhetoric as Philosophy.* University Park, PA: The Pennsylvania State University Press.

Greasser, A. C., N. K. Person and J. Huber. 1993. "Questions asked during tutoring and in the design of educational software." In *Cognitive Foundations of Instruction,* edited by M. Rabinowtiz. Hillsdale, NJ: Lawrence Erlbaum Associates.

Grimaldi, W.M.A. 1980. *Aristotle, Rhetoric I: A Commentary.* New York: Fordham University Press.

Grimes, R., J. Klaff and C. Smith. 1996. "Legal skills and clinical legal education—a survey of undergraduate law school practice." *The Law Teacher* 30 (44–67).

Grimshaw, Jane. 1990. *Argument Structure.* Cambridge, Mass.: MIT Press.

Grindal, B., and W. Shepherd. 1993. "Redneck Girl: From Experience to Performance." In *Anthropology and Literature,* edited by P. Benson. Urbana and Chicago: University of Illinois Press.

Guenthner, S., and H. Knoblauch. 1995. "Culturally Patterned Speaking Practices—The Analysis of Communicative Genres." *Pragmatics* 5 (1): 1–32.

Gumperz, J. and D. Hymes. 1972. *Directions in Sociolinguistics.* New York: Holt, Reinhart and Winston.

Gunnarsson, B. L. 1984. "Functional Comprehensibility of Legislative Texts: Experiments with a Swedish Act of Parliament." *Text* 4: 71–105.

Habermas, J. 1984. *The Theory of Communicative Action: Volume 1 Reason and the Rationalization of Society.* London: Heinemann.

Hairston, M. 1986. "Bringing Aristotle's Enthymeme into the Composition Classroom." In *Rhetoric and Praxis: The Contribution of Classical Rhetoric to Practical Reasoning,* edited by J. D. Moss. Washington, D.C.: Catholic University of America.

Hall, D. and S. Birkerts. 1994. *Writing Well.* 8th ed. New York: HarperCollins.

Halliday, M. A. K. 1994. *An Introduction to Functional Grammar.* 2nd ed. London and New York: Edward Arnold.

Harvey, D. 1973. *Social Justice and the City.* London: Arnold.

Hasan, R. 1989. "The structure of a text." In *Language, Context and Text: Aspects of Language in a Social-Semiotic Perspective,* edited by M. A. K. Halliday, R. Hasan. Oxford: Oxford University Press.

Hegelund, S. and C. Kock. 1999. "Macro-Toulmin: The Argument Model as Structural Guidelines in Academic Writing." Paper given at Ontario Society for the Study of Argumentation Conference, 13–15 May 1999, at Brock University, St Catherine's.

Heilker, P. 1996. *The Essay: Theory and Pedagogy for an Active Form.* Urbana: National Council of Teachers of English.

Higgins, L. 1994. *Negotiating Competence Schemas for Discourse: A Framework and Study of Argument Construction.* Unpublished report for Carnegie Mellon University, Pittsburgh.

Hodgins, Jack. 1993. *A Passion for Narrative: A guide for writing fiction.* Toronto: McClelland and Stewart.

hooks, b. 1993. "Eros, Eroticism, and the Pedagogical Process." In *Between Borders: Pedagogy and the Politics of Cultural Studies,* edited by H. A. Giroux and P. McLaren. New York: Routledge.

hooks, b. 1996. *Teaching to Transgress.* London: Routledge.

Hounsell, D. 1987. "Essay Writing and the Quality of Feedback." In *Student Learning: Research in Education and Cognitive Psychology,* edited by J. T. E. Richardson, M. W. Eysenck, and D. W. Piper. Milton Keynes: The Society for Research into Higher Education and Open University Press.

Hunston, S. and G. Thompson. 1999. *Evaluation in Text.* Oxford: Oxford University Press.

Hyland, K. 1994. "Hedging in Academic Writing and EAP Textbooks." *English for Specific Purposes* 13 (3): 239–56.

Hyland, K. 1996. "Writing Without Conviction? Hedging in Science Research Articles." *Applied Linguistics* 17 (4): 433–54.

Hymes, D. 1980. "What is Ethnography?" In *Language in Education: Ethnolinguistic Essays.* Washington, D.C.: Center for Applied Linguistics.

Jackson, B. 1995. *Making Sense in Law: Linguistic, Psychological and Semiotic Perspectives.* Liverpool: Deborah Charles Publications, Legal Semiotics Monographs.

Jakobson, R. 1987. "Linguistics and Poetics." In *Language in Literature,* edited by K. Pomorska, S. Rudy. Cambridge, Mass. and London: Harvard University Press.

Jameson, F. 1981. *The Political Unconscious.* Ithaca, N.Y.: Cornell University Press.

Jordan, R. R. 1992. *Academic Writing Course.* 2nd ed. London: Nelson.

Jude, C. 1995. "The report for decision making: genre and inquiry." *Journal of Business and Technical Communication* 9 (2): 170–205.

Kane, T. 1988. *The New Oxford Guide to Writing.* Oxford: Oxford University Press.

Kaufer, D.S. and C. Geisler. 1991. "A Scheme for Representing Academic Argument." *Journal of Advanced Composition* 11: 107–102.

Kennedy, X. J. and D. M. Kennedy. 1990. *The Bedford Guide for College Writers.* New York: St Martin's Press.

Kinneavy, James. 1980. "A Pluralistic Synthesis of Four Contemporary Models for Teaching Composition. " In *Learning to Write: First Language/Second Language*, edited by A. Freedman and I. Pringle. London: Longman.

Kissam, P.C. 1987. "Thinking (By Writing) About Legal Writing." *Vanderbilt Law Review* 40: 135–73.

Kolb, D. 1984. *Experiential Learning.* Englewood Cliffs, N.J.: Prentice Hall.

Kress, G. 1989. *Linguistic Processes in Sociocultural Practice.* 2nd ed. Oxford: Oxford University Press.

Kress, G. 1989. "Texture and meaning." In *Narrative and Argument,* edited by R. Andrews. Milton Keynes: Open University Press.

Kress, G. 1993. "A sociotheory of genre." In *The Powers of Literacy: A Genre Approach to Teaching Writing,* edited by B. Cope, M. Kalanzis. Washington, D.C.: Falmer Press.

Kress, G. 1994. *Learning to Write.* 2nd ed. London: Routledge.

Kress, G. 1995. *Making Signs and Making Subjects: The English Curriculum and Social Futures.* London: Institute of Education, University of London.

Kress, G., and T. Threadgold. 1988. "Towards a social theory of genre." *Southern Review* 21: 215–43.

Krueger, M. and F. Ryan, ed. 1993. *Language and Content: Discipline- and Content-Based Approaches to Language Study.* Lexington, Mass.: D.C. Heath.

Lankshear, C. 1997. *Changing Literacies.* Buckingham: Open University Press.

Lave, J., and E. Wenger. 1991. *Situated Learning: Legitimate Peripheral Participation.* Cambridge: Cambridge University Press.

Lea, M., and B. V. Street. 1997. "Student Writing and Faculty Feedback in Higher Education: an Academic Literacies Approach." Unpublished draft reprint.

Lea, M., and B. Street. 1998. "Student Writing in Higher Education: An Academic Literacies Approach." *Studies in Higher Education* 23 (2): 57–72.

Leech, G. 1981. *Semantics: The Study of Meaning.* 2nd ed. Harmondsworth: Penguin Books.

Leech, G., and M. Short. 1981. *Style in Fiction.* London: Longman.

Leech, G., and J. Svartik. 1975. *A Communicative Grammar of English.* London: Longman.

Leighton, P., T. Mortimer and N. Whatley. 1995. *Today's Law Teachers: Lawyers or Academics?* London: Cavendish.

Leith, D. and G. Myerson. 1989. *The Power of Address: Explorations in Rhetoric.* London: Routledge.

Lemke, J. L. 1993. *Talking Science: Language, Learning and Values.* New York: Ablex.

Lester, S. 1998. *Systematic Wisdom: Assessments in self-directed learning* [cited.] Available from www.devmts.demon.co.ukLRG21st.htm.

Locke, J. 1984. *An Essay Concerning Human Understanding.* Edited by A. C. Fraser. Vol. 2. Oxford: Clarendon Press.

Lynch, W. M. L. 1996. "Discovering the Ripening Functions of Argument." In *Perspectives on Written Argument,* edited by D. Berrill. Cresskill, N.J.: Hampton Press.

MacDonald, S.P. 1994. *Academic Writing in the Humanities and Social Sciences.* Carbondale, Ill.: Southern Illinois University Press.

Mackay, S. 1997. *The Engineer's Apprentice: Evaluating How Genres Impact the Professionalization of Students in a Senior Engineering Capstone Course.* unpublished.

Maharg, P. 1996a. *Contracts: An Introduction to the Skills of Legal Writing and Analysis.* Available from http://elj.warwick.ac.uk/jilt/issue1/articles.htm.

Maharg, P. 1996b. "(Re)-telling stories: narrative theory and the practice of client counselling." *The Law Teacher* 30: 295–314.

Maharg, P. 1999. "The Culture of Mnemosyne: Open Book Assessment and the Theory and Practice of Legal Education." *International Journal of the Legal Profession* 6, 2, 219–239.

Mannheim, R. 1991. *Ideology and Utopia: An Introduction to the Sociology of Knowledge.* London: Routledge.

Margulies, P. 1990. "'Who are you to tell me that?' Attorney-client deliberation regarding non-legal issues and the interests of non-clients." *North Carolina Law Review* 68: 213–52.

Marius, R. 1992. "Composition Studies." In *Redrawing the Boundaries: the Transformation of British and American Literary Studies,* edited by S. Greenblatt and G. Gunn. New York: Modern Language Association.

Martin, J. R. 1989. *Factual Writing: Exploring and Challenging Social Reality.* Oxford: Oxford University Press.

Martin, N., ed. 1984. *Writing Across the Curriculum Pamphlets; a Selection from the Schools Council and London University Institute of Education Joint Project: Writing Across the Curriculum.* Upper Montclair, N.J.: Boynton/Cook.

Martin, N., P. D'Arcy, B. Newton, and R. Parker. 1976. *Writing and Learning Across the Curriculum 11–16.* London: Ward Lock Educational for The Schools Council.

Mason, J. and P. Washington. 1992. *The Future of Thinking: rhetoric and liberal arts teaching.* London: Routledge.

Mathison, M.A. (in preparation). "Surveying Professional Engineers on the Importance of Workplace Writing," p. 3.

Matsuhashi, A., ed. 1987. *Writing in Real Time: Modelling Production Processes.* Norwood, N.J.: Ablex.

Maughan, C. and J. Webb. 1996. *Teacher Lawyers' Skills.* London: Butterworths.

Maughan, C., M. Maughan, and J. Webb. 1995. "Sharpening the Mind or Narrowing It? The Limitations of Outcome and Performance Measures in Legal Education." *The Law Teacher* 29 (3): 255–78.

Maughan, J. and J. Webb. 1995. *Lawyering Skills and the Legal Process.* London: Butterworths.

McCleary, W. 1979. Teaching deductive logic: a test of the Toulmin and Aristotelian models for critical thinking and college composition. Austin, Texas: University of Texas.

McDaniel, M. A., G. O. Einstein, R. K. Dunay, and R. E. Cobb, 1986. "Encoding Difficulty and Memory: Towards a Unifying Theory." *Journal of Memory and Language* 25: 645–56.

Medway, P. 1980. *Finding a Language: Autonomy and Learning in School.* London: Writers and Readers Publishing Collective.

Medway, P. 1984. "The Bible and the Vernacular: The Significance of Language Across the Curriculum." In *English Teaching: An International Exchange,* edited by J. Britton. London: Heinemann.

Medway, P. 1990. "Language with Consequences: Wordly Engagement for Critical Inquiry." *English Education* 22 (3): 147–64.

Medway, P. 1991. "Technology Education and its Bearing on English." *Design and Technology Teaching* 24 (1): 37–43.

Medway, P. 1996. "Virtual and Material Buildings: Construction and Constructivism in Architecture and Writing." *Written Communication* 13 (4): 473–514.

Medway, P. 1999. "Words, Signs and Things: A Linguist Looks at Architecture." Paper read at Forum Lecture, 17 March, at Carleton University, School of Architecture.

Medway, P. 1999. "Writing and Design in Architectural Education." In *Transitions: Writing in Academic and Workplace Settings,* edited by P. Dias and A. Paré. Cresskill, N.H.: Hampton Press.

Medway, P. (Forthcoming–in 2000). "Uncertain Genres: The Case of Architecture Students' Sketchbooks." In *The Rhetoric and Ideology of Genre: Strategies for Stability and Change,* edited by R. Coe, L. Lingard and T. Taslenko. Cresskill, NH: Hampton Press.

Meiland, J. W. 1989. "Argument as Inquiry and Argument as Persuasion." *Argumentation* 3: 185–96.

Miller, C. 1984. "Genre as Social Action." *Quarterly Journal of Speech* 70: 151–67.

Miller, C. 1994. "Genre as Social Action." In *Genre Knowledge and the New Rhetoric,* edited by A. Freedman and P. Medway. Bristol, Pa.: Taylor and Francis.

Miller, R. R. 1992. *The Informed Argument.* 3rd ed.: Harcourt, Brace & Janovich.

Miller, S. 1991. *Textual Carnivals: The Politics of Composition.* Carbondale, Ill.: Southern Illinois University Press.

Miller, S. 1997. "Composing the Masses: Rhetorical Reproduction in the North American Writing Class." Paper read at the Second International Conference on Teaching and Learning Argument, at Middlesex University, London.

Milroy, J. and L. Milroy. 1985. 1991. *Authority in Language: Investigating Language Prescription and Standardisation.* 2nd ed. London: Routledge.

Mitchell, S. 1992. *Questions and Schooling: Classroom Discourse across the Curriculum.* Hull: University of Hull, Center for Studies in Rhetoric.

Mitchell, S. 1994. *The Teaching and Learning of Argument in Sixth Forms and Higher Education.* Hull: University of Hull, Center for Studies in Rhetoric.

Mitchell, S. 1996. *Improving the Quality of Argument in Higher Education: Interim Report.* London: Middlesex University, School of Education.

Mitchell, S. 1997. "Quality in Argument: Why We Should Spell Out the Ground Rules." In *The Quality of Argument: A Colloquium on Issues of Teaching and Learning in Higher Education,* edited by M. Riddle. London: Middlesex University, School of Lifelong Learning and Education.

Mitchell, S. 1998. *Improving the Quality of Argument in Higher Education: trial materials.* London: Middlesex University, School of Lifelong Learning and Education.

Mitchell, S. forthcoming. "Some Speculations on Language and the Arts." In *Journal of Apsthetic Education.*

Mitchell, S., and M. Riddle. 2000. *Improving the Quality of Argument: Final Report.* London: Middlesex University, School of Lifelong Learning and Education.

Mitchell, S., V. Marks, J. Harding, and L. Hale. 2000. "Making Dance; Making Essays." In *New Contexts for Student Writing in Higher Education,* edited by M. Lea, B. Stierer. Milton Keynes: Open University Press.

Mohan, J. 1995. "Thinking Local: Service Learning, Education for Citizenship and Geography." *Journal of Geography in Higher Education* 12 (2): 129–40.

Moore, T. 1997. "From Text to Note: Cultural Variation in Summarisation Practices." *Prospect* 12 (3): 54–63.

Myerson, G. 1995. "Democracy, Argument and the University." *Studies in Higher Education* 19 (2): 125–33.

NCIHE (National Committee of Inquiry into Higher Education). *Higher Education in the Learning Society.* London: HMSO, 1997

Neumann, R. K. 1990. *Legal Reasoning and Legal Writing.* Boston: Little, Brown & Co.

Newell, G. E., and D. Swanson-Owens. 1994. "Using Intervention Protocols to Study the Effects of Instructional Scaffolding on Writing and Learning." In *Speaking About Writing: Reflections on Research Methodology,* edited by P. Smagorinsky. Thousand Oaks: Sage Publications.

Ohmann, R. 1976. *English in America: A Radical View of the Profession.* New York: Oxford University Press.

Ong, W. J. 1958. *Ramus: Method and the Decay of Dialogue.* Cambridge, Mass.: Harvard University Press.

Pacanowsky, M. 1983. "A Small-Town Cop—Communication In, Out and About a Crisis." In *Communication and Organizations—An Interpretive Approach,* edited by L. Punam and M. Pacanowsky. Thousand Oaks: Sage Publications.

Paltridge, B. 1997. *Genre, Frames and Writing in Research Settings.* Philadelphia: John Benjamins.

Pennycook, A. 1997a. "Borrowing Others' Words: Text Ownership, Memory, and Plagiarism." *TESOL Quarterly* 30 (2): 201–30.

Pennycook, A. 1997b. "Vulgar Pragmatism, Critical Pragmatism, and EAP." *English for Specific Purposes* 16 (4): 253–69.

Perelman, C., and L. Olbrechts-Tyteca. 1958. *La Nouvelle Rhetorique: Traite de l'argumentation.* Brussells: University of Brussels.

Perelman, C., and L. Olbrechts-Tyteca. 1969. *The New Rhetoric: A Treatise of Argumentation.* Notre Dame: University of Notre Dame Press.

Pinker, S. 1989. *Learnability and Cognition: The Acquisition of Argument Structure.* Cambridge, Mass.: MIT Press.

Pope, R. 1995. *Textual Intervention.* London: Routledge.

Portwood, D. 1999. "An Intellectual Case for Work Based Learning Studies." In *In Developing Work Based Learning in a University,* edited by D. Portwood and C. Costley. Birmingham: Staff and Educational Development Association, Kogan Page.

Quirk, R., and S. Greenbaum. 1973. *A University Grammar of English.* London: Longman.

Raney, K. 1997. *Visual Literacy: Issues and Debates.* A Report on the Research Project "Framing Visual and Verbal Experience". London: Middlesex University, School of Education.

Redfield, K. A. 1996. "Opening the Composition Classroom to Storytelling: Respecting Native American Students' Use of Rhetorical Strategies." In *Perspectives on Written Argument,* edited by D. Berrill. Cresskill, N.J.: Hampton Press.

Reich, R. 1991. *The Work of Nations: Preparing Ourselves for 21st Century Capitalism.* London: Simon and Schuster.

Reid, J. M. 1988. *The Process of Composition.* 2nd ed. Englewood Cliffs, N.J.: Prentice Hall Regents.

Richards, I. 1997. "White City." *Architectural Review* 1201 (March): 34–40.

Richardson, L. 1994. "Writing: A Method of Inquiry." In *Handbook of Qualitative Research,* edited by N. Denzin, and Y. Lincoln. Thousand Oaks: Sage Publications.

Riddle, M. 1996. Position Paper at the First International Workshop on Argumentative Text Processing, EARLI-SIG Writing, Barcelona.

Riddle, M. 1997. "Literacy Through Written Argument in Higher Education." In *The Quality of Argument,* edited by M. Riddle. London: Middlesex University, School of Education and Lifelong Learning.

Riddle, M, ed. 1997a. *The Quality of Argument: A Colloquium on Issues of Teaching and Learning in Higher Education.* London: Middlesex University, School of Lifelong Learning and Education.

Riddle, M. 1997b. "Evaluating Argument in Student Texts: How Can Staff Distinguish the Appearance from the Reality?" Paper read at Teaching and Learning Argument Conference, 4–6 September 1997, at Middlesex University.

Riddle, M. 1998. "Is Argument an Issue in the Teaching and Assessment of Undergraduate Research-Based Assignments?" In *Writing in H.E.: Perspectives in Theory and Practice,* edited by R. Lonsdale. Aberystwyth: University of Wales Aberystwyth.

Robinson, E. 1991. "The Enfield Experiment." In *Innovation in Higher Education,* edited by K. G. Collier. Windsor: NFER (National Foundation for Educational Research), 44–58.

Rogers, C. 1980. *A Way of Being.* Boston: Houghton Mifflin.

Rowe, A. 1972. "Human Beings, Class and Education." In *Education for Democracy,* edited by D. Rubinstein and C. Stoneman. Harmondsworth: Penguin.

Scardamalia, M. and C. Bereiter. 1982. "From Conversation to Composition: the Role of Instruction in a Developmental Process." In *Advances in Instructional Psychology,* edited by R. Glaser. Hillsdale, N.J.: Lawrence Erlbaum Associates.

Scardamalia, M., and C. Bereiter. 1986. "Research on written composition." In *Handbook of Research on Teaching,* edited by M. Wittrock. Skokie, Ill.: Rand McNally.

Schegloff, E. 1968. "Sequencing in Conversational Openings." American Anthropologist, Vol. 70-No. 6, reprinted in Gumperz and Hymes (1972).

Scholes, R. 1985. *Textual Power: Literacy Theory and the Teaching of English.* New Haven: Yale University Press.

Schön, D. 1987. *Educating the Reflective Practitioner: Toward a New Design for Teaching and Learning in the Professions.* San Francisco: Jossey-Bass.

Schön, D. A. 1983. *The Reflective Practitioner: How Professionals Think in Action.* Aldershot: Avebury.

Schriver, K. 1992. "What Can Document Designers Learn from Usability Testing?" *Studies of Functional Text Quality,* edited by Henk Pander Maat and Michael Steehouder. Amsterdam: Rodopi Publishers.

Scott, M. 1994. "The Pedagogic Relation in Accounts of Student Writers' Needs and Difficulties." In *Improving Student Learning: Theory and Practice,* edited by G. Gibbs. Oxford: Oxford Centre for Staff Development.

Scott, M. 1999. "Agency and Subjectivity in Student Writing." In *Writing in Higher Education: Cultural and Epistemological Issues,* ed. C. Jones, J. Turner and B. Street. Amsterdam and Philadelphia: John Benjamins.

Sharples, M. 1999. *How We Write: Writing as Creative Design.* London: Routledge.

Shotter, J. 1995. "In Conversation: Joint Action, Shared Intentionality and Ethics." In *Theory and Psychology.* Thousand Oaks: Sage Publications.

Silecchia, L. A. 1996. "Legal Skills Training in the First Year of Law School: Research? Writing? Analysis? or More?" *Dickinson Law Review* 100 (2): 245–301.

Singley, M. and J. Anderson. 1989. *The Transfer of Cognitive Skill.* Cognitive Science Series. Cambridge: Harvard University Press.

Smith, N. 1982. *Mutual Knowledge.* London: Academic Press.

Smith, P. 1997. "Reflections on Hunstanton." *ARG: Architectural Research Quarterly* 2 (8): 32–43.

Smithson, Alison, and Peter Smithson. 1973. *Without Rhetoric: an Architectural Aesthetic 1955–1972.* London: Latimer New Dimensions.

Smithson, A. and P. Smithson, 1982. *Alison and Peter Smithson.* London: Academy Editions.

Smithson, Peter. 1997. "Reflections on Hunstanton." *ARG: Architectural Research Quarterly* 2 (8): 32–43.

Spellmeyer, K. 1996. "After Theory: From Textuality to Attunement with the World." *College English* 58 (8): 893–913.

Sperber, D., and D. Wilson. 1982. "Mutual Knowledge and Relevance in Theories of Comprehension," in Smith (1982).

Sperling, N. 1994. "Constructing the Perspective of Teacher-as-Reader: A Framework for Studying Response to Student Writing." *Research in the Teaching of English* 28 (2): 175–207.

Spradley, J. and D. McCurdy. 1973. *The Cultural Experience: Ethnography in Complex Society.* Chicago: Science Research Associates.

Stevenson, J. and M. Yorke. 1998. *Capability and Quality in Higher Education.* London: Kogan Page.

Stockton, S. 1995. "Writing in History: Narrating the Subject of Time." *Written Communication* 12 (1): 47–73.

Stratman, J. F. 1994. "Investigating persuasive processes in legal discourse in real time: cognitive biases and rhetorical strategy in appeal court briefs." *Discourse Processes* 17: 1–57.

Street, B. 1996. "Academic Literacies." In *Challenging Ways of Knowing in English, Maths and Science,* edited by D. Baker, et al. London: Falmer Press.

Street, B. V. 1995. *Social Literacies: Critical Approaches to Literacy in Development, Ethnography and Education.* London and New York: Longman.

Stubbs, M. and S. Barnet. 1983. *Practical Guide to Writing.* 4th ed. Boston: Little, Brown & Co.

Swales, J. M. 1990. *Genre Analysis: English in Academic Research Settings.* Cambridge: Cambridge University Press.

Swales, J. M. and C. B. Feak. 1994. *Academic Writing for Graduate Students: A Course for Nonnative Speakers of English.* Ann Arbor: University of Michigan Press.

Swanson-Owens, D. 1993. Learning to "Invent the University": A Case Study of Students Acquiring and Applying Discourse Structure Knowledge in Two Freshman Composition Classes. Unpublished Ph.D. thesis, Stanford University.

Tadros, A. 1981. Linguistic Prediction in Economics Text, University of Birmingham, Birmingham.

Tadros, A. 1993. "The Pragmatics of Text Averral and Attribution in Academic Texts." In *Data Description, Discourse,* edited by M. Hoey. London: HarperCollins.

Tadros, A. 1994. "Predictive Categories in Expository Text." In *Advanced in Written Text Analysis,* edited by M. Coulthard. London and New York: Routledge.

Tannen, D. 1989. *Talking Voices.* Cambridge: Cambridge University Press.

Tannen, D. 1998. *The Argument Culture.* New York: Random House.

Tenney, D. and P. J. Annas. 1996 "Positioning Oneself: A Feminist Approach to Argument." In *Argument Revisited Argument Redifined,* edited by B. Emmel, P. Resch, and D. Tenney. London: Sage Publications.

Thompson, D. 1996. "Rescuing the Failed, Filed Away, and Forgotten: African Americans and Eurocentricity in Academic Argument." In *Perspectives on Written Argument,* edited by D. Berrill. Cresskill, N.J.: Hampton Press.

Torbe, M., and P. Medway. 1982. *The Climate for Learning.* Montclair, N.J.: Boynton/Cook.

Toulmin, S. 1958. *The Uses of Argument.* Cambridge: Cambridge University Press.

Toulmin, S., R. Rieke, and A. Janik. 1984. *An Introduction to Reasoning.* 2nd ed. London: Collier Macmillan.

Twining, W. 1994. *Blackstone's Tower: The English Law School.* London: Sweet and Maxwell.

Twining, W., and D. Miers. 1991. *How To Do Things with Rules.* 3rd ed. London: Butterworths.

Van Maanen, J. 1988. *Tales of the Field: On Writing Ethnography.* Chicago: Chicago University Press.

Van Maanen, J., ed. 1995. *Representation in Ethnography.* Thousand Oaks: Sage Publications.

Vickers, B. 1988. *In Defence of Rhetoric.* Oxford: Clarendon Press.

Volosinov, F. N. 1976. *Freudianism: A Critical Sketch.* Translated by I.R. Titunik. Edited by H. Neal. Bloomington, Indiana: Indiana University Press.

Vygotsky, L. 1962. *Thought and Language.* Translated by E. Hanfmann, and G. Vakar. Edited by E. Hanfmann and G. Vakar. Cambridge, Mass.: The MIT Press.

Walters, K. S. 1994. *Re-Thinking Reason: New Perspectives in Critical Thinking.* Albany, N.Y.: State University of New York Press.

Walton, D. 1999. "The Importance of Dialogue Theory at the Century's Turn." Paper read at Ontario Society for the Study of Argumentation Conference, 13–15 May, at Brock University, St Catherine's, Ontario.

Watson-Gegeo, K. A. 1996. "Argument as Transformation: A Pacific Framing of Conflict, Community, and Learning." In *Perspectives on Written Argument,* edited by D. Berrill. Cresskill, N.J.: Hampton Press.

Weissberg, R. and S. Buker. 1990. *Writing Up Research: Experimental Research Report Writing for Students of English.* Englewood Cliffs, NJ: Prentice Hall Regents.

Wertsch, J. V. 1994. "The Primacy of Mediated Action in Sociocultural Studies." *Mind, Culture and Activity* 1: 202–208.

White, A., J. Fitzpatrick and J. Roberts. 1996. "Similarities and differences between the care planning and care delivery skills of senior student nurses". Paper read at Annual Conference of the British Educational Research Association, at University of Lancaster.

White, M., and A. Hunt. 1999. "Citizenship and the Transition from 'Character' to 'Personality': Challenging the Contemporary Civic Revival." Paper read 22 January, at Carleton University, Department of Sociology and Anthropology.

White, S. 1989. "Teaching Novices How to Read Law Reports." *Law Teacher* 23 (2): 142–61.

Williams, R. 1973. *The Country and the City.* London: Chatto and Windus.

Winsor, D. A. 1992. "What Counts as Writing? An Argument from Engineers' Practice." *Journal of Advanced Composition* 12: 337–47.

Womack, P. 1993. "What are essays for?" *English in Education* 27 (2): 42–49.

Woods, C. 1996. "Altered Geographies: Ethnography, Rhetoric, Discourse and the Construction of Knowledge in a BA (Professional Writing and Communication)." *Australian Journal of Communication* 23 (3): 84–100.

Wrigley, C. 1989. "Review of 'Levanthal, The Last Dissenter.'" *Bulletin of Society for Study of Labour History* 54 (1): 111–13.

Wright Mills, C. 1970. *The Sociological Imagination.* Harmondsworth: London.

Young, K. M., and G. Leinhardt. 1998. "Writing from Primary Documents: A Way of Knowing in History. " *Written Communication* 15 (1): 25–68.

Zwaan, R. A. 1994. "Effect of Genre Expectations on Text Comprehension." *Journal of Experimental Psychology: Learning, Memory and Cognition* 20 (4): 920–33.

Notes on Contributors

Richard Andrews is Professor of Educational Studies at The University of York, England. He is author of *The Problem with Poetry* and *Teaching and Learning Argument* and editor of *Rebirth of Rhetoric: Essays in Languages, Culture and Education.* He directed the Leverhulme Trust research projects on argument at Hull and Middlesex Universities between 1991 and 1998.

Carol Costley is Head of Research at the National Center for Work-Based Learning Partnerships at Middlesex University. Research interests include methodologies and epistemologies in work-based learning; interdisciplinarity; using life history to reflect on previous learning; and argument in work-based learning. Current projects include links with universities in Brazil to further research on work, curriculum, and learning; business links with Cyprus to further the development of the work-based curriculum; and the continuing development of the new Doctorate in Professional Studies both in the U.K. and abroad.

Catherine Davidson is the University Writing Coordinator at Richmond American International University in London. She teaches first-year writing to students from around the world and runs the Writing Across the Curriculum program. In addition to her academic writing, she has published poetry and a novel.

Kathy Doncaster is in charge of postgraduate program in Work-Based Learning Studies and joint program leader of the Doctorate in Professional Studies at Middlesex University, England. Her current research interests are in professional education, reflective practice, discourse analysis (in which she gained her Ph.D. at Lancaster University), and the career stories of work-based learners.

Aram Eisenschitz is a Senior Lecturer at Middlesex University teaching urban studies. He has worked as planning adviser for the London Chamber of Commerce and Industry. He has published widely in the field of Urban Regeneration including coauthorship of *The Politics of Local Economic Policy.* His interests include higher education as a means of turning students into critical thinkers.

Associate Professor of English at the University of British Columbia, in Vancouver, **Janet Giltrow** teaches courses in stylistics, writing, and rhetoric. She has published articles on style in literary and nonliterary texts, genre theory, ideologies of language, and the sociopolitics of ESL instruction, as well as a textbook, *Academic Writing* (2nd ed. 1995), and an anthology of scholarly readings, *Academic Reading* (1995).

Nicholas Groom teaches academic literacy at the Institute of Education, University of London, England. He has also worked in schools and universities in Japan, Indonesia,

Australia, Vietnam, and Thailand. He is interested in literacy education, text analysis, and text-making practices.

Amanda Jacobs worked initially as an actress. After some years at home with her children she undertook a degree course at Middlesex University, graduating in 1998 in Education Studies and the History of Ideas. Intrigued by the processes of learning, her dissertation focused on mature women students and their perceptions of academic argument. Amanda currently works with students with learning difficulties.

Paul Maharg is Senior Lecturer in Legal Practice in the Law School at the University of Strathclyde in Glasgow. He is responsible for curriculum development in the postgraduate Diploma in Legal Practice, and teaches legal skills, legal ethics, and jurisprudence. His research interests include legal education, particularly professional writing skills, use of C&IT in under- and postgraduate legal education, and the use of critical and literary theory in jurisprudential enquiry.

Peter Medway has taught in schools and universities in the U.K. Currently a Professor in Linguistics and Applied Language Studies in Carleton University, Ottawa, and Visiting Professor in Education at Middlesex University, London, he conducts research in the fields of language in education, writing, design in education, and linguistic and semiotic processes in architecture.

Maureen A. Mathison is Assistant Professor in the Communication Department and a faculty member of the University Writing Program at the University of Utah, where she coordinates the Writing Emphasis/Intensive Program. Her research, which focuses on disciplinary rhetoric, has appeared in *Communication Theory and Written Communication,* and in numerous edited volumes.

Sally Mitchell is a research fellow at Middlesex University, where she has been working on the project "Improving the Quality of Argument in Higher Education." Prior to this, she investigated the place of argument in post-compulsory education at the University of Hull. She is co-editor with Patrick Costello of *Competing and Consensual Voices: The Theory and Practice of Argument.*

Mike Riddle is a Visiting Academic at Middlesex University. He formed a close association with the University's Leverhulme project on improving the quality of argument, resulting in published conference papers, and an edited colloquium on argument in higher education. His research interests include academic literacies, cognitive competences, the higher education curriculum, and innovative methods of introducing argument via workshops, course materials, and web-based programs.

Deborah Swanson is Associate Professor of English at San Francisco State University. She teaches in the Masters in Composition Studies Program and has published pieces in *Research in the Teaching of English, Kappan,* and a volume published as part of the Sage Series in Written Communication.

Doug Sweet is Coordinator of Business Writing at Santa Clara University, Santa Clara, California. He is the author of *Contexts & Choices: A Practical Guide to Writing for Business* and co-author, with Jeanne Gunner, of *Critical Grounds for Writing.*

Claire Woods is Professor of Communication and Writing and Director of the Centre for Professional and Public Communication at the University of South Australia, Adelaide. She has published on aspects of English and Language Arts Curriculum, literacy, and on writing and writing pedagogy. Her research interests are in writing and communication in education, workplace, and community.